For Jed.

May you see these things written not just
in black and white on a page, but also clear
as day in how I live.

And may you come to know the precious
gift of Jesus writing and re-writing your
own story in dazzling technicolour.

Contents

THE DNA
OF HEALTHY
DISCIPLESHIP

Letting Jesus ReCODE
Your Spiritual Life

DAVE CRIDDLE
Foreword by Alex Harris

Commendations for **The DNA of Healthy Discipleship**

The Lord is inviting His bride on a journey of transformation - He longs for His children to return to fresh encounter with Him and discover their true identity as sons and daughters. Dave writes to help us journey a life that will recode us and enable us to become disciples that make disciples. This is the very journey the Church of Jesus Christ is called to.

—**ANNE CALVER**, OVERSEER OF UNLEASHED: SEEKING TO LIVE LIKE THE ACTS CHURCH TODAY; CO-AUTHOR OF *UNLEASHED*

Dave allows the light of God's word to illuminate and ignite the joy in the calling of Jesus to every believer. This is much needed for those who are not satisfied with the status quo of Christian life and desire to see New Testament results in our world today. This is practical and inspiring and honours the great commission of Christ our King.

—**JASON KING**, LEAD PASTOR OF FAITH CHURCH, ARVADA

This book is not just about doing; it's about becoming. Dave's engaging writing style, coupled with his theological understanding, makes complex spiritual truths accessible and applicable. Whether you feel stuck in your faith, are seeking a deeper relationship with Jesus, or simply want to live out your calling more fully, *The DNA of Healthy Discipleship* provides a compass to find your way to spiritual renewal and growth.

Dave's personal anecdotes, biblical references, and practical applications ensure that every reader can find themselves within these pages, making it a must-read for anyone serious about their discipleship journey. Prepare to be challenged, inspired, and equipped to live a life that truly reflects the DNA of the Great Commission. This book is a timely call to transformation that the UK Church desperately needs.

—**ANDY GLOVER**, TEAM LEADER OF HBC CHESTER & FRESH STREAMS

The very premise of this book gets my pulse racing - what better question to be asking than, 'what kind of DNA do we need as followers of Jesus to complete the Great Commission?' The emphases on confidence and obedience addresses the two biggest issues facing disciples today. Dave's book is full of useful information and tools to help us with the greatest job that the church has been entrusted with - to go and make disciples! It's really well written and a delight to read.

—**NIC HARDING**, FOUNDING PASTOR OF FRONTLINE CHURCH; LEADER OF KAIROS CONNEXION

Dave writes with real wisdom which will help you to become disciple of Jesus and a disciple-maker for Jesus. This book will both help you help yourself and help you help your friends.

—**PHIL MOORE**, AUTHOR OF THE 'STRAIGHT TO THE HEART' SERIES OF BIBLE COMMENTARIES

Over the last decade a major discipleship void has been uncovered in many Western and UK churches. *The DNA of Healthy Discipleship* helps rectify this vacuum and encourages and equips followers of Jesus to step forwards with intentionality and confidence. Dave excellently roots his ideas in Scripture and provides great practical methods to equip each of us with repeatedly (re)aligning our lives under the Lordship of Jesus and engaged in His Mission.

—**STEPHEN WALKER-WILLIAMS**, PASTOR – TEAM LEADER, GOLD HILL BAPTIST CHURCH; EXECUTIVE DIRECTOR, AMNOS MINISTRIES

Published by Mathetes Publishing 2024.
ISBN: 978-1-0687083-0-5
eISBN: 978-1-0687083-1-2

Visit my Website
www.davecriddle.com

For more content, head to my website and sign up to my newsletter. You'll get more resources to accelerate your discipleship growth, including a Personal Learning Journal to make the most of this book, and my free discipleship training video series.

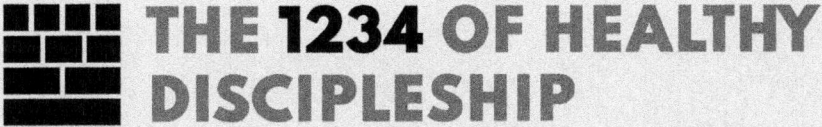 **THE 1234 OF HEALTHY DISCIPLESHIP**

A free four-part video series, unlocking four vital aspects of following Jesus:

1 Lord: why treating Jesus as King changes everything
2 Priorities: discover the true purpose of life with Jesus
3 Ways to Build: overcome imbalance and embrace the whole of discipleship
4 Threads of Discipleship DNA: The CODE of a healthy spiritual life

Available only from my website.

E: EXPERIENCE WITH JESUS

What is this book about, and why read it?

Books are an investment of time, and there are far more than you'll ever be able to read. It is important to choose wisely. So I want to give you a little bit of an idea of whether this is a book that, right now, is going to be worth the time it will take to read. Then the choice is yours!

What is this book about?

My shortest and simplest answer to that question is this: this book is about some very important aspects of following Jesus and how to grow in them.

But there is a slightly longer version.

The longer version is to do with what we normally call the Great Commission. It's a part of the Bible where Jesus gives his followers the task to go and make more followers. Disciples who go and make disciples. That's a big task, but if it's God's plan to reach the world, I want to step into it. But as I've spent more time with the Great Commission, I've come to see it not only as a command. It is also Jesus shaping the people who first heard it and, if we let it, a way he can shape us today. What does that mean? It means it is not just about what God wants us to do, but about who God wants us to *become*.

That's where this longer answer gets us. This book is about who God wants you to be as you go about doing what he wants you to do. It is about your spiritual DNA being healthy, being what Jesus always intended it to be. The Great Commission gives clues about the kinds of disciples he wants.

He wants disciples who are CONFIDENT in him. This book will

help you stop trusting flimsy things and put your whole weight on Jesus as king.

He wants disciples who are OBEDIENT to him. This book will guide you into the freedom of letting Jesus call the shots.

He wants disciples who are DEPENDENT on him always. This book will help you harness Jesus' power in your life instead of trying to go it alone.

And he wants disciples who are EXPERIENCED with him, growing over time instead of standing still, so you can thrive in every season of life.

Confidence. Obedience. Dependence. Experience. That's the 'CODE' this book is about. Some chapters dig into what all that means so we can catch a glimpse of the amazing life of a disciple as Jesus truly intended it. Others get practical, helping us take steps forward in each of those areas (because just good ideas don't get us anywhere). As a whole then, the book is an invitation: let Jesus 're-CODE' your life with healthy discipleship DNA.

So that's what it's about, but there's another question that's good to ask before you commit the money and time to read a book.

Why read this book?

There are a few different reasons I can imagine it being helpful to read this book. I have definitely found it helpful writing it... So if one of the reasons below describes you, maybe this is the book for you at the moment.

You are a passionate disciple of Jesus

You love Jesus! You can look back at the last few years of your life and point to ways your discipleship is healthy already. But instead of coasting you want to keep that momentum and pursue even deeper discipleship health. If that's you, this book contains things that will help you press on with Jesus and keep stepping forwards. As well as casting a vision for what some of these qualities of discipleship can mean, we get practical so you can keep building on the foundations you've been laying with Jesus.

You want to be passionate, but feel stuck

You are a Christian, that's not in doubt. But it's been a while since that really came alive and meant something. You honestly couldn't describe your discipleship as 'healthy' but you aren't satisfied with that and want something to change. If that's you (no judgment, it's been me plenty of times), this book can help. It will paint a picture of what discipleship can be that will excite and inspire, then give you the tools to get going again one step at a time.

You want to help others in their discipleship

We aren't meant to do this Christian thing by ourselves. We all need others to invest in us, and we are all meant to invest in others. Perhaps there's a person you know who you want to help grow as a disciple. You might already be doing that or it might be something new for you. Maybe you are a church leader looking for tools to help your people, or a small group leader, or (even better!) an ordinary Christian investing yourself in one other person to help them take steps forward. If any of that is you, this book will give you ways of thinking about the discipleship of those people, as well as things you can work through together practically. Don't just give them the book, though. Read it together, one-to-one or in a group, and journey its content through together by putting things into practice as you go.

One or more aspect of CODE jumps out

Maybe as you read the words above, one or more of Confidence, Obedience, Dependence or Experience struck home. You want deeper confidence in God, or see ways you are disobedient. You're depending on things that aren't God, or feel like you haven't grown in meaningful experience with Jesus for a while. Because we go deep on each area, you should find something that can help. While the book is designed to be read as a whole you could even jump to the relevant section if you wanted.

You want to live out the Great Commission

Maybe you are fascinated, motivated or intimidated by the Great Commission itself. We do come back to it a lot in this book. And I'm convinced that the success of the Great Commission in our lives is linked to the kinds of disciples we are. So by inviting Jesus to 're-CODE' you with healthy discipleship DNA, you'll step deeper into the Great Commission life he wants for you.

What if I'm not a Christian?

I am going to be honest. As I was writing this book and picturing the kind of person I hoped would read it, I was mostly imagining those who are already committed to Jesus. It is not an introduction to who Jesus is or how to become his follower. But, if you are exploring Christian faith and want to get a picture of what the life of following Jesus might look like, you might find some things that help inform that and even inspire you to delve deeper. So I would absolutely invite you to dig in, but I want to be up front about that first.

So that is a taste of what you can expect in this book. To get more of a flavour, the Introduction fleshes all of this out a bit more. Beyond that, it's up to you. Maybe this isn't the book for you at the moment. If so, put it down and find a better one. I'll never know! But maybe it is just what you need to kickstart a new phase in your own discipleship with Jesus, because you know your spiritual life needs him to 'reCODE' it a bit.

Foreword
By Alex Harris

I am not the only one who noticed it. I am also not the only one who is celebrating it. It was probably why I was so delighted when Natalie and Dave moved up to Sheffield and began to explore a new pattern and ethos for ministry. As Dave was commissioned into that new pioneering role in Sheffield, his friend and former lead minister Stephen described it well. How Dave had moved from being (an extremely good) pastor-teacher to more and more someone who was enabling disciples to make disciples. It's perhaps a subtle shift, but it is certainly a transformative one. Over the years I have known Dave, I have seen him embrace that shift wholeheartedly.

Perhaps Dave's own journey mirrors the essence of this book—moving away from the comfort zones of conventional church and away from the good but perhaps deficient practice of preaching and pastoring delivered faithfully Sunday by Sunday. Moving instead toward a more intentional discipleship of each other, of those we know and meet, and of ourselves. Like me, Dave loves conventional church. And innovative church. And cell church and big church and missional communities and micro-church and mega-church. This book isn't about the style of your church, but it is about the substance of your faith. Are you a growing disciple? And are you growing other disciples?

It is why I am so delighted Dave asked if I would write a brief word at the start of this great little book – it made me read it well and learn from it deeply. I am better at my job and, more importantly, at being a disciple of Jesus because of that. Thank you, Dave!

The heart of the book joins the growing clamour in the UK and beyond to help Christians and churches return to the task of disciple-making. It is a clear but very practical call to shed some of our accidental superficiality and embrace authentic, Christ-centred discipleship. From the outset, Dave challenges us to discard the veneer of cultural Christianity and instead find ways to plunge into the depths of a genuine relationship with Jesus and with others. This call is not just theoretical but practical, lived out in the daily grind of ordinary life.

If the heart of the book is that call to being a disciple, the strength of the book is twofold. First, it is very helpful around the Bible – expecting that to be the place we primarily learn from and lean into. Starting with the fundamental need for confidence in Jesus as seen in Acts 4:23-31, Dave builds a robust foundation for what it means to be a confident disciple. Dave's exposition is empowering, urging us to move beyond a passive faith to one that actively engages.

The second strength is that Dave doesn't leave us in the world of new concepts and good ideas. Rather, he jumps from the Word to the real world. The DNA of Healthy Discipleship is as practical and action-oriented as it is careful and precise around the Bible. Half the book is dedicated to what we do differently. It's an extremely helpful combination. I suspect ordinary Christians will be greatly helped by both aspects.

Finally, a word to my fellow ministers. I cannot recommend this book highly enough for the task of helping your people become fuller disciples of Jesus. Dave has given us an effective new crook and hook! We are called not just to shepherd our flocks but to raise up disciples who will, in turn, make disciples. This book offers just that. I urge you to read this book. Then, invest in the spiritual growth of your key leaders by providing them with copies too and read it together. It is one of those brilliant books that isn't complicated or convoluted but rather challenges and convicts in helpful ways. I would really encourage you to read it with your church and together implement the principles laid out here. The ripple effect of such an investment will, I am sure, be well worth it.

Rev Dr Alex Harris — June 2024
Regional Minister for Pioneering & Church Planting: Yorkshire Baptist Association
Co-Leader: Firestarters Network

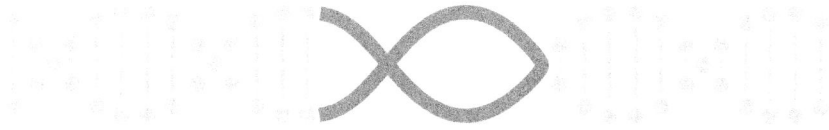

No more fake tan

What kind of person do you need to be to do the things God wants you to?

Certain tasks require skills. When someone comes to re-wire my house, I need to know they have the training and qualifications to do it. Certain tasks require time and patience. You cannot make a garden grow overnight. And certain tasks require the right tools. Ever tried to open a bottle of wine without a corkscrew? It's messy.

Following Jesus, also known as being a disciple, requires all of this. There are skills to learn—things like prayer, Bible-reading and sharing our faith. Time and patience are needed—discipleship is a lifetime, not a moment. And there are tools we need—there is a reason God gave us the Bible, other people and the church.

But I did not ask what skills, time and tools you need to do what God wants you to do. I asked what *kind of person* you need to be. That is the focus of this book.

Answering that question in our minds and hearts (and letting the answer work its way out through our lives) is very important. When Jesus kicked off what we now call Christianity, he did it by investing in exactly that, in growing healthy disciples and entrusting the whole thing to them. Alan Hirsch puts it like this:

> The founding of the whole Christian movement, the most significant religious movement in history, one that has extended through the ages and into the twenty-first century, was initiated through the simple acts of Jesus investing his life and embedding his teachings in his followers and developing them into authentic disciples.[1]

For a moment, before I introduce the central idea of this book, I just want us to pause and reflect on that for a moment. The whole movement of Christianity across the world was entrusted to ordinary people whose lives had been shaped and changed by Jesus. The plan was nothing more or less than them going and doing the same for others. At the end of his three years investing in those disciples, Jesus gives what we normally call 'The Great Commission' (Matthew 28:16-20). We will spend lots of time with the Great Commission in this book, but for now here's my summary of what Jesus says in it: "You're a disciple? Great, go and make some more!"

And that plan hasn't changed. At no point in the New Testament after Jesus gives those instructions does he take them back in favour of something else. And at no point in history since the New Testament finished has he done that either. These instructions are still the plan, and it is still God's intention that all those who follow him are the kinds of followers who can and will step into that plan.

Jesus still says, "You're a disciple? Great, go and make some more!" And if that is true, then how healthy I am as a disciple matters not just for me, but also affects the health of disciples I might *make*.

So I return to the question that underpins the whole of this book: what kind of person do you need to be to do the things God wants you to do? In May 2019, while I was praying, I believe I caught a whisper of something Jesus is saying as part of an answer. A phrase started rumbling through my mind and heart, and it wouldn't go away: *"I want to recode my church."*

Let's delve into that. To do so, we're going to need to talk genetics.

Spiritual genetic CODE

Our genetic 'code' defines who we are. I am a brown-haired Caucasian man (and a fairly pale one at that). I can dye my hair pink and apply fake tan, or even sit on a sun-lounger for a couple of months, at the end of which I won't look like a brown-haired, pale man. But I still will be. Time will prove that. As the tan fades and the hair grows out, the reality of who I am will resurface. DNA, whether healthy or not, always reveals itself.

What is the fake tan of our churches? That depends on the part of the church we're in. It could be your building, your liturgy, your services, your songs and your production values. It could be your preaching, your discipleship courses and your evangelistic programmes. It could be your staff, your budget, your constitution and your AGM. It could be your prayer meetings, your spirituality, your fasting and your tithing. 'If we could only get _____ right, then we would see the breakthrough we've been seeking.'

But this is the difference between restoring and recoding. A piece of furniture is restored to look right on the outside. The church needs to be transformed by the re-coding work of the Spirit from the inside.

Please do not misunderstand. The things I mentioned above as potential 'fake tan' are not bad things. They are all very good things, or at least can be. They matter and they need attention. It's just that none of them is *the thing*. They are all outside us, when really our discipleship DNA is a matter of what is inside us.

So I believe Jesus wants to 'recode' us by his Spirit. But in this book the word 'code' will normally be written as 'CODE' because (just as physical genes are made up of four bases—adenine (A), cytosine (C), guanine (G), and thymine (T) in different combinations) I see four basic aspects to the spiritual genetic CODE which Jesus wants to give to his disciples:

- **C:** Confidence in Jesus
- **O:** Obedience to Jesus
- **D:** Dependence on Jesus
- **E:** Experience with Jesus

Please remember, this is God's work, not ours. We can open ourselves up to his re-coding work, or shut ourselves off from it, but we cannot do it by ourselves. Try to do this without him, and it will fail. If we try to fake it, do it by ourselves or muster it up, it will start to smell of fake tan very quickly.

'Re-'

I have already said I believe Jesus wants to 'recode' his church. The 're-' is very important. I have not had a new idea for Christ's church. The pages of this book do not contain something never said before. But I do see things to be re-discovered, re-emphasised, and re-claimed.

In that sense, we are in a moment where we need to be radical, not in the common usage of the word, but the original. 'Radical' comes from *radix* which means 'root' (also 'radish'). We must go back to our roots, purpose and guiding principles. And they are found, before anything else, in Jesus.

Jesus is described in Hebrews 12:3 as the 'author and perfecter of our faith'. It was Jesus who founded the church. Jesus appointed Peter and declared 'I will build my church' (Matthew 16). Jesus gave his disciples their primary purpose in the Great Commission (Matthew 28). Jesus declared his followers to be 'witnesses' all over the world (Acts 1). And Jesus sent his Spirit at Pentecost to give power to the whole thing (Acts 2). Jesus, Jesus, Jesus. But God is gracious and knows we need not only 'authoring' but 'perfecting'. In every generation, from the church on the day of Pentecost, right through until today, we are not a perfect reflection of the body Christ calls us to be. He isn't finished with us and the work of perfecting continues as Jesus restores us back, more and more fully, to be healthy disciples.

There is beauty to uncover and rot to remove. Both are vital.

I also want to be extremely clear: this is a work in progress in my own life. I thank and worship Jesus as the author of my own faith, the one who wrote my life with him into being. I am so grateful for the wonderful things he has placed in me and around me. But I also pray, asking him to clear the rot, strip back the layers of pretence and wash me clean of the spiritual fake tan I love to cake myself in. I have not 'arrived'. No, there are many things I still need Jesus to bring to full healthiness.

'Who needs re-coding?'

I said earlier that Jesus wants to reCODE his church, but I'm not using 'church' to describe an institution. This isn't about systems, structures, denominations and movements. Remember the plan: "You're a disciple? Great, go and make some more!" So really this is about the church in its truest form: a united group of disciples following Jesus together. Paul had something to say about the church being made up of lots of individuals, didn't he?

Now if the foot should say, "Because I am not a hand, I do not belong to the body," it would not for that reason stop being part of the body. And if the ear should say, "Because I am not an eye, I do not belong to the body," it would not for that reason stop being part of the body. If the whole body were an eye, where would the sense of hearing be? If the whole body were an ear, where would the sense of smell be? But in fact God has placed the parts in the body, every one of them, just as he wanted them to be. If they were all one part, where would the body be? As it is, there are many parts, but one body. (1 Corinthians 12:15-20)

In one image, Paul shares two important principles. First, every part of the body is valuable for the specific part it has to play. Second, no one part of the body is complete in isolation. These two truths help us neither ignore the role of the individual nor elevate it too highly. Every single one of us can carry the spiritual DNA of Jesus in full, but we are not the church by ourselves.

This is important. God's church is not more or less than the disciples who are part of it, you and me. But you and I are not more or less than part of God's church. So if it's true that Jesus wants to 'reCODE the church', the only way to do that is to 'reCODE' lots of individual disciples like us. There is no such thing as a healthy church that isn't made up of healthy disciples.

So to any church leaders reading this, resist the urge to systematise and structure what you read. Fake tan that way lies. Invite Jesus to work on your own heart and to enable you to join him in that work in others. By all means consider if there are things that could change to better enable and reflect this DNA in the community you lead. But don't either start there or stop there.

And to the majority of Christians who aren't in those roles, be encouraged: you are part of the body of Christ and as you allow Christ to shape, transform and 'reCODE' you, it does impact others around you. You are connected, so it has to. The DNA you carry, good and bad, makes a difference, so tend it well and invite the Holy Spirit more and more to shape you into the likeness of Jesus, the only one who carries the perfect 'spiritual DNA'.

How this book works

Next chapter, we go big picture, showing how the four parts of CODE come together in the Great Commission as vital parts of healthy discipleship DNA.

Then, the main part of the book takes each of C, O, D and E in turn, and contains four things for each:

1. **Spotlight:** A brief look at a Bible story where all four qualities are at work, but which really shines a light on one very strongly.

2. **Big Picture:** A full chapter giving a biblical understanding of the quality at hand, asking what it is when its healthy, what can stop it being (the fake tan) and what it means to recover it again (Son-bathing, if you will).

3. **Toolkit:** A full chapter exploring what that means today. These chapters give tools and ideas, based around our HEADS (decisions) our HEARTS (character) and our HANDS (actions).

4. **Great Commission:** A return to Jesus' instruction, asking how the quality we are looking at impacts the call to go and make disciples.

I want to highlight here the importance of the third in that list. It is fair to say that if those chapters weren't part of this book, I wouldn't really be interested in writing it. It is good to see these things at work in Scripture and to delve in and ask what they really mean, but that remains academic unless we take hold of them and let them take shape in us more and more. So each of these chapters (one per quality) is a toolkit of ideas for you to work through.

In structuring those chapters, I have taken my lead from Jesus. When asked what the greatest commandment is, Jesus replied, "Love the Lord your God with all your heart and with all your soul and with all your mind and with all your strength." (Mark 12:30) He knows there are different parts of us and we are to direct all of them toward God. So these chapters are structured around three parts of who we are: our **heads** (minds, decision-making, thinking), our **hearts** (will, desires, posture toward God) and our **hands** (actions, strength, habits). The eagle-eyed might have noticed I have changed the order of these from Jesus' order. That is because more often than not I see this as the order things work out in our discipleship. A change in our thinking leads to new desires, and on into new be-haviour. There is more on this process in Chapter 8.

When we think about our heads, we will consider key decisions we can make. Paul tells us to be 'transformed by the renewing of our minds' (Romans 12:2). If we want to change, we are going to have to change our mind about a few things.

When we consider our hearts, it is about our posture before God. How do we approach him? How will he shape us? In Acts, the disciples are described as those who 'had been with Jesus' and were clearly different as a result (Acts 4:13). The way they related to him changed them. It can change us too.

And when we consider our hands, we are concerned with putting into practice what we are learning. In the New Testament James warns, "Do not merely listen to the word, and so deceive yourselves. Do what it says." (James 1:22) If we want to avoid that trap, we need to do something.

I find this structure helpful as I consider my own discipleship and I've borrowed it from Kris Rogers. As he says,

> It's when these three areas of discipleship are given over to God that we find our whole lives transformed in how we think, how we feel, and what we do to embody who we are in Christ. It's in the balance of these areas that our whole discipleship can take place.[2]

Notice the call there to 'balance'. A healthy disciple is a balanced disciple. By nature, you're likely drawn more strongly to some of these areas than the others. My simple request is that you embrace all of this, consider each part of the toolkit, ask God which area to invest in and then do it!

The book finishes, then, with a chapter asking the obvious question: will we let Jesus do this in us? I believe he wants to. It is time. But will we let him?

It is my hope that what is written here will help you to discover or re-discover the DNA Jesus wishes you to have as a healthy disciple. Whether you are new to this life of following him or have done so for a long, long time, may he instil in you a deeper and stronger core. Yes, he wishes to recode his church. But as we've begun to see, that means he wants to reCODE *your* life.

CODE – The Ingredients of Healthy Discipleship

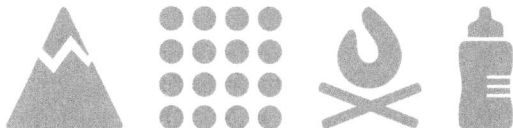

Jesus is a master of communication. It should be no surprise to us that the Son of God, described in John's gospel as 'the word' was, in fact, good with words!

Of course, good communication is far more than being able to pull together a nifty phrase. After all, 'there is a time to be silent, and a time to speak' (Ecclesiastes 3:7). Just like the rest of us, the Son of God was born into a body with two ears and one mouth and he showed interest in listening to others, not just speaking at them. Words do come into it though, and Jesus excelled here too. He knew that learning isn't just about receiving information but about having your mind and heart stretched, provoked, challenged and inspired. So he asked far more questions than he answered.[3]

When he spoke, he often used riddles and parables, because a mystery solved is far more impactful than a fact given. Jesus explains his approach in Mark 4:11-12. To the crowds, a mystery to draw in, to puzzle and intrigue. To the disciples, a mystery revealed. Of course, once a secret has been revealed, it's on you to do something about it. The closer people were, the more plainly he would speak.

And speak plainly he did! As well as explaining the mystery of parables, he gave direct teaching on all kinds of things. He gave practical advice on how to pray or to proclaim the good news in new places.[4] He revealed God's plans, explaining why he had come and teaching about the end of the world.[5] He told them what life would be like once he had gone, empowered by the Spirit and full of trials.[6] And he used strong, even sharp, language when needed, rebuking his disciples and bemoaning how slow they were to understand what they should already have grasped.[7]

In all of this, he was no slouch with words. The Bible tells us that 'the tongue has the power of life and death,' (Proverbs 18:21) and Jesus certainly used his tongue to great effect in releasing life, hope, truth and even healing to others. In long, captivating stories or short, snappy phrases, Jesus used language to great effect.[8] It is no wonder that people flocked to hear him teach and then stayed far longer than they had planned, even missing meals to listen to what he had to say.

And Jesus' words did impact those who heard them. One of the things we hear a few times about Jesus' teaching is that people were 'amazed' because he spoke with authority, not like other teachers (e.g. Luke 7:28-29). Of course the reason for their amazement was not catchphrases, good delivery and clever rhetorical style. No, it was the origin of his words. It was his authority that wowed the crowds, not his vocabulary. The divinity, not the diction. His words came straight from the heart of God who made us, so they cut straight to our human hearts.

But we must also note that this divine message was spoken through a human voice to human ears. That is the wonder of the incarnation: 'the word became flesh and dwelled among us.' (John 1:14) So the communication of Jesus comes not in spite of his humanity, but through it. God (mostly) forgoes the big, booming voice from the sky and instead draws alongside, speaking in human language. And, as we've begun to see, speaking that language extremely well and to great effect.

I begin here because I want now to introduce the central passage of Scripture in this book, a place where what I am calling 'CODE' comes together at a vital moment: The Great Commission. It's well known, but I do not want any familiarity to stop us capturing the magnitude of the moment.

You see, this moment is deeply divine but also utterly human. The humanity is clear: it is one man (Jesus) speaking to eleven other men (the disciples), in a physical way at a physical location. Even a very human experience like doubt is mentioned. But the divinity of the moment is on full display as well: this man is in fact the God-man, Jesus, and what he speaks is the divine commission to begin the movement of God's kingdom across the world. It happens in the aftermath of Jesus' resurrection, the greatest move of God in our universe's history, but to a group of men distraught, confused, weak and full of doubt. Jesus is divinity poured into humanity and this moment is humanity infused with divinity.

There are moments when we aren't really listening, when words and ideas pass us by because we're not really tuned in. This was not one of those. These disciples who Jesus comes to were on the edge of their seats. Bated breath. Hearts pounding. Ears wide open. This is a holy moment. A moment where words pack a punch. But what kind of punch does Jesus choose to pack?

He doesn't listen first. This is a time for him to speak and for them to listen. He doesn't dress up his message in riddles and parables. This was a time for plain speaking. He doesn't ask questions to help them get there themselves. No, what he has to say is what they need to hear. Clear, direct and unfiltered. That is the importance of these words, of this Great Commission. So let's have a look.

The Great Commission (Matthew 28:16-20)

I suspect that for many this passage is so familiar that you're tempted not even to read it but to skip over and just read on. Flattered as I am that you might consider my words to be of more interest, I hope we all know they aren't. So instead, why not read it several times in a few different versions?[9] By all means play a bit of 'spot the difference' as you go, but be sure to let the punch Jesus packed sink in.

New International Version
Then the eleven disciples went to Galilee, to the mountain where Jesus had told them to go. When they saw him, they worshiped him; but some doubted. Then Jesus came to them and said, "All authority in heaven and on earth has been given to me. Therefore go and make disciples of all nations, baptising them in the name of the Father and of the Son and of the Holy Spirit, and teaching them to obey everything I have commanded you. And surely I am with you always, to the very end of the age."

Amplified Bible

Now the eleven disciples went to Galilee, to the mountain which Jesus had designated. And when they saw Him, they worshiped Him; but some doubted [that it was really He]. Jesus came up and said to them, "All authority [all power of absolute rule] in heaven and on earth has been given to Me. Go therefore and make disciples of all the nations [help the people to learn of Me, believe in Me, and obey My words], baptising them in the name of the Father and of the Son and of the Holy Spirit, teaching them to observe everything that I have commanded you; and lo, I am with you always [remaining with you perpetually—regardless of circumstance, and on every occasion], even to the end of the age."

English Standard Version

Now the eleven disciples went to Galilee, to the mountain to which Jesus had directed them. And when they saw him they worshiped him, but some doubted. And Jesus came and said to them, "All authority in heaven and on earth has been given to me. Go therefore and make disciples of all nations, baptising them in the name of the Father and of the Son and of the Holy Spirit, teaching them to observe all that I have commanded you. And behold, I am with you always, to the end of the age."

New Living Translation

Then the eleven disciples left for Galilee, going to the mountain where Jesus had told them to go. When they saw him, they worshiped him—but some of them doubted!

Jesus came and told his disciples, "I have been given all authority in heaven and on earth. Therefore, go and make disciples of all the nations, baptizing them in the name of the Father and the Son and the Holy Spirit. Teach these new disciples to obey all the commands I have given you. And be sure of this: I am with you always, even to the end of the age."

The Message

Meanwhile, the eleven disciples were on their way to Galilee, headed for the mountain Jesus had set for their reunion. The moment they saw him they worshiped him. Some, though, held back, not sure about worship, about risking themselves totally.

Jesus, undeterred, went right ahead and gave his charge: "God authorized and commanded me to commission you: Go out and train everyone you meet, far and near, in this way of life, marking them by baptism in the three-fold name: Father, Son, and Holy Spirit. Then instruct them in the practice of all I have commanded you. I'll be with you as you do this, day after day after day, right up to the end of the age."

As we spend a little bit of time with these words, let's consider what exactly it is that Jesus is giving his disciples and what impact it was meant to have. Once we have, we'll be able to introduce the four qualities with which I believe Jesus wants to 'reCODE' his disciples.

Are you talking to me?

What did Jesus think he was doing when he said these words to his disciples? If he really is the communicator I've suggested, he must have had a clear purpose and must have chosen his words to meet that purpose. So what is it?

My friend and former colleague, Stephen, used to ask three questions about the Great Commission to help make people think:

1. Are we meant to take them *literally*?
2. Are they meant to be carried out by *individuals*?
3. Are they meant to be carried out by *whole churches*?

Once, these questions formed the basis of a devotional time at a meeting of our church and Terry, an eighty-something stalwart of the church, shouted out in response, "Yes! Yes! And yes!" I believe he was right, but the questions are really helpful ones because together they make us ask the difficult question: how seriously do I take the Great Commission?

So are we meant to take these words literally? Does Jesus *really* want his followers to go everywhere in the world, to 'make disciples', to baptise and teach obedience? Does he *really* have all authority? Is he *really* with us in a meaningful way. I don't feel I need to argue that the answer to all of this is a clear 'yes'. There is nothing to suggest he did not mean, in a very literal sense, what he says here. And there is no reason to think that these words had an expiry date either. This wasn't simply Jesus' plan for starting the church. This is Jesus' plan 'to the very end of the age'—if it weren't, it would make more sense to say, "I am with you, until I tell you to stop all this disciple-making and move on to stage two." But he doesn't. This is Jesus' plan. Not just then, but now. Not just for them, but for us.

Of course, we need to ask of ourselves whether our lives and churches behave as if it is literal. And that leads us on to Stephen's next questions: is the commission to be received individually or corporately? While I echo Terry's triple 'Yes!', lets unpack this a little further. Because there is a danger that we end up excusing ourselves of really following Jesus here. What do I mean?

Let's start at the corporate level because it's a slightly easier place to start. In practice this is often how we in the western church expect it to work. We put great stock in Paul's image of a body with many parts (1 Corinthians 12:12-31). 'I'm not really an evangelist,' we might say, 'but that's okay because my part lies elsewhere.' So, even though we might not say it out loud, our practices show that we believe some will do the planting ('go and make disciples'), some will get to reap ('baptise them') and some will help with growth ('teach them to obey'). And, if we're really honest, many Christians do not see any of those as their role. They 'play their part' by attending or contributing to worship services, providing finance, praying or carrying out other roles within a church.

Isn't there some truth here though? Paul said to those same Corinthians, "I planted the seed, Apollos watered it, but God has been making it grow." (1 Corinthians 3:6) When I look back over my own life, the people that have poured into me have all played very different roles. None of them has been the full package, save Jesus himself.

So yes, there is some truth here, but it is not the whole truth. If you were to say, 'my shape as a disciple seems to fit more often in training for obedience than in leading people to a decision for Jesus', then that might very well be true. But, if you were to say 'I could *never* baptise someone, that's just not my part to play' then I ask you to reconsider. We are all called into Jesus' disciple-making, baptising and obedience-teaching work as individuals, not just as part of a greater whole. This is absolutely vital. To see why, let's turn to the individual level now.

The question is: does Jesus want individuals to take this 'Great Commission' to heart and do it? There are many reasons to think he did. I'll give two.

First, *it was given to individuals in the first place*. This message was given to a group who, at this time, were not the formed 'church'. Jesus did not wait until the Jerusalem church of Acts 2 was established. Nor did he wait until the various churches we hear of in the New Testament (in Corinth, Berea, Galatia, Laodicea, etc.) were set up and then gather their leaders together to give the Great Church Commission. He chose this moment, these people and this set of instructions. He didn't start with a fully-formed church. He started with individual disciples. Like you and me.

The second reason we need to hear the Great Commission individually is because of *the language Jesus chooses to use*. The language is about individual disciples being made, not about communities and structures. The three 'results' of this commission are things that happen in the life of an individual person: they become a disciple, they are baptised and they become obedient to Christ's commands. Of course these often happen in the presence of a community and the culture of that community will 'rub off' on us, but they cannot be done *by* that community on a person's behalf. I am baptised not because I am in a church where baptisms happen but because, on March 24th 2002, I got dunked!

And consider the experience that these 11 individuals had of being discipled. Who did that in them? Not a community, but a man. One man: Jesus. The way they would have heard this is simple: as individuals, go and make individual disciples, who will then go and do the same.

We miss the individual call of the Great Commission when we leave disciple-making to extraverted evangelists and the Alpha Course. We miss it when only our clergy and church leaders perform baptisms. We miss it when 'teaching to obey' is the job of the preacher in the pulpit and no-one else. If we have adopted this mindset, we need to re-hear the Great Commission as it was initially given: to all.

If it feels like I'm labouring this point, I am, but I've done so for a reason. I want to be extremely clear: everything in the Great Commission is for you! It is a task Jesus wants you to engage with, but it is also something that should form and shape the kind of disciple you are to begin with.

The CODE of the Great Commission

So, what do we learn from the Great Commission about the kind of healthy discipleship DNA Jesus wants us to have? If this moment of formation and commissioning is for all of us to receive, how should it transform us?

This book began with a question: what kind of person do you

need be to do the things God wants you to do? In other words, what needs to be *in us* so that the life Jesus wants can flow *out of us*? I see in these words from Jesus big clues that help answer that question. There are four qualities of healthy discipleship DNA that are vital in the Great Commission. Together they are the ingredients of what I've been calling CODE, and I will introduce them now.

Confidence in Jesus

Often when the Great Commission is quoted, we launch in: "Go and make disciples…" We miss out the 'therefore'. But as many of us have been taught by someone wise (for me, an old youth worker), when you see 'therefore' you need to ask what it's 'there for'. What is the 'therefore' that leads us to 'go'?

> Then Jesus came to them and said, "All authority in heaven and on earth has been given to me. Therefore…" (v18)

Jesus' words do not begin with instruction, command or strategy. He starts on their hearts—confused, doubting and struggling hearts. Three years they spent with him, seeing his authority firsthand and learning to trust his judgment, teaching, and wisdom. Then the horror of the cross. Then the silence of the tomb. Then the questions of the reports of his resurrection. It is not a group of confident, certain and sure disciples who Jesus comes to.

But Jesus knows without a right confidence placed in him they would never be able to go on to do the things he is about to call them to. So he reminds them of what they have already learned about him: he has authority. Not just some authority but all of it. Not just in heaven where he was going ahead of them, but on earth where they were staying. The cross hadn't stripped him of it. He hadn't left it in the tomb. It was his birthright and it always would be.

This would also trigger some memories for them because this wasn't the first time Jesus had commissioned them. He had been training and preparing them. In Luke 9:1-6 we see one of these times. On that occasion, they went not to 'all nations' but 'from village to village'. The job was not to make disciples, but 'to proclaim the kingdom of God and to heal the sick'. And another key detail: 'he gave them power and authority to drive out all demons and to cure diseases'.

When Jesus sends out, he gives authority for the task at hand. He did before and he still does. The implication of Jesus is clear: all authority belongs to me, and I share it with you, *therefore* go. For any of us seeking to live a Great Commission life, we need the confidence Jesus wanted the Great Commission to give. The task is great, but the one who sends is greater! Without confidence, rightly placed in Jesus, we will either be unwilling or too timid to follow through.

Obedience to Jesus

Obedience is baked into the passage. It begins with a simple act of obedience: they go 'to the mountain where Jesus had told them to go.' A great start! Then Jesus gives them a command because, at its heart, that is what the Great Commission is:

> *...go and make disciples of all nations, baptising them in the name of the Father and of the Son and of the Holy Spirit, and teaching them to obey everything I have commanded you. (v19-20)*

It is an instruction and when we receive instruction from someone who has the authority to give it, we can do one of two things. We follow it or we do not. If someone has the authority to tell us to do something, we really have nowhere to hide. Our response to them is not just about our behaviour anymore. It is now about our relationship with them and whether or not we respect the authority they have over us. With Jesus, we've just seen there is no higher authority. So when it comes to his instruction, our choices are simple: obedience or disobedience.

But it does not stop there. Obedience to this command will lead to disciples being made, baptised and, crucially, being taught 'to obey everything I have commanded you,' including this very command! With the Great Commission, obedience is vital because it makes us useful in the gospel being spread all over the world. It creates a chain that can go from one generation of disciples to another. Reject the command and the chain gets broken.

Dependence on Jesus

Just as Jesus didn't start with the command, he doesn't end with it either. His closing words are not instruction but encouragement:

> *And surely I am with you always, to the very end of the age." (v20)*

Jesus' authority and his presence stand as two bookends holding the command of the Great Commission in place. We are to be confident because we go in the name of the one who has all authority. But we are not to go arrogantly, thinking that because he has sent us we can now go it alone.

Jesus has already taught these disciples the lesson of dependence: 'If you remain in me and I in you, you will bear much fruit; apart from me you can do nothing.' (John 15:5) Now, after giving them a massive task, he reminds them of his presence. Why? Because this task is not to be done alone but with him and in him. They are to depend on him not just for the job he has given them, but for the strength they will need for every stride.

These three great themes come together in just a few words from Jesus. And each of them needs the others in order to be complete and healthy.

- **Without confidence,** we will be timidly trying to do our best at the things we know God wants from us but not trust him for the outcomes, so will never be convinced he can help even if we ask.

- **Without obedience,** we turn in on ourselves and assume his authority is there to depend on and benefit from ourselves, confidently pursuing our own agenda and attaching his name to it.

- **Without dependence,** we will be sure Jesus can achieve anything he wants and be sure we need to work toward that same goal, but they will sit as parallel paths, never drawing on his strength as we do his work.

The final theme is, I believe, what brings these things together so we do not end up with any of these imbalances.

Experience with Jesus

It might seem like stating the obvious, but these words of Jesus were given when he was with them. They didn't just hear or read the Great Commission. No, they *experienced* Jesus giving them the Great Commission.

But the experience did not start or finish at this moment. Over the three years they had been with Jesus, they had experienced many things and had many experiences of Jesus. These informed one another. What they experienced 'out in the world' was brought back to Jesus. And their time with him helped them understand and frame that experience. After they are sent out, they come back and share experiences (Luke 10:17). Time with Jesus shaped their activity in the world, and experience of the world was submitted back to Jesus.

Likewise, once he has given the Great Commission, Jesus does not expect them to go, do it and never talk about it again. No, going in dependence on him means going, learning, growing, going again and learning again. We see this process throughout the book of Acts as these disciples and those who join them are constantly growing and learning. They find new things in the world and have to make sense of them by going back to Jesus in prayer or by examining them in light of what he has done. They have an experience of Jesus and it reinvigorates their mission to the parts of the world he has led them to.

This is why I speak about experience *with* Jesus, not just experience *of* Jesus. Having an experience of Jesus is fantastic, and we should be seeking that in our lives. But it is only part of the picture. It is meant to be a cycle, an ongoing process of life lived *with* Jesus where everything is up for grabs, not just occasional experiences *of* him that fill us up for a bit until we feel we need another one.

Someone who has more experience in a certain field (like plumbing or teaching) will normally be more competent than someone with less experience. So it should be that the more experience we have of following Jesus the more our confidence will be in him, the more obedient to his commands we will be and the more we will have learned the art of depending on him above all. Our experience with him will lead to these things, and they will then lead us into new territory, new experiences of the world, new opportunities to obey, new need for dependence, new discoveries of his authority in which we have confidence. And onward we go!

Sometimes, though, the reverse is true. Where new converts show confidence in God ('If he did it for me, he can do it for anyone!'), others can be more jaded. Where new believers seek God's will for every decision so they can be obedient, others can just settle into a pattern and stay there. Where those young in faith have a childlike dependence on their heavenly Father, others can settle into an independent attitude and stop relying so much on God. If this is true for you, if more experiences *of* Jesus and more experience *with* Jesus is not leading to a greater trust, faithfulness and reliance, perhaps it is time to consider what the nature of that experience has become.

Confidence makes us willing. Obedience makes us useful. Dependence makes us effective. And experience makes us grow.

An invitation: let Jesus reCODE your life

So the Great Commission is the launchpad for the book. These four vital parts of healthy discipleship DNA flow from it and are all needed if we are to be good at it. But while the Great Commission is where we start, it is not where we end. We will return to it many times and at the end of each section do so very fully to see how what we have discovered applies directly to it. But we will also take a much more expansive view of each theme, looking beyond the Great Commission to ask what else the Bible has to say as we ask Jesus to reCODE us.

At the start of each section in this book, we will briefly explore one story in the Bible where all four qualities are evident, but where one in particular is centre stage. There is a pattern of people experiencing God and/or situations in ways that build confidence, call for obedience and require dependence. When they follow in those ways, greater and deeper things await, so that their experience of God and in the world are transformed, stronger and fuller.

And as the people in those stories go through these events, learn these lessons, and take steps forward, they experience what it means for Jesus to reCODE them from the inside out.

That, really, is the invitation I lay before you now. I believe Jesus wants to reCODE your spiritual life with a deeper and healthier discipleship DNA. Will you let him? Will you ask him?

Chapter 1 at a glance…

In this chapter, we:

1. Introduced the Great Commission and got familiar with it.

2. Asked whether the Great Commission is intended for every follower of Jesus to carry out, and concluded it is indeed for all of us.

3. Introduced each aspect of CODE (Confidence, Obedience, Dependence and Experience), seeing how they are formed through the way Jesus chooses to give the Great Commission.

4. Began to consider how these different qualities relate to one another, considering a pattern that can be found elsewhere in the Bible.

PART 1

CONFIDENCE IN JESUS

Then Jesus came to them and said,
"All authority in heaven and on
earth has been given to me."

(Matthew 28:18)

Acts 4:23-31

Our first spotlight comes near the start of the book of Acts. The church has been born at Pentecost, and the first real episode in the life of the church is found in Acts 3—4. I recommend you go and read the whole thing, because really it is one whole story. It starts with a healing, leading to a crowd hearing the good news of Jesus. The authorities aren't happy with that, so Peter and John are hauled up and told to stop preaching about Jesus. They refuse, are threatened, but are ultimately released. Then we read this:

Acts 4:23-31
23 On their release, Peter and John went back to their own people and reported all that the chief priests and the elders had said to them. 24 When they heard this, they raised their voices together in prayer to God. "Sovereign Lord," they said, "you made the heavens and the earth and the sea, and everything in them. 25 You spoke by the Holy Spirit through the mouth of your servant, our father David:

'Why do the nations rage
and the peoples plot in vain?
26 The kings of the earth rise up
and the rulers band together
against the Lord
and against his anointed one.'

²⁷ Indeed Herod and Pontius Pilate met together with the Gentiles and the people of Israel in this city to conspire against your holy servant Jesus, whom you anointed. ²⁸ They did what your power and will had decided beforehand should happen. ²⁹ Now, Lord, consider their threats and enable your servants to speak your word with great boldness. ³⁰ Stretch out your hand to heal and perform signs and wonders through the name of your holy servant Jesus."

³¹ After they prayed, the place where they were meeting was shaken. And they were all filled with the Holy Spirit and spoke the word of God boldly.

The focus of our brief exploration of this passage will be around the *confidence* this community has and finds in Jesus, but first let's have a look at the whole of CODE at work through this episode.

The Complete CODE

This whole story begins because Peter, John and a lame beggar have an *experience* that changes everything. He asks for money but instead receives physical healing that leads to his spiritual life being restored —he heads off 'into the temple courts, walking and jumping, and praising God'. This leads many others, who recognise him, to have a new *experience* of God which challenges them. They want to make sense of it, so a crowd gathers and the good news is preached. One of the results is that the early Christian community have their first taste of persecution. The question: how will this *experience* shape them? Will they retreat or advance?

Or perhaps it starts with *obedience*. Peter and John are just doing what Jesus had taught them to do. He had sent them out to heal and proclaim the good news (in Luke 9 and 10), and they are being *obedient* to him. They see someone who is lame, they declare healing in Jesus' name and then they proclaim the good news when a crowd gathers. When persecution comes, Jesus has already prepared them for that, too: "In this world you will have trouble. But take heart! I have overcome the world." (John 16:33) So when they are arrested, the question is not what to do about it. The question is whether they will be *obedient* to what Jesus has already told them to do about it. Will they take heart? Will they trust that he is greater than their enemies and keep doing what he told them to do?

And *dependence* on God is woven throughout as well. It is there in the healing: "Silver or gold I do not have, but what I do have I give you. In the name of Jesus Christ of Nazareth, walk." (Acts 3:6) They *depend* on Jesus for the healing. They are not the heroes. It is there also in their proclamation of the good news: "Why do you stare at us as if by our own power or godliness we have made this man walk?" (Acts 3:12) This is then followed by a declaration of the power of Jesus. They do not want eyes on themselves, but eyes turned to Jesus, "for there is no other name under heaven given to mankind by which we must be saved." Jesus, Jesus, Jesus. So what will they do when they are under attack and know their enemies are too strong for them? They do the most natural thing in the world to them: they turn in *dependence* and in prayer to God.

And the result is a new, deeper and stronger…*confidence*.

Ask and you shall receive

But why is it that confidence is what they receive when they turn to God in prayer? That's very simple: it's what they asked for! The situation they faced was serious. The religious elite were against them, locking them up, and threatening them. These people were not messing around. Just weeks earlier, these same people had nailed Jesus to a cross. Very soon after, they would stand by as Stephen is stoned to death and becomes the first Christian martyr. The threat is serious.

But they do not ask God to stop the threats. In fact, the only thing they ask God to do about those threats is consider them: "Now Lord, consider their threats." The threats are, in this prayer, simply the context they are living in, to be noted but not to be changed.

What they actually pray for is an increase of…exactly what got them into this mess in the first place! They pray for two things: for God to "enable [them] to speak with great boldness," and to "heal and perform signs and wonders through the name of your holy servant Jesus." These same two things—words and wonders—were what they had done in Acts 3 to provoke the difficulty in Acts 4. And they are asking for God to do it more!

If you are thinking they are acting foolishly, that they should have just laid low for a little bit, you have God to answer to. Because God immediately endorses their prayer by answering it with a divine 'Yes'! We hear that "the place where they were meeting was shaken" (wonders) and "they were all filled with the Holy Spirit and spoke the word of God boldly" (words).

What both they and God knew they needed was not for things to get easier but for an increase in their boldness, their confidence to keep on going. I say an increase because they have already displayed a lot of confidence. In fact it was their 'courage' which made their enemies pause for thought when Peter and John were hauled up in front of them (Acts 4:13). But they pray for an increase in boldness, in confidence, because they know they will need more of it.

But it is not just that they need a greater level of confidence and courage. It is also that a greater number of them will need it. So far it is Peter and John who have borne the brunt of the kickback, but it will not stay that way. Soon, persecution and threats will hit all of them, which is perhaps why when God answers their prayer they were '*all* filled with the Holy Spirit and spoke the word of God boldly.' Just as the Great Commission is not just for the leaders, but for everyone, so this confidence was for every member of the Christian community.

There are times when what could stop us pursuing Jesus, his calling and his Great Commission will be our level of confidence. This was one of those moments. We will face those as well. Not just because of persecution or danger, but because of all sorts of things. Doubts about God's nature. Questions we don't feel we have good enough answers to. Situations we weren't expecting. Situations we were expecting but were also dreading. Time changing the way we view God, his word or the good news, perhaps wondering if it really is good news after all.

These early Christians had a degree of confidence—of faith—in God, and I suspect you do as well if you are reading this book. But that faith might be under pressure, or might get strained. Like these early disciples, we sometimes need to seek God for a greater measure of it and, vitally, look for it in the right places. So keep their story in mind as we continue on. We will return to it a few times as we now explore what kind of confidence it is that Jesus wants to inspire and grow in us.

No tiptoeing on the glacier

I am sometimes mistaken for a 'confident person'. I think it's because I can stand on a stage in front of lots of people and talk pretty coherently and clearly. For lots of people that is the stuff of nightmares and for many more it is just something they are not keen on or particularly good at. But take me off the stage and remove the microphone and I am actually quite shy. I normally find speaking to 100 strangers easier than speaking to one. I find small-talk harder than big-talk.

It goes further than that, though. On a sailing boat I can confidently know what I'm doing. Hand me a musical instrument and I have no clue. Put me in a kitchen and I can make you something tasty. Ask me to fix your car and it'll be a very different story. For every single one of us, there will be situations where we are confident and ones where we are not. If there is any such thing as a 'confident person', it is surely more to do with how we handle situations where we aren't naturally confident. Do we crumble or do we give it a good go? Do we cope out of our comfort zones or not?

Confidence is part of the spiritual genetic CODE Jesus wants his followers to have. It is a quality he wishes to infuse us with and see us live out. But what is it? I probably do not have to convince you that confidence has a few close relatives that are not so desirable, like arrogance, pride, narcissism, and just generally being a know-it-all. But if, in the desire to avoid those things, we simply become timid and unsure, we are also going to be held back. 'For the Spirit God gave us does not make us timid...' (2 Timothy 1:7)

So we are going to take a look at a few things that hang on this idea of confidence to see where it should be placed and what it is meant to look like.

Confidence in...what?

There is a danger in writing about our need for confidence. If I focus on my own confidence more than on the one in whom our confidence should rest, I've shot myself in the foot. Glen Scrivener calls this 'thingification':

> We're always making a *thing* out of things that aren't things. There's a technical term for this but I'm just going to call it *thingification*. The name's not important. What is important is that it's ruining your Christian life.[10]

But why would thinking about my level of confidence as a Christian ruin my Christian life? That sounds a bit extreme! Well, Scrivener unpacks this a little by speaking about something very much linked to our confidence: our 'faith'.

> We must constantly remind ourselves that faith is not a thing. It is not a possession by which we make claim to salvation. Faith is the absence of a thing - it is the confession of a complete lack. To even ask 'Am I having faith?' is already an unbelieving question for *faith is looking away to Christ.*[11]

I agree with this, but I want to stay with it for a moment. Confidence in and of itself is meaningless, it is nothing, it is not a thing. Whether confidence is good or bad, right or wrong, depends *entirely* on the thing it is placed in. I can be utterly confident that I can walk across a thinly frozen lake, but I will still plunge into it. I can have zero confidence placing my weight on a glacier, but I will not suddenly fall through it.

Your level of confidence does not make something true or false.

You do not have that kind of power.

The danger of making confidence into the main thing is that it all becomes about us, about you and me. How strong is your faith? How confident is your Christianity? It is all about us. This is why 'thingification' must be avoided. But that does not mean all talk of confidence must be avoided. It is true, our level of confidence does not make something true or false. But it does affect how we relate to that thing. It can mean we tiptoe around the glacier when we could be jumping, skiing or having a snowball fight. If we are to live as followers of Jesus *as fully as possible* and to be people who fulfil his Great Commission in the world, a correct kind of confidence is vital.

So, how do we focus on it without 'thingifying' it? We focus less on the confidence itself and more on what the confidence is placed in. That is what we need to know is sure, certain and will hold our weight. When we know that, confidence will follow. So, what should our confidence be in? I want to suggest three answers, all seen in those early Christians praying for boldness in Acts 4.

Confidence in God

This is not really a stunning revelation: our confidence as Christians should be in God. As we stay with this theme in the next two chapters, I hope to show how, in practice, our confidence is often found in many other things, but this is where the compass *should* be pointing. Confidence in God is our true north.

We see this over and over in the Scriptures, beautiful scenes of people placing their confidence in God. Whether it is Moses standing before the tyrant, Pharaoh, safe because he has heard God's "I am who I am", or whether it is Joshua rallying his people to be 'strong and courageous' because God is with them. Whether it is David's trust in God as he goes out to fight Goliath or Solomon's call to 'trust in the Lord with all your heart', this thread of deep confidence in God recurs again and again.[12] And we love to see it!

But we also see the opposite, people losing confidence in God and putting it in something else. Whether it is Eve listening to the serpent's "Did God really say...?", or whether it is the Israelites getting Aaron to make a golden calf to worship instead of waiting for Moses to come down the mountain.[13] Whether it is the cycle in Judges of rejecting God and coming back to him only to reject him again, or the faithlessness of the nation that would lead to their exile, this thread of confidence *not* being in God also abounds in Scripture. And if we are reading it correctly, it makes us uncomfortable because we see ourselves in it. We too often place *our* confidence elsewhere.

But the Christians who gathered and prayed in Acts 4 stand in the long line of those who make the choice to place confidence, trust and faith in God over anything else: "Sovereign Lord," they said, "you made the heavens and the earth and the sea, and everything in them." (Acts 4:24) That is a God worth praying to, so they do! If God made everything—including the place their leaders have just been imprisoned, the people who threaten them and even the heaven they trust would be their home if they are killed—then rather than turn *from* him when things get tough, they are going to draw closer *to* him.

Returning briefly to the Great Commission, we noted in the last chapter that Jesus begins his words by instilling confidence: "All authority in heaven and on earth has been given to me. Therefore…" (Matthew 28:18) This is a declaration of his sovereignty, his complete rule and reign over all things, which is exactly the same quality these believers call out as they turn to God in prayer.

It is worth us considering for a moment the nature of the God in whom we are to put our confidence. You might have noticed that these believers were praying to God the Father (we know they are not praying *to* Jesus because their prayer refers to 'your holy servant Jesus'), but Jesus has said that all authority is his. So who is our confidence in: Father or Son? The simple answer, of course, is 'yes'.

This is not the place to consider the Trinity very fully, but it is important that we understand something here: when we place our confidence in Jesus, we *are* placing our confidence in the Father and we can *only* do this through the work of the Holy Spirit in our lives. Jesus is very clear: there is not one inch of separation between him and his Father. Consider Jesus' words here:

> *Don't you believe that I am in the Father, and that the Father is in me? The words I say to you I do not speak on my own authority. Rather, it is the Father, living in me, who is doing his work. Believe me when I say that I am in the Father and the Father is in me; or at least believe on the evidence of the works themselves. (John 14:10-11)*

The authority Jesus has is given him by the Father. To look at the life, teaching, heart and personality of Jesus is to see the depths of God's being. But it does not stop there, kept in an exclusive holy huddle. No, the Spirit invites us to join and share in that as well. Jesus says, on the same evening:

> He will glorify me because it is from me that he [the Spirit] will receive what he will make known to you. All that belongs to the Father is mine. That is why I said the Spirit will receive from me what he will make known to you."
> (John 16:14-15)

Writing about these words of Jesus in his fantastic book on the Trinity, *The Good God*, Mike Reeves says:

> The Spirit takes what is the Son's and makes it ours. When the Spirit rested upon the Son at his baptism, Jesus heard the Father declare from heaven: 'This is my beloved Son in whom I am well pleased.' But now that the same Spirit of sonship rests on me, the same words apply to me: in Christ my high priest I am...adopted, beloved, Spirit-anointed.[14]

Why does this make a difference to our confidence in God? If we let it, it will make all the difference! Our confidence is in *this* God, not just in some general idea of 'god'. And *this* God is the one who invites us into an eternal relationship of love and self-giving. We are not confident in God simply because he is big and we want to be on the winning side. No, we are confident in God because he is love and he has given us himself that we might be close to his side. It also makes all the difference because it is no longer our own confidence in God that matters. It is the Son's confidence in the Father given to us as a gift by the Spirit. "No one can say, "Jesus is Lord," except by the Holy Spirit" (1 Corinthians 12:3). We do not muster this from within. We receive it from on high. That is true confidence in God.

Before we consider what this sort of confidence (or lack of it) looks like biblically, there are two other (related) places our confidence should lie. Both are gifts from God, and both are sturdy. They are God-given glaciers and we can trust them with our weight.

Confidence in the gospel

We can have confidence in the gospel, the good news of Jesus for us and for the world. In the Acts 4 prayer meeting, this confidence is expressed as well. Praying about those who crucified Jesus, they say,

"They did what your power and will had decided beforehand should happen" (Acts 4:28). They are not embarrassed that Jesus was killed because they know this was what he came to do. And they know why he came to do it. It was, after all, preaching this same message that started the threats against them:

> You killed the author of life, but God raised him from the dead. We are wit-
> nesses of this... Repent, then, and turn to God, so that your sins may be
> wiped out, that times of refreshing may come from the Lord... (Acts 3:15,
> 19)

The Apostle Paul knew this as well. He declared, "I am not ashamed of the gospel, because it is the power of God that brings salvation to everyone who believes" (Romans 1:16). The news that Jesus entered our world, lived the perfect life, died in our place and rose to grant us glorious life is not only very, very good news for those who will re-ceive it in repentance. It is solid news. There is nothing in it we need worry about or be ashamed of.

Paul also knew, though, that people would be ashamed of this very message. It is not the news everyone *wants* to hear. The Chris-tians in Corinth were becoming unsure of this gospel and wondering if there might be another one, one that casts them in a better light and is easier for others to swallow. Paul pulls no punches. He begins and ends his response with these two statements:

> For the message of the cross is foolishness to those who are perishing, but to
> us who are being saved it is the power of God. (1 Corinthians 1:18)

> For the foolishness of God is wiser than human wisdom, and the weakness of
> God is stronger than human strength. (1 Corinthians 1:25)

Paul describes the cross as foolish in the eyes of the world. What kind of 'god' would allow himself to be nailed to a cross? Everyone knows that's not what gods do! They kill their enemies because they are more powerful. A cross? Really! It is utter stupidity! Not only stupid, but weak as well. If this Jesus is weak enough to be arrested and exe-cuted, why in the world would you want to follow him? What could a weak god like that possibly do for you? So it appears to the Greeks who look for wisdom and strength, Paul reminds the Corinthians. But this is the gospel God has given us and those who are being saved know its true power. Jesus was cursed and killed so we might have blessing and life. John Stott puts it well:

> Powerless wisdom or foolish power: it was (and still is) a fateful choice. The one combination which is not an option is the wisdom of the world plus the power of God.[15]

The western world is not that different from Corinth. We also love to appear wise, and we also admire displays of strength. Add to that the fact that nobody wants to be told they are broken, sinful and in need of God's forgiveness and we see why shame about the gospel can begin to creep in. But this is the gospel we have been given because it is the gospel the world needed! It will hold our weight.

Confidence in the Bible

There's one more: the Bible. Another gift from God that we can trust. Because none of what we've thought about so far comes from us sitting down and working things out. We know what God is like *because he has told us*. We know what the gospel is (the one we need not the one we wanted) *because he has told us*. God reveals himself and, in his infinite wisdom, he has chosen to give us the Bible to do so.

Returning again to our persecuted brothers and sisters of Acts 4, they had a confidence in the Scriptures. A lot of their prayer is taken up with Scripture. They begin, "You spoke by the Holy Spirit through the mouth of your servant David…", then quote a portion of Psalm 2, see how Jesus is revealed in it, apply that to their own situation and then pray in light of it. It's a great prayer, but also a fantastic lesson in how to do theology!

Psalm 2 is a coronation Psalm, and coronations were dangerous times. Between one king and the next, a nation is weaker and enemies would often try to seize the moment to invade. The part they quote reflects that: "The kings of the earth rise up…against the Lord and against his anointed one." But they aren't praying a history lesson. They know this Psalm is truly about Jesus because *he* is the Lord's anointed one. So now they see those who are threatening them as the 'kings of the earth' trying to strike while they look weak. But they know what others do not: Jesus' death does not make them weak, and the king is still on the throne, so it is a time for boldness not shrinking back. And *all of that* informs the prayer that leads to renewed boldness.

But why such confidence in the Scriptures? Simply, it is the origin of the Bible that means we should sit up, take notice and trust it. Confidence in God should lead us naturally to confidence in Scripture.

Remember when Jesus promised that his Spirit would "receive from me what he will make known to you" (John 16:15)? Something very similar is going on when we think of what the Bible is. I do not believe the inspiration of the Scriptures is the only way he takes what the Father has given the Son and makes it ours, but it is the main way. When Paul writes that "all Scripture is God-breathed" (2 Timothy 3:16), we see this at work. The Greek word *pneuma* means both 'spirit' and 'breath' (and also 'wind'; the same is true of the Hebrew word *ruach*). If the Bible is 'breathed out' by God we must understand that as being the work of the Spirit inspiring the many human authors of the Bible. That means it comes from God. And that means we can have confidence in it.

Jesus himself reinforces this. Speaking in Judea early on in his ministry he says, "Do not think that I have come to abolish the Law or the Prophets; I have not come to abolish them but to fulfil them," going on to say that not a single part of it should be removed and warning against any attempt to do so (Matthew 5:17-19). Andrew Wilson comments:

> That's hugely challenging. Many of us, when faced with a biblical difficulty – and there are plenty of those! – conclude that the Scriptures are broken. Maybe this didn't really happen. Maybe God didn't really say that. Hardly a day goes past without some Christian, somewhere, apologising for something the Bible says, and muttering something about it being a human book, complete with muddles and mistakes.

> But if the Scriptures are the unbreakable word of God, as Jesus seems to have thought they were, then a different approach is needed. Maybe it's my interpretation, or my assumptions, that need challenging. Maybe there is something I don't know. Maybe the answer is in there, and I just need to look a bit harder.[16]

We will return to this idea further in the next chapter, but for now it is enough to state that the Bible, like the gospel, is worthy of our confidence. Because God is.

Three ways to put God first

But God knew people would find it hard to place their confidence fully in him, and many times in the Bible he gets out ahead to prepare them for it. We see this in one of the most famous parts of the Bible: the 10 Commandments. We are going to look at how these commands are given, then the content of the first three. We'll find that in them God helps his people to trust him, to have the confidence to put him first.

The 10 Commandments start not with command but declaration: "I am the LORD your God, who brought you out of Egypt, out of the land of slavery." (Exodus 20:2) God is about to give the Israelites many instructions for how to live, worship, and conduct themselves in the land he is taking them to. All of that will mean nothing unless they remember who is giving the instructions. It is the very God who *just* rescued them, demonstrating his power and his love for them. He is worthy of their trust and their obedience. And this is underscored by the same thing our Acts 4 prayer meeting experienced: the ground shook (Exodus 19:18). This is how the commandments are given and it is meant to fill them with courage and awe. They can trust the lawgiver, not just follow the law.

Let's read up to the first three commandments and dig into them a little. After that, we'll consider ways that we might need to hear them and let them guide us into a life where confidence is more squarely placed on God.

And God spoke all these words:

"I am the Lord your God, who brought you out of Egypt, out of the land of slavery.

"You shall have no other gods before me.

"You shall not make for yourself an image in the form of anything in heaven above or on the earth beneath or in the waters below. You shall not bow down to them or worship them; for I, the Lord your God, am a jealous God, punishing the children for the sin of the parents to the third and fourth generation of those who hate me, but showing love to a thousand generations of those who love me and keep my commandments.

"You shall not misuse the name of the Lord your God, for the Lord will not hold anyone guiltless who misuses his name." (Exodus 20:1-7)

1. Worship God only

The first command is the shortest and the simplest: do not have any other gods. In the extremely polytheistic world Israel was about to be led into, this was not going to be easy. Not only would every nation they meet have their own set of gods, but a lot of the different tribes or families within them would as well. Then there were the gods of harvest, fertility, rain, war, economics, family, safe travel and so on. In the everyday life of the average Canaanite there would be lots of different acts of worship to appease whichever gods the activity of that day interacted with. It was a complicated business! But for Israel, 'the Lord your God is one.' (Deuteronomy 6:5) They must not get caught up in this kind of thinking or living.

God's people were and are to worship God alone, not set him alongside or under other deities. As Christians, we know that this one God is ultimately expressed to us in Jesus and that to make him our Lord, empowered by the Spirit to do so, is pleasing to the Father. Jesus is to have that place in our lives. Nothing or nobody else. This is about having the confidence to put Jesus ahead of everything else.

2. Worship God directly

Am I the only one who, for a very long time, did not realise there were two commandments that look like they are saying the same thing? When listing the 10 Commandments, I could count them off on my hands: 'no lying, no murder, no adultery, no coveting, no idols, honour your parents…' and already I've made a mistake! 'No idols' is not one command but, in some senses, two commands.[17] Have a look back at the first two commandments again. Why are they both needed?

They say very similar things, but they are different. The first speaks of 'gods' and the second 'images'. So the first is about not having other gods at all, and the second is about not creating something as an image of the one true God and then worshiping that. This is because of another very common practice they would encounter. Because all of these 'gods' (harvest, tribal, etc.) were invisible, people found it helpful to make a statue or carving to be a physical representation of them. Of course what ends up happening is that the statue *becomes* the object of worship, not the god it is there to represent. God does not want his people to do that. He would give them various things to connect them to him (priests, temples, the Law, sacrifices), but they must never let those things become the focus of their worship. That is only ever God.

If the words about God being 'jealous' here are uncomfortable, remember that jealousy is not always a bad thing. There is a kind of jealousy that is awful and paralysing for a relationship: the kind that means your children, spouse or friend cannot even speak to another person without paranoia setting in that their love and devotion to you is in question. But if a commitment is made that is actually broken, that is a different story. If someone's spouse breaks commandment seven (adultery), jealousy is a healthy response not a wrong one. It is the same with God. He is not looking to catch us out and punish. He is looking to bless. That is why faithfulness has a reward far longer-lasting ('a thousand generations') than unfaithfulness.

3. God first, you second

This is another commandment we often don't notice or think about. God's people were not to 'misuse the name of the Lord'. What sort of 'misuse' did God have in mind? Nowadays we often think the biggest violation is using 'God', 'Jesus' or 'Christ' as swear words. That is misuse of God's name, even though it is so common that 'Oh my God!' has become almost just part of the English language. God is God, and we should be careful with his name.

But that is not really the focus I see in God giving the third commandment. It is a lot closer to forging someone's signature, putting their name to a document or agreement that they are not choosing to make. A very normal way to use the name of a god (Baal, Marduk, Yahweh, or any other) was to swear oaths in their name. It is saying that your god will back up your promise, bringing them into the deal you are making with somebody else. So why is God against that? Very simply, it gets God and his people the wrong way round. It is not for me to set the agenda and then put God's name down as a signatory so it carries more weight. No, it is for God to set the agenda and for me to put my name to it, following in his plans.

A similar thing happens when Christians take Jesus' encouragement to 'pray for anything in my name' and assume we are now in the driving seat. I can get what *I* want so long as I tack on 'in Jesus' name, amen' to the end of my prayer. No! To truly ask for something in Jesus' name means it must be something he will put his name to. It is an invitation to conform our will to his as much as it is a promise of fruitful prayer when we do. The third commandment is about this: do we have the confidence in God's purposes to put our name to his plans instead of trying it the other way round?

So these three commands, given as God gathers his people up from a place of slavery and sets them off in the direction of the new life he is leading them to, share a similar heart. God wants his people to know they can place confidence squarely and securely in him. They need no other god. He is enough. They do not need to build a go-between. He is theirs. They do not need their own agenda. His is far better.

He is the glacier, and this is how to avoid the temptation to tiptoe.

The problem of idols: what has your heart?

So far, as we've thought about what confidence in God looks like, we've looked at it positively. We've considered the God in whom we can place our confidence, the good gospel worth staking our lives on, the very word of God given to us. And we've considered three ways God gives us to keep our confidence in him.

Of course, there is the other side too. We've already mentioned a few people in the Bible who *didn't* place their confidence in God and the fact these three commands are given means God must know we'll be tempted to live another way and need a warning. So it is worth us spending a little time considering things negatively, the opposite of confidence. And, as is already clear from these three commandments, this means looking at the idols in our lives.

So what is an idol and how do we spot them in our lives? The late Tim Keller describes them like this: "It is anything more important to you than God, anything that absorbs your heart and imagination more than God, anything you seek to give you what only God can give."[18] It is a helpful description, and it should prompt us to look inward and ask some big questions of ourselves, inviting the Holy Spirit to help us answer them. Questions like:

- What did I spend the first few minutes of my day thinking about, dwelling on and doing today? And likewise for the last moments of the day before sleeping?

- If I were to look back at the last month of my calendar, how would I find that I have spent my time, efforts and energies?

- What does my bank statement say about my priorities?

- When I am daydreaming, waiting for the kettle to boil, walking the dog or standing in line to pay for my shopping, where does my mind wander?

- What does my internet browsing history or use of social media reveal?

- What gets me excited and energised, or angry and despairing?

- When I am with those closest to me, where does the conversation go? What always comes up and what never comes up?

If our aim is to place absolute confidence in Jesus because 'all authority in heaven and on earth' belongs to him, then we should be asking these sorts of things. We should be looking for things we might have allowed to have too much authority over us. And we should be taking steps to dethrone them.

Of course, some of these 'idols' in our lives will be very specific. The sports team you spend all your time thinking about, the person your whole life centres on, the hobby you pour all your disposable income into, the career you do anything to advance, or the popularity you crave above all else. Others, though, are going to be more general. Here are a few big ones I see operating in the Western world, so much part of the air we breathe that they feel more like how the world works than like a choice we are making ourselves:

The accumulation of stuff (consumerism & materialism)

As I write this in 2024, the global advertising market is very soon expected to tip over the $1 trillion mark.[19] That means that companies across the world will spend a total of a million million dollars trying to get us to buy new things (I had to look up what a trillion is when I read that, just to make sure.) Of course, these companies are not stupid. They know it will be worth their while doing so, which means the amount of money we'll give to them for those new things will be even more staggering!

Our world loves to spend money on things because our world

loves things. New things. Shiny things. Better, more up-to-date things. Do I *need* to upgrade my iPhone. Probably not, but it feels a very natural thing to do. Do I have more clothes than I can actually sensibly wear? Yes, I do. Do I have a really good reason for that? No, I never thought to come up with one, it's just normal.

Jesus warns us, 'where your treasure is, there your heart will be also' (Matthew 6:21). Paul had something similar to say: 'Command those who are rich in this present world not to be arrogant nor to put their hope in wealth, which is so uncertain, but to put their hope in God, who richly provides us with everything for our enjoyment' (1 Timothy 6:17). We can focus on accumulating more treasure, more stuff, here on earth. Or we can place our treasure with God and find our heart has got caught up with him too.

Stuff isn't bad. Possessions are not evil. Extra money in the bank does not condemn us. But they can be symptoms and indicators that our life is lived to the beat of the world's drum, not God's. It's worth at least asking the question, right?

#YOLO, #FOMO and 'living your best life' (hedonism)

You only live once, so don't miss out! Tomorrow doesn't matter as much as today, so live in the moment and make every second count! This is the mantra of thrill-seekers, of those living life to the full, of people who aren't one of the worst things you could possibly be… boring. Who wants to be boring, steady, perhaps even consistent, when instead you could be edgy, spontaneous and exciting? Add into this a paralysing fear of missing out on the fun others are having and the recipe is complete for a life focused on gaining maximum pleasure from every moment.

I might be slightly over-exaggerating here, but probably only slightly. This idea is very much out there and we all buy into it to one degree or another. It isn't great for us in the parts of life that are important but mundane. Things like work, which can be a slog no matter how much we love our job. Or marriages and parenting, hugely valuable but also hard work if we want to do them well. If the deep centre of your life is a pursuit of happiness, you'll discard anything that doesn't bring it. If it doesn't 'spark joy' (in the words of expert de-clutterer Marie Kondo), it has to go.[20]

The Bible tells us a different story. Instead of joy being rooted in our situations, we are told that 'the joy of the Lord is your strength' (Nehemiah 8:10). God is not anti-fun! Just before these words, the people are told to 'enjoy choice food and sweet drinks'. But ultimately, their strength is not to come from joy in a wonderful meal, but from God. They are weeping when Nehemiah says this, but instead of comforting them with something temporary and fleeting, he points them to an endless source of joy. I can live my best life, but as long as it's *my* best life, it won't be God's best life.

Thank God it's…Sunday (religiosity)

This one isn't as pervasive in our world because it only really applies to those of us who follow Jesus. And it falls into the area of the second commandment, about making an image of God instead of seeking God himself. In our day, the pastor, the sermon, the church service, the worship songs or the building can do that. These are all good things, designed to lead us in community to God. But they can, if we're honest, become the focus of our devotion if we are not careful.

It looks like consuming sermon after sermon, never missing a message from our favourite preacher, but not listening deeply to what God is saying through them and doing something with it. It looks like using the Sunday service as a tick-box to convince ourselves our faith is still going strong. It looks like disengaging in corporate worship times (normally singing) because the song, style or band are not to our liking. It looks like behaving as though God is more interested in what we do in a certain church building than in our workplace, home or school.

It even looks like an unhealthy relationship with the Bible. Jesus says that. When he is challenging the Pharisees, the religious elite of his day, he says:

> You study the Scriptures diligently because you think that in them you have eternal life. These are the very Scriptures that testify about me, yet you refuse to come to me to have life. (John 5:39-40)

The Bible does not contain eternal life. Neither does your pastor, a preacher, a building, a ritual, an event, a song or an experience. Only God does. These things can all lead us deeper and closer into a love for and confidence in God and they are beautiful when they do. But we can also use them to keep us at arm's length. And that is a pretty ugly thing before a God who welcomes and embraces us with open arms.

Who sits on the throne?

At this point, it's important to offer a word of caution: you cannot dethrone an idol by yourself. The reason for that is simple. You can't find a solution for a problem by relying on what caused the problem. And the cause of the idols in your life is, at its root, you. This doesn't sound like good news and it isn't really. The good news is this: the thing which causes us to place confidence in anything other than God is the exact things Jesus has dealt with already. Sin, which leads to confidence in idols instead of God, is no match for the gospel of God!

But sin is real and it is what leads to these idols in the first place. Sin is often described as being 'curved in on oneself'.[21] Instead of 'Jesus, Jesus, Jesus', a sinful life is all about 'me, me, me'. Where do my materialism and consumerism come from? A desire for *my own* riches and success. Why does a hedonistic desire to 'live my best life' appeal? Because *I* want *my* pleasure. What turns religious activity unhealthy? When it becomes about *me, my* preferences and what *I* can enjoy or get out of it.

As long as you stay on the throne of your own life, idols will spring up. In your desire to look out for number one, God becomes an obstacle to overcome, not the focus of your worship and confidence. Jackie Hill Perry is right when she says,

> We are thoughtful with our rebellion. There is a level of reasoning within us when we decide which golden calf we'll love on any given day … We [sin] when we have made the decision not to believe, trust, acknowledge, or depend on who God has revealed Himself as in some way.[22]

God is better. Consumerism? God has revealed himself to be of greater worth than any treasure or riches in this world can be. Hedonism? He promises greater joy than even the most thrill-seeking, daring and complete life can give. Religiosity? The way he makes himself available to us is far purer and more intimate than any religious system we might create that boxes him in or keeps him comfortably at a distance. If we truly wish for him *and nothing else* to be at the centre of our lives, to put him first in reality not just in theory, we have to ask ourselves a question: "Who is on the throne in my life?" It cannot be God if it is already me.

But let's be honest: the world is telling a different story, and it is one we are starting to believe. In his thought-provoking book *The Big Ego Trip*, Glynn Harrison tracks some trends about people's views of self. One example is about a poll asked every year about whether "quality of life in Britain is best improved by (a) looking after the community's interest instead of your own or (b) looking after ourselves, which ultimately raises the standards for all." These were the findings:

> Before the year 2000 the overwhelming majority had chosen (a). Most people thought that the best way to improve the quality of life for everybody was to put other people's interests ahead of their own. But as a new millennium dawned, the gap began to close. And just six years later a majority (53%) of those interviewed chose option (b). For the first time in the history of the poll more people believe in looking after 'me' first.[23]

Hold onto that for a moment as we look at another, which found that:

> …in the early 1950s, only 12% of teens aged fourteen to sixteen agreed with the statement: 'I am an important person.' By the late 1980s, however, a staggering 80% claimed to feel important in this way.[24]

The trend, according to these and other bits of data, is clear: over time, we have learned to think more and more highly of ourselves, to value our own flourishing more and more. Put another way, we believe more and more that we do in fact belong on the throne in our lives.

On one hand, there is something to be celebrated here. The message of the Bible is not that you are a pathetic, worthless maggot who should count yourself lucky if you are ever noticed. Far from it! You are a person, made in God's own image, loved and cherished, so much so that he stepped in to die in your place, win you for an eternal relationship he delights in, and who he chooses to live in by his Spirit and lead into a life of flourishing. You *are* important!

But on the other hand, there is something to be cautious about. If we embrace this too strongly, place too much confidence in ourselves, we risk taking the wrong road to get to the right destination. The road to fulfilment is not self-focus, self-confidence or self-esteem. Instead, Jesus says it is self-denial.

> *Then Jesus said to his disciples, "Whoever wants to be my disciple must deny themselves and take up their cross and follow me. For whoever wants to save their life will lose it, but whoever loses their life for me will find it."* (*Matthew 16:24-25*)

Jesus knew the path to our life, our true life, was shaped like a cross. He embraced that, and invites us to as well. The destination is good, so good, but the path is not quick and easy. He is clear: we must deny ourselves. As long as your ideas, desires and comfort are the ruling principle in your life, full confidence has not been placed in Jesus. Some of your ideas are wrong. Some of your desires are not God's desires for you. Some of the things you see as comfort are not what's best for you. Sin will do that. A life curved in on yourself will make things appear different than they actually are, and we need God to pull us out of that.

But make no mistake, this talk of self-denial is not a negative! Harrison is clear to point out that,

> The gospel *is* about flourishing, of course, but it is also about repentance, self-denial and the way of the cross. And we shouldn't duck that painful reality any more than a decent doctor would try to help her patient by ignoring the symptoms of a deadly disease.[25]

We need the good God who gives himself to us freely and gladly. We need his good gospel, which might appear foolish and weak (who would deny themselves in order to find themselves?). We need his good word that tells us what is true when our own hearts lie to us. We need it to be about him, not an idol, not a go-between, not attaching his name to a promise he never made. Just him, pure and simple. We need our confidence to be squarely and firmly on him.

So, as we turn now to consider how we can grow in that confidence with our head, our heart and our hands, what we will really be doing is answering this question: how can I get off the throne so that Jesus can sit more fully upon it?

Or put another way: if we know the glacier can hold our weight, how can we stop tiptoeing?

Chapter 2 at a glance...

In this chapter, we:

1. Introduced the idea of confidence, considering what it is, and the fact that what really matters is what it is placed in, not just how strong it is.

2. Considered things that, as disciples, Jesus wants us to place confidence in:

    *   God himself—Father, Son and Spirit.
    *   The gospel, because it is the good news that God has given us.
    *   The Bible, because it is how God has revealed things to us.

3. Looked at the first three commandments as biblical instructions about how to place confidence squarely in God:

    *   Commandment 1: nothing coming before God.
    *   Commandment 2: no go-betweens that become 'gods'.
    *   Commandment 3: letting God set the agenda, instead of asking him to follow ours.

4. Explored some of the big 'idols' of our world today, in particular those of consumerism/materialism, hedonism, and religiosity.

5. Concluded by looking at a potential root cause of different ways we do not put confidence in God: a wrong focus on ourselves.

A CONFIDENT
DISCIPLE'S TOOLKIT

How to get off the throne

In each section of this book, we are not just interested in how these qualities of a disciple are *supposed* to look. We are also interested in how we can *actually* look more and more like the ideal. So this chapter is a toolkit of sorts, with five specific steps that can be taken to help you grow in confidence toward God. As mentioned in the Introduction, this toolkit is based around our **heads** (minds, decision-making, thinking), our **hearts** (will, desires, posture toward God) and our **hands** (actions, strength, habits).

HEAD: Confident Decisions

Our thinking defines so much about who we are and how we'll behave. In fact it is a core part of a word Christians use quite a lot: 'repentance'. To repent is more than just 'saying sorry'. It involves a total change of direction—stopping one thing in order to start another. But the word itself means something significant. In Greek, 'repent' is *metanoia*, made up of *meta* ('change') and *noia* ('mind'). So to repent is, at its root, to change our mind. Unless our thinking about something fundamentally changes, it's unlikely anything else will and we'll keep on going with the same actions, same idols and same mistakes.

If it's true that Jesus wants to shape you as a disciple who has deep confidence in him (not yourself), there are two 'decisions' I want to suggest you can make.

1. 'I will see idols for what they are'

"It's just a hobby!" But it's a hobby you devote 20 hours a week to, lots of disposable income and a massive amount of mental energy thinking about. "I need those savings, they're for a rainy day." But just how rainy a day are you anticipating? And is building up more and more as a buffer for that uncertain future stopping you using the money God has entrusted you in a very concrete present? "They're my kids, I just want them to be happy." But is a desire for your child's (or partner's) happiness (or success, or security, or…) becoming more important than their godliness? "Right now I'm focusing on my career, what's wrong with that?" But if it's at the expense of your discipleship or marriage, might it have a place in your life it was never meant to have?

We are great at justifying our actions, to others, to God and—perhaps most often—to ourselves. Of course hobbies, savings, children and careers are not bad things. They are, though, examples of good, God-given things that can become our 'god', at which point it is no longer good.

You might be familiar with the story of the rich young ruler who came to Jesus asking how to get eternal life. Jesus could see what he himself was blind to, that his wealth was what he worshipped and, until he could dethrone that idol and demonstrate it by selling all he had and giving it to the poor, he was never going to enter God's Kingdom. We are told that 'he became very sad, because he was very wealthy' (Luke 18:23). At some level this man knew following Jesus was worth it, or he would not have been sad. But wealth had such a grip on his heart that he just couldn't let it go.

I pray you do not make the same choice. Whether it's money like it was for this man, or whether it is popularity, exercise, food, beauty, a person, or anything at all, I do not want you to go away from God sad because something else is of greater value to you than him.

But we can make a choice. We can take up arms against those things that threaten to become 'god things' instead of just 'good things'. We can decide to see an idol for what it is. And when we do that, we can begin to interrogate ourselves, taking different aspects of our life in turn (relationships, work, how we spend time, money and brain-space, things we have, hopes and dreams) and ask probing questions. You might also invite someone to work through these things with you, someone who you trust enough to be kind to you, but also not let you off the hook!

As you interrogate different parts of your life, ask these sorts of questions:

- Why is this important to me? (Perhaps, like a persistent toddler, you need to keep asking 'Why?' to all your responses till you get to the bottom of it!)
- How much time, money or energy do I give to it compared with other things I know are probably equally or more important?
- Is this something I can imagine praying about? What do I think God might say if I did?
- What would my reaction be if this was taken away or radically altered?
- Have I considered whether the Bible has something to say about it?
- How does it impact on other areas of my life and am I content with that?

In lots of parts of your life, you'll ask these questions and find something is not an idol at all! If you are married or a parent, your family *should* take a large amount of your time, energy and finance, you *should* be devastated if you were to lose them and it *should* have an impact on your career and pastimes. That's healthy! But in some cases, you might find yourself on shaky ground. You might discern things that are too important, too dominant or too close to having the space of devotion only God should have.

The question is what to do with that. We'll consider that more when we come to a suggested 'confident action' later in this chapter, but for now I simply want to acknowledge one thing: it won't be easy. By definition, if something has taken on this kind of place in our life, it matters to us. It might even be a very good thing that matters to us, just too much. Some of the things Paul wrote to the believers in

Corinth were very hard-hitting because they had a lot of their confidence misplaced, so he called them out on it. Then, after hearing they had taken it on board, he wrote again saying:

> Even if I caused you sorrow by my letter, I do not regret it. Though I did regret it—I see that my letter hurt you, but only for a little while—yet now I am happy, not because you were made sorry, but because your sorrow led you to repentance. For you became sorrowful as God intended and so were not harmed in any way by us. (2 Corinthians 7:8-9)

When we spot an idol in our life, it is hard and should lead us to sorrow. When we then seek to dethrone it, that can be even harder and increases the sorrow. I can remember my wife and I both in tears during a phone call where I told her I had realised I needed to give up a hobby I loved because it took up too much of my energy, time and focus. I was in tears because I didn't want to let it go but knew I had to. She was in tears because (though she'd never understood why!) she knew how big this was for me.

But sorrow leads us to repentance, a change of mind. And this change of mind lets us put God first in the ways the first three commandments tell us to. It starts with a decision to see idols for what they are.

2. 'I will trust God's word not my own'

Another vital decision we can make is about how we will decide what is right and what is wrong, what is wise and what is unwise. Jesus says that 'all authority' belongs to him, and that includes the authority to tell us something is acceptable or off-limits.

Our world is asking so many questions, and they aren't bad questions! There are questions about identity, gender, race or sexuality. There are those about our world, the environment and the movement of people across the globe. There are economic questions, as the gap between the richest and poorest becomes greater while the global population growth accelerates. There are questions of life, death, abortion, assisted dying and medical ethics. There are questions of technology, artificial intelligence, and how (or whether) to regulate it all. And there are, of course, spiritual questions of whether religion is good for the world, whether any of it is true, or whether at the end of the day all of it is saying the same thing.

Closer to home for us, though, are the choices we make about our own lives. Should I marry or remain single? Does the answer to that change if I've been married before and am widowed or divorced? What about having children? How should I dress? How should I vote? How should I spend or save my money? What about giving money away to churches or charities? What should my relationship be with food? Or alcohol? Or drugs? How should I use my home? How should I treat my body? Is it ok for me to get a tattoo?

Every single one of those questions matters! What's more, I believe God cares about them, and that—through the Bible—he gives instruction or guidance on each and every one of them. *If we'll look and listen carefully.* Often though, if we're honest, we don't take that time to look and listen. We have a view or opinion and we go with it, whether or not we're sure that view lines up with God's. True and total confidence in God looks different from that. It looks like making the choice to trust God's revealed truth to us, not go with our gut.

To help us, I want to suggest four 'levels' of theological thinking we can engage in. Theology is simply the way we think about God and the things of God. We all do it. The question is how we do it. As we go up through these levels, we place more and more confidence in God, and less and less in ourselves. I'll illustrate each with examples from the last of my list of questions: "is it ok for me to get a tattoo?"

Level 1: Intuitive Non-theology

Examples: "I have no problem with tattoos" or "I think tattoos are gross."

We start with, essentially, our own gut reaction. This is what you think, without any consideration of anything beyond a mixture of your own preference, opinions, and experiences. Yours might be different than mine. We are different people and we won't always agree. That's just how it goes.

Of course, this doesn't display any confidence in God because he's not even in the picture. That's why I call it 'intuitive *non-theology*'. On this topic (whatever the topic is), you don't need his input because your own intuition is surely right and surely good enough.

Level 2: Intuitive Theology

Examples: "I reckon God has bigger things to worry about than ink on my skin" or "Well, God made my body this way so maybe he doesn't want me to change it."

We have taken a step forward here because God is now part of the equation. You know some things about God, so you work it out from there. If God is X, then I can assume he'd think Y. It is still intuitive though, in that it's not thought through to a great depth and is still your own thinking, just with God in the mix.

This displays much greater confidence, because you are now recognising that it is not your view that matters, but God's. That is great! But it lacks a fair amount of confidence because it's still your assumptions about what God's views are, instead of really taking the time to explore them more fully.

Level 3: Inherited Theology

Examples: "My parents say not to get a tattoo because it says not to in Leviticus" or "My pastor preached about it once and said tattoos are fine today."

In moving from 'intuitive' to 'inherited' theology, we have made another step. Not only is God still part of the equation, but our own opinions no longer are! We are stepping out of the frame and replacing ourselves with someone whose spiritual guidance and authority we trust.

Now we are placing more confidence in God because we are getting off the throne ourselves in a real way, and we are looking for guidance in a way that God chooses to give it. Whether it is the authority of godly parents, church leaders, or others we respect, we can look beyond ourselves as we work things through. Not all can look to parents for this and we must be sure those in leadership over us are rooted biblically not just spouting their own Level 1 or 2 thinking. We can also 'inherit' well from mentors, friends who have followed Jesus longer than us and trusted books or online sources.

(Of course, for this to be a step forward not back, they have to be a trustworthy source, so choose wisely. And for it to be genuine, you need to go to a trusted person, not shop round till you find someone who gives the answer you wanted when you were still at level 1!)

Level 4: Investigated Theology

Examples: "I've concluded that the verses in Leviticus about tattoos are bound to a culture where tattoos were a sign of bondage or worship of foreign gods, but that is not the case today, so it's ok, so long as the tattoo glorifies

God" or "God values my physical body, even dwelling in me as a temple, so I shouldn't take lightly what I do to it and I'm not sure a tattoo sits well with that."

Did you notice that the examples were much longer this time? That's because they are much more thought through. If we really want to know what God has to say about a particular topic, we need to investigate it for ourselves, seeking every tool at our disposal to get to the bottom of it. That means praying about it, getting your Bible open, investigating what others have said about it (including differing views), asking probing questions and then piecing it together until you settle on a conclusion.

This can be hard work, but if we truly want to trust God's word instead of our own, this kind of work is part of that. It places absolute confidence in him. We will never be able totally to ignore our own preconceptions, baggage and thoughts, but as we seek God's heart instead of our own we can seek to keep them in check.

Some bad news: we will never be able to have fully investigated level 4 thinking about everything! And the good news: that means we don't need to try! But what we can decide to do is to prioritise where we need to do that work and what we'll do where we can't.

I didn't always have an investigated theology of divorce and re-marriage. Then I was divorced and considering remarrying. At that point, confidence in God and faithfulness to him meant I couldn't settle for anything less than level 4 thinking. The same was true for my wife and I when we experienced the pain of infertility and began to explore fertility treatment. Prior to that, I had an inherited theology from people I trusted, but before deciding what we were happy to do or not do, we needed to investigate those questions theologically.

So, will you make the decision to trust God's word over your own? To show him that kind of confidence? Perhaps you could think through a few areas of your own life or the world you inhabit. Big issues, important decisions or ethical questions. Then ask what level of thinking you've done so far, and whether trusting God more would look like stepping that up a level.

HEART: Confident Postures

It is good for us to examine our thinking and decision-making. But people are not purely rational beings. And I'm not just talking about other people—this includes you and me! We are emotional beings, with wills, desires, dreams, fears, baggage and all kinds of inward and outward responses to things. When Jesus says we are to love God with 'all our heart', this is the sort of things he was talking about.

In our day, we talk about our hearts as being where our emotions live. We know it is symbolic because our hearts physically have nothing to do with our emotions, but it's an agreed-upon symbol. In Jesus' day, it was also understood that our heart was the symbolic home of part of our being, but that part was the will. More than just our emotions, this was about the centre of our being, the part that drives us, defines who we are and what we'll do. If our hearts are right with God, aligned with his heart, we will become more and more faithful as his followers. So in these 'Heart' sections, we will consider important 'postures' to cultivate before God as we seek that kind of alignment.

3. A posture of submission

The first posture is all about submission to God. Now, if when you saw that word 'submission' you immediately pictured a muscle-clad WWE wrestler tapping out because an even more muscle-clad WWE wrestler had got them in an inescapable grip, that's not quite what we're talking about here! It's understandable though. In our world, often the reason someone would 'submit' is because they know they are beaten and, in effect, they don't really have another choice. It's the only way out, so they may as well take it.

That isn't the way with God. There is always a choice. From the Garden of Eden right up to today, the choice is always there: love and follow God, or don't. It is a genuine choice, freely given and freely made. God does not have you in a headlock! You can choose to go his way, or not to. What he wants with you isn't a robotic, programmed response that always gets the results he desires. No, what he wants is a relationship. And for a relationship—for love—to be meaningful it has to be free. Otherwise it is a manipulative or abusive relationship and God is no manipulator or abuser.

So you are free to go your own way. But to display true confidence in God is to go his way even so. And that is what true, healthy, submission looks like.

And it's needed, isn't it? We've just explored the idea of deciding to trust God's word (having investigated our theology) instead of ours (settling for our own intuition). Let's be honest, though. Sometimes those things will not match up. We will find that what God has to say about something is not what we would want for him to say. And that presents us with a choice: deny our own opinion and trust that God's must be better, or deny God's so we don't have to budge.

If we have built a heart toward God that is willing to submit, the choice is made: we go God's way. If we haven't, the choice is made too, but it's the other choice, the one that keeps ourselves on the throne, and leads to bad places.

In fact that choice—questioning God's way instead of willingly submitting to it—is the source of sin in the first place. What is the first tactic of the serpent in the Garden of Eden? "Did God really say…?" (Genesis 3:1) If Eve had been able, simply, to answer with 'Yes, God *did* say, and that's good enough for me!' then all that came next would be stopped before it had a chance to start. But she didn't and that gave space for the rest of what the serpent says:

> *"You will not certainly die," the serpent said to the woman. "For God knows that when you eat from it your eyes will be opened, and you will be like God, knowing good and evil." (Genesis 3:4-5)*

The serpent flat out denies that what God has said is true, and then challenges his motivations. 'Did God really say…?' leads onto 'God is lying to you' and 'God doesn't want the best for you.' Fast-forward to today and the tactics haven't changed. This is a danger for us, but a choice to submit—freely, willingly and quickly—to God, can stop it in its tracks.

Not to mention, submission is just the obvious choice! When we really think about it, it just makes sense. The prophets of the Old Testament could sometimes be a pretty gloomy lot, which sometimes makes it tricky to spot when they're using humour to point out how silly something is. But Isaiah has a few amusing words to say about those who choose to pick a fight with God:

> *"Woe to those who quarrel with their Maker,*
> * those who are nothing but potsherds*
> * among the potsherds on the ground.*
> *Does the clay say to the potter,*

'What are you making?'
Does your work say,
    'The potter has no hands'? (Isaiah 45:9)

It's a silly image! It's meant to make us laugh and then realise we're laughing at ourselves… It's a picture of someone who chooses to quarrel with God, and tell him he's wrong. Maybe it's his actions that are wrong, or his ethics, or his choice to forgive someone we think is beyond the pale. It doesn't really matter. But the picture likens this person to a piece of pottery shouting at the potter who made it, criticising what it is he's making.

There is some debate over how that last accusation, 'The potter has no hands,' should be translated. Some word it 'Your work has no handles'. Either way, it's a very silly thing to say. It is either an accusation that the one who made us didn't have hands in the first place so doesn't know how to make anything right, or that he has missed something out and got the pottery wrong. One says that the God who made me can't make anything and the other says that the God who made me can only make things wrong.

Of course, all of this is ridiculous! If the potter had not made the pot, it would not even exist. As Andrew Wilson puts it, "the pot and the potter are not on a level playing field. Pots cannot criticise or argue with potters; it is only through the potter's creativity and wisdom that they exist at all."[26]

There are times when God's creativity and wisdom will offend our own. We will not always agree, or always like how God acts. But cultivating a posture towards God of submission means it will no longer be about what we like or whether we agree. It will be about him and we will become alright with that.

Pastor Mike Winger, when discussing ethical questions, often asks people this question: "Does God have the right to correct your lifestyle?"[27] It's a probing question, but an important one. If our heart's answer is 'No' then it doesn't really matter what theological conclusions we come to. If we don't like what God says, we won't do it. If our heart's answer is 'Yes' then it opens the door for God to mould, shape and build us. But the key that unlocks it is a heart that submits.

4. A posture of trust

Another posture toward God we need if we are going to place confidence in him is trust. We cannot submit to someone fully, letting them sit on the throne of our lives, if we don't trust them. We don't jump up and down on a glacier unless we're sure it can hold our weight.

But trusting God is not always easy. The world we live in can be a mess, with all manner of things in chaos. Couldn't God sort that out? Situations in our lives can be a mess, with relationships, health and events going in directions that terrify us but that we can't control. But God could control them, right? And we ourselves can be a mess, making mistakes, getting confused and just trying to make it through. If only God would make it just a little easier…

I am not here to give the answer to that, to tell you something that means we will always trust God in the midst of that mess. Not that there are no answers, but actually when it comes to a question of our heart (we trust with our hearts), an answer for our mind is not the full solution.

Instead, I want to suggest four ways we can cultivate this posture of trust. All of them are real about the messiness of life and real about who God is. Each is based on a Psalm in the Bible. We can be sure God is on board with these postures toward him because he inspired them and chose them to be included in the Bible.

i. Remind yourself of what God has done (Psalm 103)

It is quite trendy, these days, to try to 'live in the moment'. It's strange when you think about it because that's the only option we have! You cannot choose to live in the past or the future. You have to exist *now*. But right now, this moment, you can choose where to put your focus. You can focus on now, whatever it is that is going on, what you have to do today, the good and the bad, or you can choose to lift your focus from now to another time. That could be the future, planning and dreaming (or fearing and retreating), or it could be the past.

Looking back to the past is so helpful in building a posture of trust towards God. In Psalm 103, David (who wrote it), starts like this:

> Praise the Lord, my soul;
> all my inmost being, praise his holy name.
> Praise the Lord, my soul,
> and forget not all his benefits (Psalm 103:1-2)

David tells himself to do two related things: praise God, and remember (or 'forget not' because that sounds more Psalm-like) all the benefits about who God is and what God has done. These are related because by doing the remembering, it leads him to praise and in fact is an act of praise and worship itself. In the rest of the Psalm, by my count, David then calls to mind 19 'benefits' of God. This then overflows back into praising God in the last few verses of the Psalm. A decision to remember what God has done and what he is like leads to a deeper ability and desire to trust and praise him.

I remember a church prayer meeting which was feeling a little slow, there was not a lot of energy and it all felt like effort. Then my friend Stephen, who was leading the meeting, asked people to give examples from the Bible (or their own lives) of times when God has moved in power. The list came, slowly at first, but then gathered momentum. "He parted the Red Sea." "He fed five thousand." "He healed my mum." "He tore the curtain in two." "He forgave me." "He shook the room when the people prayed." Then Stephen encouraged us back into prayer and the atmosphere was different.

One way to build trust is to remind yourself of God's greatness, what he *has* done, what he *is* like and to let that be bigger than the particular situation you are in.

ii. Become ok with waiting and not knowing (Psalm 130)

A lot of us find waiting hard and it's even harder if we aren't completely sure of what will happen when the waiting comes to an end. If I know something will be good, waiting for it is easier. When I'm not sure, waiting becomes fearful. We've just thought about looking back, but now we turn to looking forward. And it can be an uncomfortable direction to look, precisely because we *don't* know what the future will hold.

Whether it is waiting for a result, journeying through unwanted singleness or childlessness, plodding on in a job because we can't see another option, or any other of life's waiting times, it can be really tough. And in particular, really tough to keep trusting God in those times because, deep down, we don't know if what is coming will bring joy or further sorrow.

We don't know who they were, but whoever wrote Psalm 130 seemed to have cultivated a trusting heart in the middle of uncertainty. They start with 'Out of the depths I cry to you, Lord', so there is something they're seeking God for. But they can also say:

I wait for the Lord, my whole being waits,
   and in his word I put my hope.
I wait for the Lord
   more than watchmen wait for the morning,
   more than watchmen wait for the morning. (Psalm 130:5-6)

The key here is what it is the Psalmist waits for. Not just a good out-come, happy ending or certain victory. No, they 'wait for *the Lord*'. A deep yearning with their 'whole being', a deep longing like a watchmen who longs for the safety that morning's first light signals. That's how much they want God. They understand that they cannot see everything from God's point of view, so simply wait for him. Uncomfortable maybe, but full of faith. Andrew Wilson captures this well.

> If God is all-knowing and I am not, there are all sorts of things I would expect God to know and to do that I cannot understand. It is simply to say that I am ignorant... *Living with that ignorance can be un-settling and sometimes deeply troubling, especially when suffering strikes us personally.* But questions, paradoxes, and mysteries are part of the fabric of Christianity. There is a limit to how far creatures can understand the Creator. Ignorance is built in.[28]

If we are able to find satisfaction in God, to seek him not just an answer to our question or a change in our circumstances, we can begin to learn to wait. We won't know what the outcome will be, if or when things will shift, but we can wait. And do so with trust.

iii. Direct the pain toward God (Psalm 88)

The weekend I found out my wife (now ex-wife) was having an affair was the darkest, hardest weekend of my life. I was at the lowest I have ever been. I did not know how to pray, so I didn't. It felt too painful. I knew that if I started to tell God I needed his help that it would be even harder if I didn't get it. I knew that if I told God I trusted him I might be lying. Things were just too hard. I knew that I couldn't ignore what was going on because it was all I could think about, but I didn't know how to talk to God about it in a way that was acceptable.

Then I called my brother to tell what was going on. He was gut-ted, expressed his love and support and all the things I already knew but still needed to hear. Then he pointed me to something I hadn't known before. I knew there were lots of Psalms where people expressed anger, pain, confusion and doubts toward God, but I thought they all ended with an expression of trust. Like Psalm 13 which starts with 'How long, Lord? Will you forget me forever?' (v1) but ends with 'I will sing the Lord's praise, for he has been good to me.' I knew I could pray the first bit, but couldn't get myself to the last bit.

I thought that it was only ok to direct my pain towards God if I could also muster up some kind of praise or thanks or positivity. But my brother encouraged me to go and read Psalm 88. I'd encourage you to do the same thing. It is pretty heavy stuff, in which God is blamed for suffering, the depth of that suffering just keeps sounding worse and worse, God is told he is distant in the midst of it all. And then it ends like this:

> You have taken from me friend and neighbour —
> darkness is my closest friend. (Psalm 88:18)

No positive end. No 'but I still praise you.' Nothing like that. My brother pointed me to this Psalm at the hardest time of my life and summed it up like this: "Life is rubbish, full stop. That is a prayer in the Bible." Now I had a prayer I *could* pray.

What makes this prayer a good prayer? What makes it an expression of trust? Simple: it's directed to God. We can take our pain and direct it inward, further and further into the sadness inside. We can take our pain and direct it outward, telling others or taking it out on others. We can take our pain and direct it nowhere, just trying to ignore it but actually bottling it up uselessly and destructively. Or we can take our pain to God and tell him. Just doing that is a step of trust and, like me that weekend, it might be the only one you can honestly take today. So take it.

iv. Celebrate what you can (Psalm 30)

But life is not all valleys and pain and sorrow. There is also good and we should not let that pass us by. Sometimes there are things to celebrate and when there are we should definitely celebrate them!

The same David who famously wrote in Psalm 22:1 the words Jesus quoted from the cross ('My God, my God, why have you forsaken me?') also wrote Psalm 30, which starts like this:

> I will exalt you, Lord,
> for you lifted me out of the depths

and did not let my enemies gloat over me.
Lord my God, I called to you for help,
*   and you healed me. (Psalm 30:1-2)*

David is delighted and rightly so! He can see the ways that God has moved, has answered his prayers in real, tangible ways and he celebrated it. God could have left him in hard places and given his enemies the victory. But he didn't! David prayed for help and he was healed by God. How wonderful! But instead of just moving on with life, he pulls out his harp and composes a song, this Psalm we now have in the Bible, just to say thank you.

If we are going to take our difficulties to God, let's also do it with the blessings, the good things, the wins. Celebrate everything that can be celebrated. It shows we know it comes from him.

Which one of those could you do? There have been times in my life when all four have been possible, and others when I simply have not had the strength, or the faith, for some of them. There are times when celebration will be harder than lament and times when it will be the other way round. That is ok. That is why God has given all of it to us.

And this is important: *each of these* is evidence of trust. It may feel as though waiting patiently is more faithful than directing your questions at God? Maybe. Maybe not. Sometimes these will feel like a small amount of faith and that is ok. Jesus says that even 'faith as small as a mustard seed' can achieve a great deal (Matthew 17:20). So whatever size and shape of faith—of trust in God—you have today, plant it before him and see what starts to grow.

HANDS: Confident Action

Heads and hearts determine much of who we are, but it doesn't end there. So far we've thought about the kind of repentance that starts with a change of mind and is backed up by a posture toward God that can sustain it. The final stage is to consider what actions we can take. John the Baptist urged people to 'produce fruit in keeping with repentance' (Luke 3:8). What starts in us must come out of us. Confidence in God must look like something.

5. Give authority back

There is just one action I am suggesting in this area. (For each of this book's four qualities there will be five tools in the toolkit, but divided up differently among Head, Heart and Hands.) The action is this: give any authority you have assumed for yourself back to Jesus.

You might have taken authority back for yourself in a number of ways, touching on different things in this section so far. You might have:

- Realised too much of your identity, worth or security comes from an 'idol' in your life, and need to relinquish it in order to put God first.

- Put God's name to something that is really your own desire, and are claiming a kind of spiritual authority there that isn't yours to have.

- Subtly adapted the message of the gospel to make it more palatable, either to yourself or others, perhaps downplaying your own sin.

- Given yourself too high a status and God too low a status.

- Come to your own conclusion about important topics without really giving God's word enough of a say.

- Adopted a posture that does not submit or trust, but retains the power for yourself, unable to relate to God unless you have all the answers.

All of these, in one way or another, is taking some of the authority Jesus should rightly have in your life and claiming it for yourself. I would be amazed if none of that is going on your life—it certainly is in mine. Even as I wrote that list, I felt God highlighting areas for me to work on. But please, this is not a shame thing, but a call to action.

There are three ways you could give that authority back. You could *reduce* something, *remove* something, or *re-align* something.

Some things might simply need to be *reduced* in our lives in order to restore the kind of balance that's right before God. If your career has become all-consuming as an idol in your life, you do not necessarily need to quit yourjob. But you might need to set firmer boundaries, not take the promotion you've been offered, or put in a request for a reduction of hours or responsibility. If money has a grip on you, the act of reducing your spending by starting (or increasing) sacrificial giving can begin to get this back in order.

When we choose to reduce something that would otherwise fill more and more space in our life, we're placing more of our confidence where it should be. This honours God by allowing him to set the balance of our lives. You have 168 hours a week, a finite amount of money and only so much space in your brain. How you choose to spend those resources tells a story and reducing your expenditure in one area can alter that story for the better.

But there are times something simply needs to be *removed*. If you have discarded an element of God's teaching because it does not sit well with your own view on things, that thinking needs to be removed. If you are caught in a pattern of behaviour that is just wrong, it needs to go. If you are dominated by a heart that is materialistic, hedonistic, selfish and totally un-submissive to God, you need to ask God to remove your heart of stone, give you a new heart and put his Spirit into you to sustain that change (Ezekiel 36:26-27).

There are also times to remove something not because it is bad but because we know as long as it stays it will have a hold we don't want it to have. Like the rich young ruler who was told to sell everything, maybe there is something you know just reducing will never be enough. Maybe you do need to quit the job, end the relationship, or stop the hobby. Of course none of these things are easy, but it is another way of giving back the authority Jesus should have.

A final way to give authority back is to *re-align* an area of our lives. This can be more of an internal thing because it does not immediately lead to change. But it will over time if we are serious about it. Perhaps you realise you are more worried about your children's grades or careers than their faith in Jesus and know you need to re-align that. It's an internal shift, but it will change how you pray for them, how you speak with them, and how you react to their grades. Ultimately, this is a re-alignment with God. It lets his priorities become ours, not the other way round.

So, where have you claimed too much authority, and where can you choose as an intentional, deliberate action, to give it back? One or more of those three steps could be the key to living with more confidence in God.

This toolkit does not only work in one order. You have been given five places to start in growing more confident in God, but it is up to you to take out a tool and use it. They also overlap and lead into and out of one another. If you decide to start with action and remove something from your life, it will be tough and you might find yourself wrestling with God over it. That can lead to developing your posture of submission, which in turn leads you to have to direct some of your new-found pain in his direction. You'll also be going on a journey of seeing that particular idol for what it really is. Wherever you start, you might need to explore more than one tool from this toolkit. But you have to start somewhere.

If you are not sure where that is, my encouragement would be to pray. God knows the state of your heart better than you do, so invite him to highlight what a good next step for you could be. Tell him you want him to occupy the throne of your life, and see where he guides you.

My other encouragement is to start that work before delving into the next section. We will shortly be moving from confidence to our second quality: obedience. But obedience will come a lot more naturally and fully if we have already allowed God to increase our confidence in him.

Chapter 3 at a glance...

In this toolkit chapter, the five tools we explored together were:

1. [HEAD:] Seeing idols for what they are, committing to digging out the idols in our lives so we can dethrone them.

2. [HEAD:] Trusting in God's word instead of our own ideas, and using the tool of the four 'levels' of theological thought to assess what is really forming our thinking.

3. [HEART:] Building a posture of submission, so that we will go God's way instead of ours when they are at odds.

4. [HEART:] Building a posture of trust, where we looked at the Psalms as examples of how to do that in very different seasons of our lives.

5. [HANDS:] Giving authority back to God in just one area of our lives by either reducing, removing or re-aligning it.

Becoming Willing

Let's go back to the Great Commission, in Matthew 28:

> *Then the eleven disciples went to Galilee, to the mountain where Jesus had told them to go. When they saw him, they worshiped him; but some doubted. Then Jesus came to them and said,* **"All authority in heaven and on earth has been given to me. Therefore go and make disciples of all nations***, baptising them in the name of the Father and of the Son and of the Holy Spirit, and teaching them to obey everything I have commanded you. And surely I am with you always, to the very end of the age." (Matthew 28:16-20, emphasis added)*

This is where we started this book and we will keep returning. As we discover the four qualities of a disciple Jesus seems to be forming in these words, as we then dive into those to see what they mean and try to bed them as strong principles in our lives, we will then return once again to where they all started. Yes, there is a call for confident faith in Jesus found beyond these words, but let's not forget what this confidence is meant to inspire. This confidence in the wonderful truth that Jesus has all authority leads somewhere and it leads us into mission.

There seems a link between what the disciples can rely on and what they can do with it. Jesus, who has '*all* authority,' sends us off to 'make disciples of *all* nations'. We can do exactly what Jesus asks only because of exactly what Jesus encourages us with. No authority, no disciples in no nations. Some authority, some disciples in some nations. But *all* authority? Well, now we can dream big dreams!

The idea of disciples being made of every nation sounds extraordinarily large and unrealistic. To most, anyway. According to the Joshua Project (at the time of writing), the approximately eight billion people in the world break down into 17,313 people groups.[29] Of these, 7,278 are 'unreached', meaning 'a people group among which there is no indigenous community of believing Christians with adequate numbers and resources to evangelise this people group without outside assistance.'[30] Those 7,278 people groups add up to about 3.4 billion people. So the task is huge!

But remember, we are not starting from scratch! Globally, more people are followers of Jesus now than at any time in history. The church may not be growing in the part of the world I live in, but the church of Jesus Christ across the world is *not* in decline! No, we are not starting from scratch. Jesus already did that when he gathered his disciples around him, blew their minds with wonderful and strange teaching about the Kingdom of God, demonstrated the power of that Kingdom, sent them out, gathered them back, died for them, rose again, appeared to them and then gave them these instructions. That was Jesus starting from scratch. And the result, two thousand years later, totals in the billions! Our task is to join in what he has already started.

It must also have sounded crazy when Jesus, not long after, told these same disciples 'you will receive power when the Holy Spirit comes on you; and you will be my witnesses in Jerusalem, and in all Judea and Samaria, and to the ends of the earth' (Acts 1:8). Again, spot the link between who they can rely on (the Holy Spirit) and what they can do as a result (be witnesses). But it must have felt a ridiculous statement. Jerusalem was where they were, and was already opposed to them: impossible to start with! All of Judea, though? There were only a few of them… And Samaria? The enemy! But Jesus doesn't stop with places that are too impossible, too large and too hostile. He then adds in 'to the ends of the earth'!

But what happens in the book of Acts? They witness in Jerusalem, and thousands follow Jesus (Acts 2–7). Then the church is scattered by persecution, and they are able to witness across Judea and Samaria, again to great effect (Acts 8–12). After that, the gospel goes beyond the Jewish parts of the world all the way to the very heart of the Roman Empire (Acts 13–28), the key to the known world at the time. If the gospel was going to get to the ends of the earth, it would need to go through Rome. Unimaginable for this small band in Acts 1. A reality by Acts 28. Perhaps we could let that inspire Great Commission Confidence in us, too?

This is not too big for God. It just isn't! Disciples being made of all nations isn't a silly idea he had one day that he quickly came to regret. It is Plan A.

And the bigness, authority and power of Jesus is up to the task. Which means we can *confidently* step in and play our part. He has the authority, so we can join him in the mission.

How? Here's a thought. The scope of the Great Commission is 'all nations'. I will never visit all countries or meet people from all people groups. I do, though, have influence in some places, with some people. And so do you. That could be your street and your neighbours. Or your workplace and your colleagues. Or your pub and the regulars. Or your school and your classmates. You have a sphere of influence and there are others that occupy that sphere with you. What if you were to think of that sphere as one of the 'nations' and those there with you as the people who Jesus wants you to 'make disciples' of?

The great news: Jesus has 'all authority', including authority over that exact place you are thinking of. It may not seem it. It may be the darkest, most 'godless' place imaginable. Your workplace, home, street or school will be chasing after all sorts of idols of their own. Your colleagues or family members will have built their lives on a thin sheet of ice, thinking it is strong enough to hold them. There will be all kinds of wrong thinking, ethics and activities going on. The darkness may seem too dark to penetrate. But the 'light shines in the darkness, and the darkness has not overcome it' (John 1:5).

At this stage, I simply want to ask you to let the truth of the authority of Jesus in the places God has put you do one thing: make you *willing*. I believe that is what Great Commission Confidence is meant to do. Jesus reminded his friends of his authority simply so they might be up for stepping out and giving it a go. There was more to come that would make them useful and fruitful, but for now he just wants them to be willing.

These people who were worshiping and doubting needed to know that what he was asking them was not too big. And the only reason it wasn't too big is that he isn't too small. Far from it!

So, will you take a moment to pray a prayer declaring two things? First, to declare the authority of Jesus over the places you live, work and play, that they belong to him, that he belongs there and that you want to see them won for him. And second, to declare your own willingness to go into them with intentionality, with boldness and with him.

PART 2

OBEDIENCE TO JESUS

"Therefore go and make disciples of all nations, baptising them in the name of the Father and of the Son and of the Holy Spirit, and teaching them to obey everything I have commanded you."

(Matthew 28:19-20)

Luke 1:26-38

As we shift our focus now, we begin with a story from the beginning of Luke. In it, we see all of CODE at work, but the climax highlights the focus of our next few chapters: obedience. First, a word of caution: as part of the Nativity, this story is likely *very* familiar! That can mean we glaze over, thinking we know the story already. So try to read it with fresh eyes, spot the different parts of CODE at work, and see what lessons there are to learn.

Luke 1:26-38

26 *In the sixth month of Elizabeth's pregnancy, God sent the angel Gabriel to Nazareth, a town in Galilee,* 27 *to a virgin pledged to be married to a man named Joseph, a descendant of David. The virgin's name was Mary.* 28 *The angel went to her and said, "Greetings, you who are highly favoured! The Lord is with you."*

29 *Mary was greatly troubled at his words and wondered what kind of greeting this might be.* 30 *But the angel said to her, "Do not be afraid, Mary; you have found favour with God.* 31 *You will conceive and give birth to a son, and you are to call him Jesus.* 32 *He will be great and will be called the Son of the Most High. The Lord God will give him the throne of his father David,* 33 *and he will reign over Jacob's descendants forever; his kingdom will never end."*

34 *"How will this be," Mary asked the angel, "since I am a virgin?"*

35 *The angel answered, "The Holy Spirit will come on you, and the power of*

the Most High will overshadow you. So the holy one to be born will be called the Son of God. ³⁶ Even Elizabeth your relative is going to have a child in her old age, and she who was said to be unable to conceive is in her sixth month. ³⁷ For no word from God will ever fail."

³⁸ "I am the Lord's servant," Mary answered. "May your word to me be fulfilled." Then the angel left her.

The Great Commission is a story of 11 men given a mammoth, seemingly impossible task and sent out to do it. The words you just read are even wilder! This is the story of one teenage girl given a mammoth, physically impossible task and invited into it. Don't let familiarity blind you. This is huge!

The Complete CODE

Mary does not say or do much in this story. We're told she's 'troubled', she 'wonders' what's going on and she 'asks' how it will happen. These all point to the same thing: she knows this is all too big for her! But the way she responds demonstrates real *dependence* on God. Unlike Zechariah a few verses earlier, who questioned a similar message from Gabriel, asking how he can be sure of it (Luke 1:18), Mary's response is full of faith. She doesn't ask *if* it will happen. She asks *how* it will happen: "How will this be, since I am a virgin?" Instead of taking control of the situation by needing to fully understand it, she puts the ball back in God's court. If this is what he wants, fine, but it can't rest on her. She knows that, and seems alright with relying on him.

Gabriel's response is that God will do it, through his Holy Spirit: this will be God's Son, not just Mary's. It is one of a number of ways he seeks to build Mary's *confidence* in God, not in herself. It starts when Gabriel calls Mary 'highly favoured'—this may be scary, but it is really a blessing, so embrace it! He reminds Mary God is with her, tells her not to be afraid and doesn't hold back with talk of thrones and everlasting kingdoms when talking about the Son she'll bear. Yes, it is a huge thing God is going to do through her, but he is up to the task and will be with her every step. He even gives courage in the form of a companion, her relative Elizabeth, who she can share this journey with. And he caps it off with a bold promise: "no word from God will ever fail." What God says, God does, so put confidence in it.

This episode also shows us something about how *experience* with

God can work. This is a supernatural encounter ('God sent the angel Gabriel' to Mary), impacting her in profound ways. But her experience of the world is also brought into it. The facts of her life matter: her name, hometown, status and situation are all named (v27). What she knows about the world—virgins don't have children—comes into play too. The encounter with God is powerful, but her own experience still counts. They inform one another, ask questions of one another, make demands of one another. The faith she displays means God's word answers the questions, not the other way round, but the questions are there. Mary seems to continue taking stock of her God-and-life-experiences, holding, weighing and cherishing them. As Jesus grows up, we hear twice that she carefully notices what's going on around her and 'treasured all these things in her heart' (Luke 2:19, 51), choosing to grow in and through her experiences, instead of letting them pass her by.

And the climax of this story is one of the purest and most beautiful expressions of *obedience* to God. Mary says, simply, "I am the Lord's servant. May your word to me be fulfilled." Wow.

Rapid response

What's so deeply impressive to me about Mary's answer is that it is *both* really faithful *and* really fast! An ambulance can have all the best equipment, but if it takes 6 hours to arrive what's the point? Or if it turns up in minutes but no-one on it is trained, that's no use either. Mary's response doesn't fail on either front. She demonstrates a *quality* of obedience to God's word I find inspiring, and does so at a *speed* I find challenging!

Let's start with the quality of her response. "I am the Lord's servant. May your word to me be fulfilled." She says 'yes' on two levels.

The first is a general 'yes', declaring herself to be 'the Lord's servant'. A servant will do what their master says simply because they have committed to serve. So whatever instruction comes, they've already decided they'll do it. It's like anyone who's ever signed a job description that finishes with 'And any other duties as agreed with line manager.' You might have a specific set of tasks within your job, but really the job is to do what's needed. If the boss says it's needed, it's now the job! I wonder if Mary said these words partly to herself, reminding herself of her general 'yes' to God in the past, so the rest of what she says comes more easily.

Because the rest is her specific 'yes' to the actual task he has given: "May your word to me be fulfilled." She has heard the task and now she says yes. Not yes to an abstract concept, but yes to *this*. This very specific, very particular, very invasive, hard and sacrificial thing. Yes. She is giving up control of her womb, giving consent for the pregnancy that will come, agreeing to the scandal and controversy she must have known would be on the way. She is committing to whatever it will mean for her and Joseph, for her and her family, for her and her community. The 'yes' may have started off general, but 'yes' never stays abstract: a real 'yes' lands somewhere, and where it landed for Mary was here.

But she has become willing, which opens the door for this staggering statement of obedience. And for its speed! She doesn't seem to hesitate. Obedience is her instinct and that is something to strive for. We get the sense from Gabriel's greeting that God chose her for a reason and I wonder if knowing she had this kind of rapid response in her heart was part of that. Was Mary perfect? Absolutely not. But in this moment, her obedience plays a part in one of the most spectacular truths in history: God became one of us. He chose to do that through the willing cooperation of a teenager. Again, wow.

I will forever be in awe of Mary, but one thing I want that to lead me to is a deeper level of what she had. A stronger, fuller, quicker obedience to God, and that's what we are going to explore for a while now.

How do you play Twister?

My parents own a copy of the game Twister and I remember a time I was playing it with my 4-year-old nephew. In case you aren't familiar, it's a sheet you lay on the ground with lots of coloured circles on. You spin a dial, which gives an instruction for a hand or foot to be placed on a circle. Right hand on red, left foot on green and so on. Someone spins the dial and calls out instructions and everyone else has to follow along, becoming more and more contorted and tangled till they fall over and are out of the game. Fun for all the family.

It's a game of obedience. Instruction leads to action and any violation is against the rules of the game. The instructions are random, of course, not based on any kind of greater good, moral framework or big plan. So it isn't an awful lot like obedience *to God*. It's just blindly following pointless commands.

Except my parents' copy of Twister is broken. At some point along the way the dial broke, so now the instructions aren't random. They are chosen by the person calling the shots which, when playing with my nephew, was me! So I could now see what would be easy or difficult, fun or boring and decide what instructions to give. Now, this game of obedience does have some kind of higher thinking to it. Do I give him an easy ride? Do I make it hard for him? Do I try to 'win' and assert my authority? As much as those questions might reveal a lot about me, I'm more interested in it from my nephew's point of view. In this version of Twister, he is not just playing a game, but choosing to obey or disobey his uncle.

(For what it's worth, I didn't try to 'win'. Competitive as I can be, I don't get much joy from asserting dominance over a 4-year-old who isn't as tall as a Twister mat is long. Also, 'winning' the game would just mean playing another game. And since one long game with him 'winning' is about as fun for me as many short games with him 'losing', I was happy to let him have his fun. So I picked the commands to twist him up a bit and then let him unknot, repeated that till he was clearly getting bored, and then gave him a series of impossible tasks to close out the game. You don't attain 'fun uncle' status without thinking these things through.)

But let's imagine an even more broken game of Twister. One where I have left the room entirely but my nephew plays on. Now there is no-one calling the shots and he can decide whether his right hand belongs on blue or yellow, where he would prefer his left foot to be placed. It's entirely up to him! It's a terrible game now, of course. Now he's just a small boy doing slow and unrhythmic breakdancing in my parents' living room. But if I've learned anything about small children, it's that most things can be a game if you really want them to be. And, zooming out to our question of obedience to God, I wonder if this is how we'd often like it to look…

So let's think about that for a moment. Which of these three games of Twister does our concept of obedience to God look most like?

Are you playing the classic game of Twister? You know there are rules, commands and principles given by God but they feel like a spinning of the dial. It all feels random, disconnected, pointless. There's no rhyme nor reason to it, which makes it feel hard to want to obey. Perhaps this is a bit of a confidence question from the last few chapters: do you really trust that God's ways are good?

Or are you playing the broken game of Twister, with the dial replaced by a person. In our relationship with God, this is where the sweet spot should be. We do not just follow a random pattern, an impersonal force, or 'the universe'. God is personal, coherent, consis-

tent. His commands are good. His rules are for our good. His principles are wise. True obedience is to listen not just for the rule, but for
his voice, to learn to hear and obey, hear and obey, hear and obey. In
fact, the Hebrew word translated 'obey' literally means 'hear the
voice'. Hear and obey.

But it might be that you've slipped into the final, voiceless game.
The Twister mat of your own life is controlled by your choices and
yours alone. You have no need or desire for outside input. You know
what shape you need to be. You know what level of comfort or challenge feels best right now, so you can decide for yourself.

In truth, the distinctions are not always that clear cut. There are
likely elements of all three in your life, just as there are in mine. But
as we focus now on how the Bible shapes our understanding of obedience, keep these images in your mind. We will see them at work in
different ways at different times.

Will we ever learn?

Obedience is perhaps the most obvious discipleship quality to draw
from the Great Commission. After all, it is a command, with things
we're told to do: go, make disciples, baptise and teach. A command
can either be obeyed or disobeyed. And the last part of the command
points to obedience again because Jesus doesn't simply instruct that
they 'teach [new disciples] everything I commanded', passing on
what he has said. No, the command is to 'teach them *to obey* everything I commanded' (Matthew 28:20).

Jesus is deliberate in making sure obedience is woven into the
very fabric of his instruction to his disciples. He wanted to leave no
doubt at all: if you are to be his disciple, obedience to him is *always*
part of the package. It may seem obvious (and it is!), but it's not hard
to see why Jesus underlined it so strongly. The story of the Bible reveals that obedience has never been something we are good at. We
won't arrive at obedience by ourselves, so we need to be guided into
it very clearly.

The very beginning

In fact, the roots of this long story of obedience (and disobedience)
start in the first few pages of the Bible. What is it that determined
whether the world would stay 'very good' or descend into darkness

and death? A command:

> *And the Lord God commanded the man, "You are free to eat from any tree in the garden; but you must not eat from the tree of the knowledge of good and evil, for when you eat from it you will certainly die." (Genesis 2:16-17)*

This tree they are not to eat from does not contain apples or lemons. It contains knowledge, specifically knowledge 'of good and evil'. Surely a good thing? Why is it that they are not meant to know what is right and wrong? To us that sounds like it might be helpful… But think about their situation at the time. They have a close, perfect, personal relationship with God who walks with them in the Garden. If they want to know what is good or evil, they can ask. When they ask, they will hear and once they've heard they can do. There is nothing broken about that.

Decisions about what is good and evil, right and wrong, are up to God, not us. He decides. He knows. The way things were meant to work, people were to trust God instead of trying to cut him out of that to get that knowledge for himself. In some sense, the desire to have that knowledge is actually a desire to get to make that choice ourselves, asking the divine Twister-caller to leave the room so we can do what we want to. John Goldingay puts it this way: "Distinguishing between good and bad is an insight that belongs to God, so God claims the right to decide whether and when to give it… To insist on taking it is to push your way into God's realm, to attempt to be like God."[31]

But that decision was made. They did insist on taking it. The fruit was eaten. We did try to make ourselves like God, deciding good and bad for ourselves. And the story from there on in is a story of that decision repeating itself again and again.

A new beginning

After several cycles of disobedience (including the first murder, countless failed generations, a flood-sized reset and a tower-shaped attempt to be like God),[32] hope comes afresh in the form of a new beginning and a new man: Abram.

> *The Lord had said to Abram, 'Go from your country, your people and your father's household to the land I will show you.*

"I will make you into a great nation,
    and I will bless you;
I will make your name great,
    and you will be a blessing.
I will bless those who bless you,
    and whoever curses you I will curse;
and all peoples on earth
    will be blessed through you." (Genesis 12:1-3)

The first 'Go' command is not the Great Commission, but these words to Abram. To go to a place he'd never been, to start a great nation, to bless the whole world. It was a new dawn of hope. And Abram does go. He does begin a great nation. And through him the whole world will be blessed. But in none of those three things does Abram demonstrate much obedience…

I do not think it a coincidence that the first episode of Abram's journey is a huge failure! He goes to Egypt, where he immediately (and pointlessly) lies to Pharaoh, gets lots of people very ill and gets unceremoniously booted out (Genesis 12:10-20). As we read the story, we are not meant to see Abram as the hero. He is not faithful to God, but God is still faithful to his promises. The great nation that comes from Abram isn't a roaring success either. Worried it won't happen because his wife is too old, he takes matters into his own hands and sleeps with a servant, Hagar (Genesis 16). She does have a son, but not the son God meant, so there's another set of broken lives left in the wake of Abram's life. And the blessing for the whole world that came through him? It does not come through some heroic act of his, or his son, or his grandson. It comes through his descendent many hundreds of years later: Jesus, the only one of his line who ever demonstrated the kind of obedience God desired. We'll come to him soon.

Abram wasn't all bad, of course! He did go when God called and he had some moments of remarkable trust and obedience. He believed what God said when he said it (even if he then wobbled). We are told that 'Abram believed the Lord, and he credited it to him as righteousness' (Genesis 15:6). But the big picture is not of God's purposes being worked out through an obedient, faithful life. The big picture is God faithfully working out his purposes *in spite of* a disobedient life.

Choices to be made

This new people had a choice to make. Hear and obey? Or hear and disobey? They grew from Abram's small family to a proper nation and found themselves as slaves. As we saw a couple of chapters ago, God brings them out of slavery with mighty acts and the very first thing he does is…give them commands. The Ten Commandments are given at this moment of rebirth as a nation so they know he has a way for them to live in the new land he will take them to.

It goes beyond the big ten, though! Most of the second half of the book of Exodus and almost all of Leviticus, is taken up with commands and principles for almost every area of life. Blame cannot be pinned on God for not telling them how to live. Humanity has eaten the fruit of the knowledge of good and evil and knowledge has been given. They do not have the excuse of not knowing. The Twister-caller has not left the room. He continues to guide, but will they listen?

The simple answer is…no. On the brink of entering the land God has for them, they take matters into their own hands. So instead of enjoying their first 40 years in a beautiful new land, they spend them wandering in circles. When you refuse directions, you end up lost. After forty years, about to enter the land, after giving the Law to them a second time their leader Moses puts the choice to them again:

> See, I set before you today life and prosperity, death and destruction. For I command you today to love the Lord your God, to walk in obedience to him, and to keep his commands, decrees and laws; then you will live and increase, and the Lord your God will bless you in the land you are entering to possess.

> But if your heart turns away and you are not obedient, and if you are drawn away to bow down to other gods and worship them, I declare to you this day that you will certainly be destroyed. You will not live long in the land you are crossing the Jordan to enter and possess. (Deuteronomy 30:15-18)

It's a choice: Hear and obey, or hear and disobey. They've heard, so there's no excuse and the choice is with them. Obedience is the way of life and disobedience the way of death. We can hear echoes of the Genesis story here, can't we? Because this is one story, written large over all of humanity, repeating and repeating and repeating. Of course the people have good moments, where they experience the way of life as they stick close to God's ways. And many moments where they don't. The cycle continues…

Let us rule ourselves!

Fast-forward through many generations of ups and downs and now the people come to God's representative at the time, Samuel, with a demand: "We want a king over us. Then we will be like all the other nations" (1 Samuel 8:19-20). What is it that makes Israel distinctive: they follow the one true God, following him and not behaving like everyone else. But what do they want? To be like everyone else, not having to follow God but having a king. In a way it's a second-commandment violation, wanting a go-between that will become their God. Samuel is troubled,

> so he prayed to the Lord. And the Lord told him: "Listen to all that the people are saying to you; it is not you they have rejected, but they have rejected me as their king." (1 Samuel 8:6-7)

They are asking God to leave the room, to stop calling the shots so a king can rule them instead. But a king would always be one of them, so what they are really asking is that they can rule themselves, like our third and most-broken game of Twister. They are told it will lead to ruin, because their kings will fail, mistreat them and rule selfishly. But their mind is made up and God grants their wish.

It doesn't take long before everything falls apart. The first three kings are Saul, David and Solomon. While two have redeeming features, all fail to rule with the purity, justice and goodness of God. Then in the fourth generation a contest for the throne leads the nation to split in two.

From there, both nations fall deeper into disarray. The reign of each new king is summarised in one of two ways: either he 'did what was right in the eyes of the Lord' or he 'did what was evil in the eyes of the Lord'. The numbers aren't good. Out of the 39 kings after Solomon (across both parts of the divided kingdom) only six 'did what was right'. Thirty are described as doing 'evil' and three get a mixed report. If we think we can do a better job than God at calling the shots, this should give pause for thought.

The results include defeats, increases of idolatry, watering down of God's laws and, ultimately, being exiled from the land God had given them. They chose the path of death and got what they asked for.

So the story of the Old Testament is a repeated lesson: obedience does not come easily to us. We love our own way, even when told and shown again and again that our way leads not to light and life but to darkness and death. Will we ever learn?

Fleshed out obedience

Left to ourselves, no! Of course we would never learn. But we aren't left to ourselves. Someone came who wasn't like those who came before. He would show us true obedience, but also teach it and grant it to us. Unlike Abram, unlike every generation, unlike every king, Jesus embodied obedience perfectly.

I mean that literally: he embodied obedience. When he took on a body, the Son of God showed in a real, physical and 'fleshed-out' form what obedience to God looks like. A number of times Jesus said things like, 'the Son can do nothing by himself; he can do only what he sees his Father doing, because whatever the Father does the Son also does' (John 5:19-20). This was at the root of Jesus' life, in lock step with his Father, never disobeying, never going his own way. Never once did he wonder if his Father was just spinning the dial and calling out random commands. He knew the voice of his Father, trusted that voice and followed it.

That obedience confuses people many times in the Bible! He doesn't dance to the tune of religions leaders, Roman rulers, or even his own disciples or family. He is marching to the beat of a different drum and it shows. Jim Packer writes:

> The rock-like integrity of Jesus in refusing point-blank to fit into Jewish stereotypes and expectations, and insisting instead on following with complete consistency his own path … strikes readers of the Gospels, as it struck Jesus' own contemporaries, as awe-inspiring; it was clearly the outworking of his entire submission to the Father's will, immediately known every moment in each situation.[33]

Next time you're reading from the stories of Jesus' life in the Bible, look out for all the times Jesus does something that confuses, offends or upsets people. It isn't hard because it happens a lot! Every single one is an example of Jesus displaying obedience to God instead of to other people, ideas or systems. Hearing and obeying. Hearing and obeying. Hearing and obeying. What an example!

Can we obey like Jesus?

But just having an example isn't enough. If we cobble together the best bits of Abram, Moses, Ruth, David, Solomon, Esther, Daniel and a few others, we could make ourselves a pretty good example, but that's not the purpose of their stories. And as great an example Jesus is, that is not the main purpose of his story, either. There is something bigger and deeper going on which is worth diving into.

There are a couple of times in the New Testament where this obedience is written about in ways that can seem strange. Paul describes Jesus as 'becoming obedient to death—even death on a cross!' (Philippians 2:8) and in Hebrews we are told that 'he learned obedience from what he suffered' (Hebrews 5:8). The ideas of 'becoming' and 'learning' sound like a process, as if once upon a time Jesus wasn't obedient and he learned it over time. So what is going on?

What is going on is a great reversal. Remember the Garden of Eden, and the tree of the knowledge of good and evil? It was God's domain entirely and eating that fruit and learning that knowledge was an attempt to take what was God's and make it ours? Well, the cross—the suffering and death of Jesus—is the reverse. It is not God's domain to die. It is ours. It is not God's domain to suffer. That is the domain of those who have rejected God's life-giving rule. Yet he takes what should be our domain and makes it his.

Jesus learns what it is to suffer, what it is to die, all in obedience to the purposes and plans of his Father to restore the disobedient back to himself. In taking on our flesh, Jesus experienced new things, things that should never have needed to be his to experience. That is his learning, an experience of what obedience requires. And it requires his suffering and his death.

So Jesus doesn't 'become' obedient because he once wasn't. No, these phrases are about Jesus truly embracing the depth of where that obedience would take him. Let's pick up the verse in Hebrews and keep on reading:

> Son though he was, he learned obedience from what he suffered and, once made perfect, he became the source of eternal salvation for all who obey him (Hebrews 5:8-9)

We see it all there, don't we? Since Jesus is Son of God, what follows in some way doesn't make sense, but he embraced it, plumbed the depths of humanity's darkness and the cost of obedience, making the plan perfect so that salvation might rain down! But who does it rain down on? The answer is given: 'all who obey him'. To follow Jesus is to commit to follow where he goes, to learn along with him the cost of obedience, to experience along with him a life lived hearing and obeying.

But we do not muster that ourselves. The very obedience of Jesus can only be granted to us by the Spirit. Not our own flesh. Our flesh is what gets us into difficulty, what Jesus had to enter so it could be restored. No, it is the Spirit in us that will lead us where we cannot go by ourselves. Paul puts it this way:

> Therefore, brothers and sisters, we have an obligation—but it is not to the flesh, to live according to it. For if you live according to the flesh, you will die; but if by the Spirit you put to death the misdeeds of the body, you will live. (Romans 8:12-13)

It sounds a little like Moses, doesn't it? Presenting the people a choice: obedience that leads to life or rebellion that leads to death. Only now a new dimension is at play. It is not *my* success or *my* failure that matters. It is *my* work (the effort of my flesh, doomed to fail) or *the Spirit's* work in me (destined to be perfected) that are contrasted. This is the work of the Spirit known as 'sanctification', meaning simply 'becoming holy'. Through the obedient sacrifice of Jesus, our unholiness is dealt with. And through the Spirit's residence in us, we too may begin to 'flesh out' holy obedience.

Not because we can. Because he can. And he did.

An important change of gears

So we return to where we started, with the emphasis placed by Jesus on obeying his teaching and his commands. It's there in the Great Commission, but we've seen we can't get there by ourselves. Once we've turned to him, though, obedience starts to open up to us, but we still need to choose it. We still need to choose what kind of Twister our life will play.

And here we need to consider an important distinction. Is our discipleship based on knowledge or on obedience? Knowledge is good. Teaching is good. Learning is really good! But, I want to suggest knowing things *about* God has never been the point of being a disciple, even if sometimes we have made it that way. Simply having good doctrine and correct theology is not what Jesus wants of his disciples.

There is a higher gear than that and it goes from knowledge to obedience, from understanding to doing.

In the last chapter, I suggested four 'levels' in how we do theology. Here is a fifth. Higher than having an 'Investigated Theology' (as good as that is), is having an 'Incarnated Theology'. Remember, it was through becoming one of us, suffering and dying as one of us, that Jesus fleshed out obedience. He did not send a book, sermon or message. He came. He acted. He did. Whatever we know of God, there is a gear he calls us to shift into: do something with it.

This seems to matter a lot to Jesus. The kinds of disciples he was interested in forming were active and obedient, not just knowledgeable. Let's look at that in four quick ways: what he taught, how he trained, what he said about his own teaching, and how it was all taken on by those who came after him.

What Jesus taught

At school, I remember being taught 'pure maths' and 'applied maths'. Pure maths was all theory, going deep into how maths works, different theories, processes and rules that governed it all. Applied maths is when you take that and use it for real situations, working out what speed something can go or the likelihood of something happening. I liked both, but my favourite was pure maths. I didn't want the hassle of real-world situations getting in the way of the neatness of theoretical ideas and abstract concepts.

With what Jesus teaches, I sometimes find myself thinking the same things: give it to me pure! He definitely teaches a lot of things we might think of as 'pure theology'. He talks about what his relationship with the Father is like and what the Kingdom of God is like, discusses things that will come as the end times draw near and why it is that he needed to come to rescue us.

But let's make sure we notice two things here. First, as big as these concepts are, they are not just 'pure'. They should be applied! If Jesus' relationship with his Father looks like something, and we are adopted into his family as brothers, sisters and co-heirs, what can *our* relationships with our Father look like? If I am a citizen of God's Kingdom, knowing what it's like should change *everything* about how I live. Because the end of the world is coming, Jesus encourages us to be alert, ready and active. The fact Jesus needed to come and rescue me means there is a response for me to make. This is all applied the-ology. There's no other kind.

Second, Jesus *also* teaches intensely practical things. He teaches about marriage, money, praying, fasting, anger, lust, dealing with conflicts, dealing with enemies, serving one another, how to trust God and many other real-life things. He told people what to do, not just things they could know. And if Jesus taught like this, it makes sense that he wanted people to learn like this. Not just know, but obey. Not just investigate what is true, but incarnate that, flesh it out, in their lives.

How Jesus trained

Let's also consider how Jesus actually trained his disciples. In our day, we often think that 'training for ministry' is done by going off somewhere to learn (maybe a theological college or conference) and then coming back to apply it. That has been the traditional model for much of Western Christianity for a long time. There are great things about it, but by itself it lacks something of how Jesus operated. Commenting on the strength of how Jesus trained his disciples, Alan Hirsch notes:

> We do not…leave our thinking behind when we are doing our ac-tions. We think while we are acting and act while we are thinking. In fact, this is precisely the way that all of us learned to walk, talk, so-cialise, and rationalise in the first place. Why would we assume that our mode of learning should change as we grow older?[34]

Jesus made no such assumption. He knew how people learn, and he knew what it was he wanted people to learn. That is why so much of his teaching with those closest to him happens 'on the way'. Some-thing happens and as they travel on from it, they reflect together, de-briefing and learning from it so that next time they are better equipped. What they do informs what they need to know and what they know inspires what they do. It's how people are apprenticed across so many different industries today, but often isn't how we as-sume discipleship works. A sermon on a Sunday can achieve lots of good things, but it cannot achieve all of what Jesus intended for those who follow him. It is good at knowledge and inspiration, but not at all designed for obedience.

One of the most formative times for Jesus' disciples was when he sent them out in pairs ahead of his visits to various towns. You can read about it in Luke 10:1-20, but really Jesus is doing what any good teacher would do. He sets a task, inspires them for it, gives clear guidance, and then sends them off to have a go. Then, once they have, he brings them back together to reflect on it and responds to some of what they've experienced by explaining it. It isn't rocket science! But how often do we take that kind of approach in our own discipleship? If it was important for the first followers of Jesus, it probably should be for us as well.

According to Jesus...

We also don't have to wonder how it was that Jesus teaching was meant to be treated, because he tells us! At the end of one of his longer sections of teaching, Jesus challenges his hearers by asking, "Why do you call me, 'Lord, Lord,' and do not do what I say?" (Luke 6:46). Ouch! Jesus sees his mega-fans, those who come out to hear his words, soak them up and nod along at all the right moments and he cuts straight to their hearts: what's the point of that devotion if you don't do anything differently as a result? Another time he says these famous words:

> *Therefore everyone who hears these words of mine and puts them into practice is like a wise man who built his house on the rock. The rain came down, the streams rose, and the winds blew and beat against that house; yet it did not fall, because it had its foundation on the rock. But everyone who hears these words of mine and does not put them into practice is like a foolish man who built his house on sand. The rain came down, the streams rose, and the winds blew and beat against that house, and it fell with a great crash. (Matthew 7:24-27)*

What is the rock that protects the house in the storm? Not *knowing* all that Jesus teaches. No! Jesus says the wise builder is the one who "hears these words of mine and puts them into practice". He's very explicit here. There is a word for those who hear what Jesus teaches—reading the Bible, studying it, listening to preaching—and don't put it into practice. Jesus' word for those people is 'foolish'. I'll say it again: ouch!

Is your engagement with Jesus' teaching changing you? Can you point to some ways it has? Not just years ago when it was all fresh, but recently, in the last year. What habits have formed or changed? How has your character shifted? How are your relationships, your finances, or your outlook different? Those things are not the whole of the purpose of Jesus' teaching and God's word in the Bible. But they are a part of it according to Jesus himself. We'd be foolish to ignore that.

In Jesus' footsteps

Those who first followed Jesus seemed to get this message loud and clear. Jesus' brother James does not mince his words on this:

> *Do not merely listen to the word, and so deceive yourselves. Do what it says. Anyone who listens to the word but does not do what it says is like someone who looks at his face in a mirror and, after looking at himself, goes away and immediately forgets what he looks like. But whoever looks intently into the perfect law that gives freedom, and continues in it—not forgetting what they have heard, but doing it—they will be blessed in what they do. (James 1:22-25)*

Mirrors are very common today, so it's unlikely we'll ever forget what we look like! But in James's day, a rare glimpse of your own reflection told you what you were like. Sometimes that would surprise you, sometimes please you and sometimes make you realise you need to work on your grooming. But to do nothing with it is a wasted opportunity. Likewise, James says, if we merely listen to what God says through his word, we are missing out, even deceiving ourselves. The Bible acts as a mirror for our lives, showing us not just what God is like, but what we are like, giving us an opportunity to do something about it. Hear and obey, hear and obey, hear and obey.

It wasn't just James, though. Paul, leading into words about the nature of love, has this warning to give:

> *If I have the gift of prophecy and can fathom all mysteries and all knowledge, and if I have a faith that can move mountains, but do not have love, I am nothing. (1 Corinthians 13:2)*

Knowledge, however it has been revealed by God, is 'nothing' if it isn't backed up by love. And love is a doing word in the Bible, not just a feeling (it definitely is here, given how Paul will describe love a couple of verses later). Even 'faith', a deep trust and confidence in God, must be backed up by love, he says. We should note that in the next verse Paul also condemns empty actions—faking it isn't what Jesus is after either! But action filled with God and in response to God absolutely is something he wants for us.

So in what Jesus taught, how he trained, what he said about his own teaching and how his followers led onward, there's a really clear thread. Jesus is calling those who follow him to step up a gear. From knowing to obeying.

Beware the pendulum swings

Before we move on to our Obedience Toolkit, considering how our heads, hearts and hands can step toward fuller obedience, I want to give two gentle words of caution. I've been encouraging a shift from knowledge-based discipleship to an obedience-based discipleship. I stand by this! But with this shift, there is a danger the pendulum might swing too far and into unhealthy places. Two come to mind.

Danger 1: A gospel of works

Your obedience to Jesus is not what saves you. As we've already seen, it was *his* obedient life, suffering and death that achieved that. But we are really good at writing stories in ways that make ourselves the heroes, so when we try to focus on being obedient disciples, there's a danger we'll start to do just that. Over time, we can slip into the idea that maybe we weren't so bad to start with, maybe we didn't need as much of God's grace as we thought.

Don't ignore obedience. Jesus commands it, several times. But don't let it trick you into thinking you could ever have saved yourself. You couldn't.

It doesn't have to be that way, though. Paul was insistent in his writing that 'a person is justified by faith apart from the works of the law' (Romans 3:28). The only way we access the saving sacrifice of Jesus is by faith—believing it, trusting it and placing our confidence in it. But that does not stop Paul writing about good works. Writing to the Ephesians, he said this:

> *For it is by grace you have been saved, through faith—and this is not from yourselves, it is the gift of God—not by works, so that no one can boast. For we are God's handiwork, created in Christ Jesus to do good works, which God prepared in advance for us to do. (Ephesians 2:8-10)*

Paul sees no contradiction. In one breath he reminds us that we can never boast about our works because they weren't enough to save us. The gospel on which we stand unashamed is one of grace, he says, accessed through faith. And then in the next breath he declares that we have been made to do good works, indeed good works that God himself has planned out for us. Obediently doing good works is, according to Paul…good.

So as you seek to pursue obedience, really pursue it! But don't boast about it. Remember faith *and* works, but also remember they aren't in the same category. Faith is what you need to be saved. You don't need good works for that. But good works of obedience to God's word are what is needed to make you faithful and fruitful as you work out that gracious gift of salvation.

Danger 2: A slave mindset

A second pendulum swing to be on guard against is a warping of the way we view our relationship with God. Normally, the kinds of people we think of 'obeying' are bosses, superiors, or angry schoolmaster types. When we think of obeying Jesus, then, we can slip into a mindset where he is the master and we are the slave. It is not a personal relationship, but a transaction. He doesn't care for us, just wants to boss us about. We don't care for him, just know we have to do what he says. But, though he is indeed Lord of the universe, that is not the way Jesus speaks of the kind of relationship he wants. This is part of his farewell meal with the disciples:

> *My command is this: Love each other as I have loved you. Greater love has no one than this: to lay down one's life for one's friends. You are my friends if you do what I command. I no longer call you servants, because a servant does not know his master's business. Instead, I have called you friends, for everything that I learned from my Father I have made known to you. (John 15:12-15)*

Just as Paul did not see faith and works as contradictory, Jesus is happy to use, side-by-side, the language of commanding and the language of friendship. He shows his commitment to that friendship by dying for them within a matter of days. And he invites them not just to obey his commands, but to respond to his love and friendship with a love and friendship of their own. Directed toward him and toward one another.

Jesus makes it very clear: they are not to think of it purely as a master/servant relationship. The reason he gives is simple: he has let them in on his plans and invited a partnership. Rather than just barking out orders and waiting for them to comply, they are brought into his purposes. While I might follow a command from a boss, I make plans with my friends. Jesus, astonishingly, wants to work *with* us, not just through us. His hands are interlocked with ours, not pulling strings to control us.

Another aspect of the 'slave mindset' to avoid is to think of obedience as being the opposite of freedom. If I have to obey Jesus, that means my freedom to choose is being limited and I just have to do what he says. But obedience and freedom are not in fact opposites. In this chapter, we've seen that the opposite of obedience is disobedience, also known as sin. And as Jesus points out, "everyone who sins is a slave to sin." (John 8:34) Sin traps us and dominates us like a slavedriver unless we are rescued from it.

And Jesus does rescue us from it, by dying for us and also by releasing us into a new life of obedience to his teaching that is good for us, in fact the very best for us. He says, "If you hold to my teaching, you are really my disciples. Then you will know the truth, and the truth will set you free." (John 8:31-32) Obedience does not remove freedom. It leads us *to* freedom. Freedom to actually choose the things that make us flourish and thrive, to be who we were made to be, instead of being trapped in the sin that holds us back from that.

So we must be wary of a pendulum swing. A heart of obedience mattered deeply to Jesus. We've seen that. If that challenges you, as it does me, let that challenge sink in. But don't let it push you farther than it should. Don't let it push you to start to believe it is your works, not your faith, that count in your standing before God. Obedience is an expression of *faith*fulness, not just hard work. And don't let it push you into a slavery mindset before God. Obedience is the response of a friend not a robot, a person truly free instead of trapped in rebellion.

So as we move on now to considering practically how we might cultivate this quality of obedience, really we are asking this question: how can I be a faithful friend of Jesus?

Chapter 4 at a glance...

In this chapter, we:

1. Used three different versions of the game Twister to open up the idea of obedience, concluding that it is to hear God and follow his voice.

2. Took a trip through the Old Testament, seeing that disobedience to God has been a constant characteristic:

   • Adam and Even taking the fruit in the Garden.

   • Abram, and a life marked by both faith and failure.

   • The choice the people had: life or death.

   • How the desire for a king was really so they could rule themselves and a rejection of God.

3. Considered the life of Jesus, and how he perfectly embodied obedience, but also asked whether we can obey like him? We took heart that through what Jesus has done being given to us by the Spirit, the possibility of actually growing in this is open up to us.

4. Thought about a 'shift of gears' from a discipleship based on knowledge to one based on obedience. We saw this biblically in:

   • Jesus teaching things that were designed to be obeyed.

   • Jesus training people for action, not just filling heads with truth.

   • Jesus plainly telling people that obedience is his aim.

   • Those who followed Jesus and writing the New Testament letters also having a strong emphasis on obedience.

5. Warned of two possible pendulum swing over-corrections as we focus on obedience:

   • Slipping into a gospel of works, where we think we are earning a standing before God by doing what he says.

   • Adopting a slave mindset where we think obedience is about being enslaved, when in fact submission to God is true freedom.

AN OBEDIENT
DISCIPLE'S TOOLKIT

How to be a faithful friend

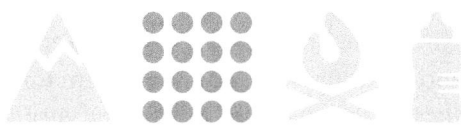

In the New Testament, it is probably James (Jesus' brother) who is most famous for waging war against the kind of faith that is disconnected from good works. In the last chapter, we saw his instruction not just to be 'hearers' of the word, but to 'do what it says'. At another point in his letter, he gives a challenge to anyone who isn't convinced of the importance of obedient action resulting from our faith. His challenge goes like this:

> *But someone will say, "You have faith; I have deeds." Show me your faith without deeds, and I will **show you my faith by my deeds**. (James 2:18, emphasis added)*

That is what this chapter is all about. We should not be interested merely in an activist attitude, choosing outward obedience over inward faith. But we should be hugely interested in our faith in Jesus being shown by obedience to all we receive from him. As before, we will consider our thinking, our being, and our doing.

HEAD: Obedient Decisions

Our minds are crucial in growing in obedience. Let's say I am training for a marathon and I have a training plan in place. One day I am tired, my legs are sore and I skip a training run. While I might blame my legs as the 'reason', my legs didn't make the decision to stay in that day. Legs don't make decisions. It is always our minds that do that. And there are at least a couple of important decisions to make if we want to live in real obedience to Jesus.

1. 'I will let God call the shots'

This might seem so obvious that it doesn't need saying, but if we are going to be obedient to him, we actually need to value what he says. But more than that, we need to value what he says *over* whatever other competing voices we might otherwise listen to. Imagine my nephew's Twister game again, but this time there are ten other people all giving instructions. He knows only my voice counts, but he has to filter the others and choose what to do with them if he wants to win.

I find this reflection from Jackie Hill Perry very helpful, but also very challenging:

> As for us, we might say Jesus was a good man worth emulating, but what does "good" mean to us, really? To many, He is good insofar as He fits within the moral standards of society. Well-mannered, generous, fair, nonviolent, tolerant, vegan, polite, and inclusive… [In] response I must say that holiness (and goodness) should never be determined by the whims, wishes, and standards of a created thing or even a whole culture. Especially when that culture's ideas are so easily influenced by the deceitful hearts within it.[35]

If the ways in which we admire Jesus, the ways in which we will follow him, are limited to the ways we or our society wants to behave anyway, that is not true obedience. True obedience is to take God at his word, let him call the shots—all of them—and follow no matter what. In every single part of our lives. John McGinley points out the all-encompassing nature of following Jesus like this:

> The lordship of Jesus Christ extends over our finances, our family, our work, our play, our ambitions, our politics, our sexuality and everything in between.[36]

To ignore the Lordship of Jesus in a certain area of life is to treat him as less than he really is. Imagine you pick up your phone and see six notifications. One is a message from a family member asking you to run an errand. One is clearly spam. One is a message from your boss asking you to give her a call. Two are from friends, one arranging a date to catch up and the other with a link to a hilarious video of a dog on a ski slope ("Not even lying, I lol'd so hard!!!"). The last is from an employee requesting some advice on a project they're working on.

What you do with each of these tells you something. It tells you something about how you view the message, yes, but perhaps more than that it tells you how you view the person sending it. If you ignore the employee but return the boss's call immediately, it might say something about the way you view power dynamics in the workplace. If you immediately arrange a catch-up with the friend but do not get round to the errand for your family, it reveals your priorities. Or if you are more interested in the spam message than the ("honestly, best thing ever") ski dog… Actually, the jury is out on that one. It might be the correct decision.

Do you see the point here, though? What we do when someone says something to us shows how we view them. In Chapter 3, we touched on having a 'Posture of Submission'. This is related, but now we aren't just interested in what we *think about* what God says. As we look toward fleshed out obedience, it is what we *do about* what God says that really counts. If we truly view Jesus as who he is, Lord of all, then this kind of obedience makes sense. McGinley goes on to say:

> A reduced and limited Jesus doesn't require everything from us and is much more manageable than the Lord of the universe. The problem is that it just isn't Jesus. And Jesus refuses to be contained. He demands that we accept his divine and sovereign claim upon our lives as Lord.[37]

So what if we add a seventh notification to our list, only this one is from Jesus? That's less likely to come as a notification on your phone. But it should be coming as you spend time in the Bible, as you open it up with others, through times of prayer and as you pause to listen to God's guiding voice. 'What is he saying?' is a great question! 'What will you do about it?' is vital too. Will you jump to it? Ignore it? Schedule it? Question it? Dismiss it out of hand? Will you value it?

Fear it? Draw comfort from it? Tweak it? Rationalise it away?

God speaks and it should change our thinking. That's submission. When we do something with it, that's obedience. Jesus' cousin, John the Baptist, put it this way: "Produce fruit in keeping with repentance" (Luke 3:8). What begins in us as God moulds and changes us inwardly, must come out of us as we allow him to change us outwardly.

So the decision is a simple one but a vital one. What voices dominate when you make choices about how to live and what to do? Do you only follow God when he lines up with other voices you agree with (including your own)? Or will you decide to let him call the shots and commit to your actions following suit?

2. 'I will not value knowledge over obedience'

A second decision we can make is about the order in which we value things. Deep down, what matters most to you: learning more of the wonders of God, or living more faithfully as his friend and follower? I know that for me, the tendency and temptation is toward knowledge. I love learning things because I love knowing things! When I finish a book, I will very quickly reach for the next one, whether or not I've really sought to bed into my life what I've read in the first one. When I hear a sermon, I will often be challenged about something in my life, but how often do I take that to its conclusion and change something?

I should be clear: part of the purpose of God's word, studying it, and preaching, is to encourage. As we are reminded of the gospel, our hearts are warmed as we come back to our Father God in renewed wonder, love and commitment. That is vital if we are to avoid the pendulum swing toward a wrong obsession with works. But simply knowledge has never been the point.

It is sometimes said that "If your output exceeds your input, then your upkeep will be your downfall."[38] It is both obvious and true! If we are constantly trying to do things for God but never receiving from him, we will run out of steam. If we seek obedience to God's word but never engage with God's word, a crash is not too far into our future. But in Western Christianity, often the reverse might be the bigger danger. What happens when your input exceeds your output? When you are filled up on teaching, on doctrine, on truth, but rarely get to a point of that teaching, doctrine or truth working its way *out* through our actions and lives? Then our downfall will not be our up-keep. Our downfall will be that we get full, stuffed with good things, but stuffed nonetheless. The truth that goes in also comes out.

Sometimes truth will come out of us when we just manage to keep on going with hope in the midst of suffering and pain. Sometimes truth will come out of us in the gentleness of our voices when every-one else is harsh. Sometimes truth will come out of us because we have prayed for someone instead of just giving our opinion on their situation. But the truth that goes into us is meant to come out of us. Being passive and accumulating knowledge has never been the point. Michael Frost and Alan Hirsch, in their excellent book *ReJesus*, put the challenge like this:

> We cannot be disinterested spectators when it comes to Jesus. In fact, in the encounters described in the New Testament, the desire of peo-ple to remain neutral observers is in a real sense the real sin (e.g., the rich young ruler or Pilate). It is those who allow Jesus to change them who end up entering the kingdom.[39]

Do you value the input more than the output? If you do, join the club! There are enough of us that we could get T-shirts made. But after we've joined the club, why not try to disband the club? It's a club Je-sus never really wanted to exist, so if this is you, definitely acknowl-edge where you are, but don't try to stay there. On second thoughts, maybe the T-shirts aren't a good idea.

But we could decide to try out some other T-shirt slogans. How about, 'When I read the Bible, I let the Bible read me' as a slogan? That could be a lot more healthy! Remember James's words about not just hearing but doing, and then comparing God's word to a mirror so we can see what we're really like? (James 1:22-25) Taking that seri-ously is a great way to value obedience over knowledge. When we do that, we'll not just be inspired by the nature of God and what he has done. No, we will be caught up in the story of God, see ourselves within it and ask how we can play our part more fully.

Or a T-shirt could say, 'Built up, not puffed up!' That would be taken straight from the Bible itself, as Paul tells the (rather arrogant) Corinthians,

> *We know that "We all possess knowledge." But knowledge puffs up while*

love builds up. Those who think they know something do not yet know as they ought to know. But whoever loves God is known by God. (1 Corinthians 8:1-3)

The Corinthians were obsessed with attaining higher levels of understanding. On the lookout for impressive teachers with new ideas, they were caught up with the desire to be in the know. Paul uses their own words back to them: 'We all possess knowledge'. It seems they used these words as a badge of honour, satisfied and a little smug in their own cleverness. Paul does not say what they know is wrong. Instead, he points them toward a higher goal: love. Their desire for knowledge above all else makes them 'puffed up', proud and arrogant. In fact, Paul says, it is making them blind to the things they don't yet know. But if someone loves, then it is clear they have been 'built up', really become solid not just over-inflated.

Why love? Paul is taking his lead from Jesus. When asked what the greatest commandment was, Jesus summed it up as love for God and love for others (Mark 12:24-31). And when he gathered his disciples together for their last meal before his death, he told them love would be the clearest sign of the community they would form in his name: "By this everyone will know that you are my disciples, if you love one another" (John 13:35). Love is an action, and to love in Jesus' name is the highest form of obedience to him. It builds us up and shows we are built up. Love trumps knowledge.

Returning to Frost and Hirsch, they carry on by saying:

Theoretical knowledge of spiritual truth is never commended in Scripture… Obedience is the evidence that knowledge of God has been received and understood. In the Bible, the real test of what you know is how you live. Something goes seriously wrong with our capacity to integrate or even comprehend Scripture if we do not obey but just study it.[40]

And that is why I was blown away by the children in my old church during the Covid lockdowns. They led the way in 'integrating' and 'comprehending' Scripture in a way that will stay with me and inspires a final T-shirt suggestion: 'S.O.S.'

Like many churches, we recorded content that people could engage with together during that time and put it online. The children of our church started a weekly online 'Kids Church'. (It was aimed at kids, but in truth I think many adults were more blessed by it than the online content I was involved in putting together, which I'm totally fine with!) It contained lots of things, but the best bit for me was a weekly 'S.O.S. Bible study'. Every week, a different child would read a bit of the Bible out and then answer three questions. S: What does it Say? O: What will I Obey? S: What can I Share?[41]

Week after week, these children were modelling for us a brilliant way of engaging with the Bible. Yes, we need to know what it says, of course we do! But if we stop there, we fall well short of the purpose of the whole thing. We also need to decide what we will do in obedience to what it says and how we will not just keep it to ourselves but pass it on to others.

If we love knowledge too much and obedience too little, we won't behave like that. We'll be too interested in gaining more information to do anything with the information we have got our heads around already. So what T-shirt do you want to wear? Which club will you be a part of? It has to be an active decision, so will you make it?

HEART: Obedient Posture

What kind of heart is needed toward God to fuel a life lived in obedience to him? If we go back to the notifications on our phone, it was the attitude toward the one who sent the messages that determined the way we responded. If you are quick to respond to someone, it could be because of love, loyalty, fear or a whole host of other things. But we don't respond quickly from a place of neutrality.

Remember, these parts of the toolkit are about our posture, the stance we wish to adopt toward God with our whole lives. It might take some gestures to get there, but it is the settled position with him that we are aiming for. I wish to suggest just one posture that marks an obedient life.

3. A posture of response

We started our exploration of obedience by zooming in on the example of Mary, and we saw how what stood out was her 'rapid response'. Not only did she say 'yes', but she said it quickly and completely. She demonstrated the kind of posture toward God that obedience is all about. She heard and she responded.

How we respond when God has said something is what makes the difference. But remember, we aren't interested in robotics here. Jesus invites us to work with him as his friends and that means questions are ok! Mary asked one, remember. She heard what Gabriel said and then asked how it was going to happen. She did not refuse to be involved, but she did ask for a greater level of understanding about what that involvement meant. There is nothing unfaithful in a response to God that says, 'Yes, but how?' Or 'Yes, but I'm confused, I'm scared, I'm going to find this hard.' Those are the kinds of things a friend can say freely. Loyalty is a key to obedience, but because Jesus has 'made known' his plans to us, it is not a blind loyalty.

Of course there are responses and questions that aren't obedient or faithful at all. Maybe we try to *bargain* with God: 'Ok, I'll do this, but only if…' When we do that, it is a transaction we are looking for, not a friendship. And God has already done more than enough for us. Perhaps our response is *cynicism*, questioning God's motives and assuming he might not have our best interests at heart. That is a trust question and perhaps some of the suggestions from the Psalms in Chapter 3 could be useful. Or maybe our response is one of *apathy*: 'Does it really matter if I follow God in this or not?' It all just feels rather pointless, so why not do the easy thing? Maybe especially in things that feel small.

But if we want an obedient heart, a posture of faithful response to God, we need not to let those attitudes dominate. We must push back on them, choose to stand straight instead of slouching. We need some obedient gestures. Here are three.

i. Respond to the little things

This could be the beginning of the answer to the issue of apathy. Jesus once told a story about people trusted with different amounts of money by their master who show different levels of trustworthiness. The punchline is this:

> *Whoever can be trusted with very little can also be trusted with much, and whoever is dishonest with very little will also be dishonest with much. (Luke 16:10)*

The principle is really obvious, isn't it? If I cannot even show trustworthiness in a small act of obedience, I'll never settle into a full posture of faithful response to God. If I'm selfish with a pound, I'll be selfish with more. If I can't keep a small and unimportant secret, I shouldn't be trusted with something bigger. If I break a simple promise, why would you take me at my word when I promise something huge? So part of cultivating a lifestyle of obedience is to start with the pennies, not the pounds.

So what are the little things in your life? They add up, but they also set us up to be able to handle the big things. Perhaps the little thing is the fifteen minutes you have at the start of the day before others wake up. How will you use it and does it belong to you, or to God? A small thing most of us have with us all the time is our phone, so is it something you are trustworthy with? Or do bad habits, like wasting time endlessly scrolling or searching out things you shouldn't, creep in? Then there is money, which is what Jesus speaks about after the words above. We'll say more about this in a future chapter and perhaps for you this isn't a little thing but a big one. But changing how you choose to spend, save or give away the resources God has trusted you with could be a gesture in service of a healthier posture.

There is biblical wisdom that can be applied to each of these things, along with so many other 'little things' in our lives. There is also common sense! But if we've decided to let God call the shots, will we respond in these small areas of our lives, doing things differently as he leads us?

ii. Respond to the clear things

There are also things that might not be little but are extremely clear in the Bible. The Dutch philosopher and theologian Søren Kierkegaard wrote:

> The matter is quite simple. The bible is very easy to understand. But we Christians are a bunch of scheming swindlers. We pretend to be unable to understand it because we know very well that the minute we understand, we are obliged to act accordingly.[42]

You might be thinking, 'What?! The Bible is *not* very easy to understand!' And in part, I'd agree! There are weird and wonderful things within it, and a great big sweeping story with so much richness, beauty and depth that we'll never be able to wrap our heads and hearts fully around it. But don't let that become an excuse! Because there is also great truth in what Kierkegaard says here. Much (maybe even most) of the Bible is not a riddle or a mystery. There is so much that is laid out plainly to us that our response is simple: obey, or disobey.

Maybe you could start with the Ten Commandments and their instructions about honouring parents, keeping a Sabbath Day of rest, murder, adultery, theft, lying, and wrongly desiring things that are not our own. No confusion is needed in approaching these commands. We can even look to Jesus for how he then took them, lived them and unpacked them in his teaching. They are clear, meaning there is no smokescreen for us to hide behind. We've heard, but will we do?

Or perhaps it is Jesus' teaching on giving, praying and fasting in Matthew 6:1-18. Is prayer a mysterious thing? I certainly find it so. But are we left with any doubt from Jesus that we should be doing it? Absolutely not! And he even gives practical, actionable guidance in how to approach it. The same thing can be said about his words on fasting and giving. We might like to dress these things up, clothe them in more mystery than they require, and ponder them at length. But before we do all of that, let's make sure we're responding to them by…doing them.

And as you spend time reading the Bible, be on the lookout for other 'clear things', where there is no nuance or ambiguity needed. If I mumble as I call out Twister commands to my nephew, he has an excuse for getting things wrong. But God is not a divine mumbler. His voice is clearer than we often give credit for. Much as we might prefer otherwise, that means the ball is in our court.

iii. Respond to one big thing

One last gesture for you to consider as you examine your posture of response is to do something a little bigger. If you want to turn a boat round 180° you can get there with lots of little 1° shifts. That might be the 'little things', and they are so important for correcting a course. But don't reject the idea that God might want you to make a much larger shift than that.

It might be that God wants a career change for you. Maybe the relationship you're in is unhealthy and it either needs to change or end. Perhaps your finances need a major shake-up not just a small tweak. There could be a habit or hobby that is so deeply embedded that losing it feels like losing a limb, but it needs to go anyway. God could be calling you to step into a new kind of leadership, or to use a certain spiritual gift in ways you never have before.

Sometimes in the Bible, God knew someone's life was going to change so much in response to him that he gave them a new name to signify the size of the shift. So Abram becomes Abraham. Sarai becomes Sarah. Simon becomes Peter. Saul becomes Paul. A big ask. A big 'yes'. A new name.

How will you know if God has one big change for you? It might be because it is one of the 'clear' things we've just explored. If you have become a habitual liar, or if you treat sex as cheap, or overindulge with alcohol, the clear teaching of Scripture is calling you to make a big shift and inviting a response to that. Or it might be that through investigating an area of life, faith or theology, you have settled that something is or is not right and you need to make the shift to 'flesh that out' with your own life. Perhaps that is in the area of financial giving and you know you need to put your money where your theology is.

Or, through listening to God in prayer, or by receiving wisdom or prophetic insight from trusted people, God might lay heavily on your heart the need for a big leap. Sometimes, when you know you know. Be cautious here, because none of us is infallible, but don't write it off either. Entrust it to God in prayer, ask for the Spirit in you to give clarity and conviction and seek wisdom from others.

But once you know there is a 'big thing' that is right for you to do, do not delay. If you've heard, respond!

At this point, I'll just give you a little reminder that if you put this book down, it'll still be here when you're ready to pick it up again! If any of those three things struck a chord, pause. The next couple of tools in the toolkit are about how we can practise obedience through the relationships in our lives, but the deep work in your heart is where it starts. If there's something you need to do, or commit to do, pause a moment to do that before you carry on.

HANDS: Obedient Actions

Part of growing in anything is about putting the right things around us to set us up for success. To get fitter, you don't just adjust diet and exercise. You also find ways to keep that going, track it, make it stick. Maybe you use an app to track your exercise or calorie intake, or you get a personal trainer. Both set the conditions so fitness is more likely. I want to suggest two of those kinds of actions we can take so that faithful obedience to our Lord and friend Jesus is more likely, and both involve other people. Obedience works better in community.

4. Imitate someone worth imitating

The first is to be really deliberate about who you will become more like. Good role models make a huge difference, not just for those who are young but for all of us. If obedience is to be fleshed out, lived out in real ways, it really helps us to see that in the life of someone else so we can then apply it to our own. Obviously nobody we meet this side of Heaven will be the perfect role-model, but where we see a likeness and obedience to Jesus in someone, let's learn from it!

Paul was very happy to encourage this kind of attitude. Writing to the Corinthians, it was not just his words but his life he wanted them to follow: "Follow my example, as I follow the example of Christ" (1 Corinthians 11:1). Paul does not claim perfection here, but he does believe there are Christ-like things about him that others can learn from. That isn't arrogance on his part, but a sign of maturity in Jesus. Or consider this in his words to the Thessalonians:

> You know how we lived among you for your sake. You became imitators of us and of the Lord, for you welcomed the message in the midst of severe suffering with the joy given by the Holy Spirit. And so you became a model to all the believers in Macedonia and Achaia. The Lord's message rang out from you not only in Macedonia and Achaia—your faith in God has become known everywhere. (1 Thessalonians 1:5-8)

Did you spot the sequence? The Thessalonians imitate Paul and the others who had first led them to Jesus. As they do this, they are also imitating Jesus. Just as Jesus had and just as Paul had, that meant they were able to accept and cling to the good news in the midst of great suffering. They saw that and they then did it themselves. 'And so [they] became a model' to others, those nearby in Macedonia and Achaia and, ultimately, their (fleshed out, obedient) faith became known 'everywhere'. There's a ripple effect, and it starts with a decision on their part to become 'imitators' of Paul and the others.

The word translated 'imitators' is the same word that we get 'mimic' from. It is the act of copying the exact actions of someone else so you look just like them. And for that to work, at least two things need to be true: they need to be worth copying and you need to be close enough to copy them.

When choosing who to 'imitate', make sure they are worth it! There is no point in having a mentor you can learn nothing from. Paul was a good one, but only in so far as he was imitating Jesus. Who do you see who is a little more mature than you, has experienced things that will be helpful for you and shines Jesus in ways that you are able to see? That could be someone worth imitating. Perhaps there is someone who has worked in the same industry or sector as you for years and has served in it as a faithful Christian. Perhaps, if you are married, there is an older couple in your church whose marriage you admire and you want to learn from. Or if you are single, perhaps you know someone who has lived single for many years and you see flourishing. These might all be brilliant people to be something of a role-model or mentor for you.

But the second component is crucial too. You need to be close enough to be able actually to see what makes them tick and how they really embody obedience and faithfulness to Jesus in real ways. Remember, this isn't about theory. It goes beyond that and that means getting up close and personal. To the same Thessalonians, Paul reminds them that,

> *"we loved you so much, we were delighted to share with you not only the gospel of God but our lives as well." (1 Thessalonians 2:8)*

These people actually *knew* him, not just from his writing but because he had opened up his life to them in real ways. They knew his routine, his habits, what his unguarded words were like. They saw how he acted and reacted, how he spoke and listened, how he prayed and fasted. They saw it all because they were close enough. A virus can be really infectious, but unless you are close to a carrier you will never catch it. Proximity is key!

You might already have the kind of closeness with someone who you want to learn from. If you do, brilliant! What have you seen in them? What is it about them that shines Jesus? What does obedience to God look like in real terms in their life? And then the big question:

what are you doing to imitate those things?

In all likelihood, though, you might not have that kind of relationship yet. But you could ask for one! Once, at a small gathering of church leaders, I met someone who I very quickly came to respect. I saw things in him that I wanted in me, that I knew would make me more like Jesus as a disciple and as a leader myself. So I approached him during one of the breaks and told him that. I then asked if he would consider a mentoring role in my life.

Two things about his response confirmed that I had asked the right person! First, he didn't give me an answer straight away. He noted it down, took my details and said he'd be in touch after both praying *and* really considering if he had capacity. I learned something just from that which I have imitated since. Second, when he did say yes and we began meeting monthly, he asked me who I was going to do this kind of thing for. If I was 'imitating' him, who was it that I could invite to 'imitate' me? A really good challenge!

The moral of that story is that if you don't ask you won't get. So perhaps you need to make that ask. A monthly conversation where you can discuss real things and learn from them. Time with them and their family on a regular basis, so you can see how they function and what life is like below the surface. There's vulnerability in making that request, because you are admitting you can't do it by yourself and that they are in a position to help. Unless you are particularly mean, I am sure that if someone came to you and admitted that, you would neither judge them nor mistreat them because of it. So if the person you're considering asking is worth asking (and therefore not particularly mean!), you are in safe hands!

Some people call this mentoring. Others discipling. Others just friendship. I don't really mind what you call it, but it is a really good thing to do. I am pretty sure this was the main way the gospel was always meant to be passed on and fleshed out. Not from pulpit to pew, but from one life to another life.

5. Become accountable to someone

A few years ago, I started running. It was hard! I did it because of a sermon my friend Stephen preached, in which he spoke about the value God has given our bodies and how, as a result, we should honour and care for them. It was a great message and I knew that honestly I wasn't looking after my body as well as God wanted me to. So I did something about it! I downloaded an app that gets you from the couch to your first 5k and started out.

At this point in this story, I'd let God call the shots, valuing obedience to what God said through that sermon over just learning knowledge through it. So far, so good! I'd also demonstrated a posture of responsiveness, downloading the app and lacing up my trainers a few times a week. But I am not the hero of this story. The hero of this story is...my friend Stephen. Not because of the sermon, but because of what came next.

What would I do once the 5k goal was achieved? I didn't know because I hadn't ever done this before, but Stephen was a marathon runner so he must know. He was worth imitating, so I asked. He asked a few questions and listened to what I said and then he said, "I think you should train for a 10k." Outwardly I probably nodded, but inwardly I was thinking, *'No way! That is double what already feels like my limit, dream on...* But then he said, "Let's sign up for an event and we'll run it together." At which point my thinking shifted. *'Well I guess now I can't say 'no', and he'll know if I back out so I'll have to follow through...'* Stephen knew me well enough to know a goal that stretches me would motivate me, but also knew something true of all of us: we need accountability.

It was accountability that changed it all for me. If I consistently skipped training runs, Stephen would know. If I backed out of the event, Stephen would know. I had to do it! Not because Stephen is an ogre breathing down my neck waiting to point out every time I failed. But because Stephen is an encouraging friend, giving me strength and helping pick me up any time I failed. Without him, I might have kept up the 5k I'd got to myself, or I might have given up... But with him, I got there. We ran the race together, and his family were waiting on the finish line with my wife. His kids even made a banner!

I share this because, while what I asked for was advice and maybe a mentor, what I got was a friend alongside. And that is what I really needed. In faith, too, we are not able to do it alone. But that is alright, because we were never meant to! In the book of Proverbs, we read:

As iron sharpens iron,
  so one person sharpens another. (Proverbs 27:17)

If you want to be sharp, not dull, you need others alongside. It is the friction as two lives rub up against each other that really creates the energy to hone every part of our lives. If you want to grow in obedience to Jesus, get yourself some friends to do it with, or really dig in deep with the friends you have. Open up not just at a surface level, but deeper than that. Become accountable, sharing the victories and confessing the failures. Do not do this with everyone. That isn't safe and is called 'oversharing'. But do it with one or two people.

What might this look like? It needs to be regular. Weekly, preferably, otherwise you will spend so much time on catching up and small talk that you'll not get to the heart of the matter. It also needs to be planned. What will you use that time for? That could include sharing highs and lows from the last week, reflecting on Scripture and how you will apply it together, confession of sin, prayer, and setting goals for the coming week.

If 'confession of sin' sounded a bit heavy there, you are not alone! In many circles, we don't use that language much at all. Or if we do, we think of public prayers in a church service (often before communion) where we confess sin in a general sense and remember our need for forgiveness. Good as that is, the confession of specific sin in our lives is a really healthy practice. Richard Foster helpfully writes:

> A generalised confession may save us from humiliation and shame, but it will not ignite inner healing… It is far too easy to avoid our real guilt in a general confession. In our confession we bring concrete sins.[43]

How can we do that? Depending on what you find most helpful, you can start with questions or with answers. To start with questions would mean asking one another specific things to give space both to share progress and confess those 'concrete sins'. You might agree upon a list of questions (perhaps like those suggested by Neil Cole,[44] see note for details) as a starting point and then go from there. Or to start with answers is simply to give freedom to share whatever comes to mind when you meet. This is less structured, which has advantages, but gives greater ability to ignore things that need to be brought into the light.

Why do this, though? I want to suggest three simple reasons. First, being honest to this level with someone (and having them be honest in return) is an accelerator for spiritual growth and deeper obedience. Having a regular time to stop, take stock, celebrate and recalibrate is a game changer. Wherever it is that you need to take a step forward, this can be a place to discover it and decide it, which makes it far more likely you will actually do it. Whether it's your prayer life or your sex life, your finances or your sharing of faith, your words or your actions, all of it can be brought up, turned over, examined and brought to greater health. And the more honest you are willing to be, the greater the impact.

The second reason is that you cannot achieve the same thing in other ways. A church service is wonderful for lots of things, but deep openness and honesty is not normally one of them. A preacher can preach a great sermon, but cannot then go round the room and individually help each person apply it. There isn't the time and that individual doesn't have the permission in everyone's life to do so. As Bobby Harrington and Alex Absalom note:

> Deep personal transformation happens in close relationships with just a few, because only a few people can earn the trust it takes to be vulnerable, open, and honest in life-on-life situations.[45]

The final reason is that accountable friends can help you avoid the pendulum swings we considered at the end of the last chapter. When we open up to others about our sin, they can remind us of how great the grace of God is and declare his forgiveness over us. We are far more likely to slip into a gospel of works if we are working at things alone, but others can point us back to this wonderful truth "If we confess our sins, he is faithful and just and will forgive us our sins" (1 John 1:9). And we are far more likely to remember Jesus as friend not just master if we embrace our life with him surrounded by friends.

As the African proverb says, 'if you want to go fast, go alone; if you want to go far, go together'. 10k is farther than 5k and I didn't get there by myself. Committing to deeper obedience to your friend and saviour Jesus is a greater thing than settling wherever you are. And you will not get there by yourself either. So pick up the phone, send a message or organise a coffee. Give permission to someone in your life and ask for permission in theirs. Go far and go together.

So which of these tools will you take from the toolkit? Which step do you need to take? Is it a decision to take, an act of a responsiveness, or a relationship you need to add to your life?

If there has been anything useful in these words, there would be a sad irony if you simply read them and left it there. These chapters are included in this book to try to avoid making that mistake. If obedience is a key part of the kind of disciples Jesus wants to form, these kinds of steps are absolutely vital.

Of course, we achieve none of it without him! After we have taken a moment to return to the Great Commission and consider what obedience to it specifically can look like, we will turn to that idea: dependence. But for now, if any of these steps is something you know is right for you, do it. Speak to God about it and commit it to him in dependence and with trust.

Chapter 5 at a glance...

In this toolkit chapter, the five tools we explored together were:

1. [HEAD:] Letting God call the shots, committing to receiving what he says as a matter of deep importance to us.

2. [HEAD:] Not valuing knowledge over obedience and letting that transform how we then engage with Jesus and the Bible.

3. [HEART:] Building a posture of response, whether by responding to little things, clear things or one big thing that God is highlighting.

4. [HANDS:] Imitating a mentor or role model, someone who inspires us, and who we are close enough to for their example and lifestyle to rub off on us.

5. [HANDS:] Becoming accountable to someone so you can spur one another on in your character and actions.

Becoming Useful

Since the Great Commission is itself a command to be obeyed, let's return to it and ask what obedience to this particular instruction means:

> Then the eleven disciples went to Galilee, to the mountain where Jesus had told them to go. When they saw him, they worshiped him; but some doubted. Then Jesus came to them and said, "All authority in heaven and on earth has been given to me. **Therefore go and make disciples of all nations, baptising them in the name of the Father and of the Son and of the Holy Spirit, and teaching them to obey everything I have commanded you.** And surely I am with you always, to the very end of the age." (Matthew 28:16-20, emphasis added)

With each area of the spiritual genetic CODE, we are interested not just in how they work generally, but how they apply specifically to the Great Commission from which they spring. The command at the centre has four parts, so let's dig into each and consider what obedience to them might look like today.

'go…'

There is an assumption from Jesus that to step into this great mission he has for them will mean to go somewhere. They cannot simply wait for everyone to come to them or cross paths with them. Since 'all nations' are in mind, not just 'those you already know' or 'those who are already part of this movement', the onus has to be on the disciples to go to whoever still needs to be introduced to Jesus.

For us as disciples, this means we need to go, not just wait for 'non-disciples' to come to our church. According to the 2022 *Talking Jesus* report in the UK,[46] just 6% of the country are 'practicing Christians'. The good news is that most of those who are not in that category know someone who is. The even better news is that they like us! When asked what the Christian they know are like, the top answer was 'friendly', with 62% of people giving that answer. But when asked what 'the church' is like, that number plummets to only 22%. According to those around us who don't know Jesus, Christians are friendlier than churches. Churches, though, are more hypocritical and narrow-minded (the top two answers, both at 26%), even though individual Christians aren't (just 9% and 10% respectively).

What does all this mean? Not only was it Jesus' plan for us to 'go' instead of waiting for people to 'come', but it is also just going to be more effective! The people you know are likely warmer to you than to your church. So instead of inviting them to church or hoping they'll come, pray for them, go to them, serve them where they are and strike up a conversation with them. That's where this starts.

'…make disciples of all nations…'

The call is to make disciples, not to make converts. A convert has agreed and has received Jesus (fantastic, by the way!), but a disciple is active as an apprentice of Jesus, always learning and growing. That begins before a moment of conversion and continues on afterwards. This may feel like a big ask and in lots of ways it is! But also let it take the pressure off. Your job is not all about 'getting someone over the line', but is about nurturing and encouraging them forward as they take steps along their journey with Jesus. Perhaps small, faltering, baby steps, or perhaps big, exciting leaps, but they are all steps forward.

According to the example of Jesus, that involves a deep investment of time in a few people. That time might be spent in conversation, asking probing questions and responding to the questions you are asked. It might be spent praying and expanding the spiritual horizons of the person you are discipling. It involves the exploration of Scripture, both understanding and applying it. It involves serving them and leading them to serve others. It involves giving them a big task and then coaching them through that to help them learn and grow. All of these are a part of how you—yes, you!—can make and grow a disciple of Jesus.

Remember as well that 'all nations' are in mind and sometimes that adds an extra dimension to the command to 'go'. It might be God does want you to go farther than to those you live, work and play with already. If so, may God bless you as you go off and seek those disciples waiting to be made wherever he calls!

'...baptising...'

Churches don't baptise people. People do. If you are a disciple, a follower of Jesus yourself, you can baptise someone. All you need is someone who has turned and followed Jesus and some water! I've had the privilege of baptising a number of people in my life, but honestly some of them I shouldn't have. Not because they shouldn't be baptised, but because there were better people to do it than me.

The way Jesus gives the Great Commission, it seems that he has in mind that the same people who make the disciples will then baptise them (when they come to a moment of conversion) and then continue leading them on. Sometimes church systems and structures get in the way and leaders do the baptising even if they aren't the ones who have really discipled them. I have been that leader a few times, while a faithful disciple-maker has stayed out of the pool, but I don't think that is right. Also, the public nature of it all can make it into a spectacle for others instead of a simple act of commitment and obedience for the disciple involved. There is of course *nothing* wrong with baptisms as part of a church service, or of celebrating them publicly. But if those things get in the way, that's not right.

So if you are the one discipling someone and they turn to Jesus in faith, it is absolutely your place to baptise them. Do it 'in church' if you'd like, or head to the swimming pool, the seaside, a river or a bathtub. Disciples make disciples. They also baptise them.

'...and teaching them to obey...'

Since discipleship does not stop at conversion, you are also called to share and demonstrate what the life of obedience to Jesus is like. It is not primarily the job of the church service, the pastor, or the sermon to do this. They can encourage, teach biblical truth, inspire and challenge. But teaching obedience is best done life-on-life. The best-placed person to teach someone obedience to Jesus is another disciple they are close to, perhaps someone a little further down the road than them.

How? You show it with actions, as you are responsive to him in your own life. And you share it with your words, encouraging that same responsiveness in others. You open the Bible together and invite God by his Spirit to lead you into both truth and response. Perhaps this looks similar to what Paul said to those he discipled, inviting people to imitate areas of your life where you have grown more like Jesus. Perhaps it is through those accountable relationships where you spur one another on. Yes, you need those things for yourself, but those you invest in also need them from you.

When we looked at the Great Commission through the lens of confidence, we saw how Jesus' absolute authority can make us *willing*. If we are indeed willing to step into it, we have seen how obedience to it can make us *useful*. There are of course lots of other useful things we can do with our lives motivated by faith. But this is Jesus' Plan A for spreading life and good news across the whole world and into all people's hearts. And to be useful in that, we need to be obedient to it.

So can I ask you to consider which parts of this command you have seen as your job and which you've assumed are for other people? Is there someone you have been 'going' to for years and years, building connection and relationship, but have assumed your part to play is to get them into church so others can teach, baptise or train them?

Take a moment to think through the people you know who haven't made the steps with Jesus you have. Having seen what obedience to the Great Commission is, what do you think God might want your role in their life to be? Pause and pray, confirming your willingness before God and asking that he would make you truly useful to them in their own journey of faith and discipleship.

PART 3

DEPENDENCE ON JESUS

"And surely I am with
you always, to the very
end of the age."

(Matthew 28:20)

Matthew 14:22-33

We are now shifting our attention again. We wish to be useful in Jesus' plans and purposes, opening ourselves up to him in obedience. But deeper than that, we wish to be really effective in them. And for that, we need to look beyond ourselves and dig deep into the resources that come from God, not from ourselves. This is at the heart of our focus on the next part of the spiritual genetic CODE which Jesus wanted to inspire through the Great Commission: dependence. As before, we start by shining a spotlight on this trait, this time through a story during the ministry of Jesus and an interaction he had with Peter.

Matthew 14:22-33

22 Immediately Jesus made the disciples get into the boat and go on ahead of him to the other side, while he dismissed the crowd. 23 After he had dismissed them, he went up on a mountainside by himself to pray. Later that night, he was there alone, 24 and the boat was already a considerable distance from land, buffeted by the waves because the wind was against it.

25 Shortly before dawn Jesus went out to them, walking on the lake. 26 When the disciples saw him walking on the lake, they were terrified. "It's a ghost," they said, and cried out in fear.

27 But Jesus immediately said to them: "Take courage! It is I. Don't be afraid."

²⁸ "Lord, if it's you," Peter replied, "tell me to come to you on the water."

²⁹ "Come," he said.

Then Peter got down out of the boat, walked on the water and came toward Jesus. ³⁰ But when he saw the wind, he was afraid and, beginning to sink, cried out, "Lord, save me!"

³¹ Immediately Jesus reached out his hand and caught him. "You of little faith," he said, "Why did you doubt?"

³² And when they climbed into the boat, the wind died down. ³³ Then those who were in the boat worshiped him, saying, "Truly you are the Son of God."

This is a very dramatic story! It follows another dramatic story in the Bible, the one where Jesus feeds a crowd of over 5,000 people with five bread rolls and two fish. That story is a miracle that affects thousands, playing out on a grand scale. In this story, the camera lens zooms in. It is still a spectacular story (in some ways even more so), but it is also an intimate story between Jesus and just one man: his friend Peter. Let's look at how the whole of CODE plays out, then focus on how Peter's dependence is stretched and challenged.

The Complete CODE

This story starts with the disciples, including Peter, in an uncertain state, battered and frightened. I don't know if you've ever been on a boat in the middle of a storm. I have and it is extremely scary! But the storm isn't why they are 'terrified'. Seeing Jesus walk on water is why. He has come to help them, but his coming to them like this is so impossible they grasp around for the only thing that might make sense: he is a ghost! But Jesus—who is decidedly not a ghost—has some simple words for them: "Take courage! It is I. Don't be afraid." Jesus knows who he is and knows that once they recognise him their fear will melt away. His true identity, combined with his presence, breeds *confidence* even in the fiercest storm.

This confidence has a great impact on Peter. He goes from cowering at the 'ghost' Jesus to asking for an invitation to join the man Jesus on the water, and it doesn't take him long at all! But notice what he says, because what he says is brilliant! He does not just announce that he's going to walk on the water as well. He does not assume he is invited to join. No, he says, "Lord, if it's you, tell me to come to you on the water." And then he waits for Jesus to say, "Come" before he moves. Peter isn't just trying to be cool and do fun things. Peter is trying to be *obedient* and to do the things Jesus invites him to. He sees his friend and master on the water and wants to follow, to imitate, to go where he goes, so he asks for the invitation. And when he hears it, he does it. Rapid response!

The next part of the story is where we will focus in a moment, but the result of it all is a lesson for Peter, a moment of worship for the whole group and a deeper realisation of who Jesus is: "Truly you are the Son of God." This *experience* works in a lot of the ways an experience with Jesus in the world should do. It stretched them. And almost certainly it stretched Peter the most because he was the one who stepped out the farthest. It taught them. Something of the nature of faith is discovered in this little episode with Jesus, but it was discovered not just through words but through action. And it inspired them. What begins in fear ends in worship. They were different as a result, and that difference will stick with them.

But the deepest moment of learning and growth is for Peter, who starts so well but then gets a little shaky, giving an opportunity to learn a lesson about what *dependence* on Jesus really means.

What are you looking at?

At the high point of the story, Peter is actually walking on water! It's a remarkable thing and is one of the reasons Peter is my favourite disciple. He's often the first to speak or act, rushing in headfirst without thinking. Often that doesn't do him any favours, but it means he's the one who gets moments like this. This is simple for him: he follows Jesus and Jesus is walking on water, so why can't I? He asks, gets the nod and just like that the water is holding his weight. It started with Jesus' voice to him and that was enough.

But then Peter gets in his own head. What started as simplicity begins to feel like stupidity. Where it started with Jesus' voice being enough, now there are other things creeping in. Where do we see this in the passage? "But when he saw the wind, he was afraid and, beginning to sink, cried out…" The wind wasn't new! It's what they'd been battling against for hours. But when Jesus arrived, he stopped looking at it. The wind was just as real when Peter stepped out of the boat as it was now he was walking toward Jesus, but now his attention had shifted off Jesus and onto the wind. Big mistake!

When our focus is on the size of the problem instead of the size of Jesus, we will start to sink. The reason is simple: when we look only at the problem, we start to think things like, 'I can't manage that' or 'that's too big for me'. Peter's version would have been, 'I can't stay afloat in this!'. But that was never the point, was it? Peter wasn't able to do this because *he* could do it. Peter was able because *Jesus* could do it… So the question really is: where are you looking? In a moment, Jesus would question Peter's faith and what he means is, "Why did you stop trusting me?" He started off trusting, but then stopped for no good reason…

What happens next shows that, while he had this blip, Peter was at his core still a person of faith and dependence. When he started to sink, what did he do? Not try to scrabble back to his feet, not flail around, not give up and start treading water. No, his knee-jerk reaction was this: "Lord, save me!" Yes, he wavered, but then he looked straight back to Jesus when it started to go wrong.

Our faith, a core part of which is about depending on Jesus, will never be perfect. We might have moments of brilliance, stepping out and looking Jesus in the eye as we trust in him for every stride. But we will also have moments of sinking when we look at everything except him. But take heart, he is there ready to catch us when we turn back to him. We're going to spend some time around this theme of dependence, asking what it looks like and how we can build it in our lives. Not just in storms, but in fair weather too, because things won't always be as dramatic as Peter's example here. But sometimes, steadier is better!

A fire needs fuel

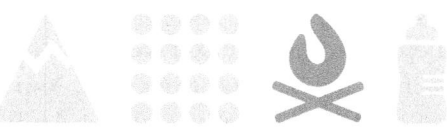

Picture the scene: you are camping. (If you're immediately thinking, 'No I'm not, I don't camp!' then please just go with it for a little while.) You're camping, it's evening and though it's dark and cold you aren't ready to head to the tent and sleep for the night yet. The dark is making things scary for some of your group and the cold is making everyone uncomfortable. You know it will be even harder to warm up when it is time to get to bed if you let the cold get into your bones for much longer. (And if you're now thinking, 'See, this is why I don't camp!' then by all means you have a very good point.)

But you aren't worried because you know exactly what is needed: a fire. A blazing fire that can give light to those who are afraid and make it possible to see one another as you talk long into the night. A warming fire that will bring comfort back to your cold bones, sending you off for a deep sleep, full of dreams of tomorrow's adventures. You know what you need and as soon as you have it all the problems of the campsite will fade away. That certainty is like the confidence in God we've already explored. When we have him, we have all we need. When we hear him, we hear what is true. There is no night too dark or too cold that his light and warmth cannot break through.

You also know the fire won't build itself. It's all very well knowing a fire is what you need, but that knowledge isn't what will warm you up. The fire will. So you set about gathering wood and kindling, assembling these pieces of wood so they will catch and burn. You also gather extra wood so you can keep the fire going after the initial kindling burns up. You know you need lots of different shapes and sizes to set the fire. You strike a match, light the fire and keep careful watch, adjusting and tending. You blow on those first gentle sparks to make sure they have the oxygen they need and move things around to keep the air flowing until it is ablaze with heat and light. This stage is like the obedience we need toward God. Theory isn't the point. Putting what we know into action is vital.

So, here's a question: where did the fire come from and what kept it burning? On one level, you did. You imagined a fire, took steps to build it and obediently tended to it so it would keep on going. But on another level, the fire didn't come from you. You weren't the firewood, you had to find that from elsewhere. And as much as you might have blown on the fire, it wasn't the air in your lungs that gave life to the fire. It was the air all around, and all you did was move it around where it needed to go. The fire needed a builder, yes. But it also needed fuel. You might have found it, but you didn't make it. The energy didn't come from you. It came from wood you had to find, and air you did not make.

I find this a useful image as we dive deeper into this idea of dependence in God. In all the discussion of confidence in God and obedience to him so far, we could be tempted to think that it is *our* confidence and *our* obedience that are where it all starts. But no! It is not just that we should not try to live life as disciples without relying on God. It is that we *cannot* do so. In the Great Commission, Jesus reminds his disciples, "I am with you always, to the end of the age." (Matthew 28:20) He did not just send them off on their own, hoping they would find their own strength and resources. No, he promises to stay with them, knowing they would need to lean on him forever.

If the life we live with God is to be a blazing fire, giving light and warmth in a dark and cold world, we need God's fuel, not our own clever assembly of logs. So one reason I find this image useful is it reminds me that while I might look for and use fuel for my faith, it does not originate with me. And the other reason is that it points to two different *kinds* of fuel, both of which are vital if we are truly to build a life lived in dependence on God.

The first is the wood. I can see wood, find wood, chop wood, and arrange wood. In a very real sense, I control it, make decisions about it, and decide how it will be used. I didn't give the wood the ability to be fuel for fire, but I can accept that it can and let it. Likewise, there are very real, practical things I can do and make use of to help me draw on the divine resources Jesus wants to give. I can decide whether and how I will pray. Or fast. Or give, worship, gather with others, meditate on God's word and a whole host of other things. I can ignore these pieces of firewood, or I can go out, seek them, gather them and build them into something that can sustain me.

And then there is the wind. A fire needs oxygen to keep on burning. Stop the flow of oxygen and the fire will die. A fresh breeze and the fire bursts to life. A lull at the wrong time and it will falter and die. But unlike the firewood, I cannot see the air, cannot control the wind, cannot capture it and make decisions about where it will be and how it will go. Jesus said, "The wind blows wherever it pleases. You hear its sound, but you cannot tell where it comes from or where it is going." He then follows that up with: "So it is with everyone born of the Spirit." (John 3:8) Part of dependence on God falls into the realm of things we cannot nail down, define, control or decide upon. But if we are to be Jesus-following, Spirit-led disciples, we need to embrace not just the wood we can control, but the wind we cannot.

Keep these two kinds of fuel in mind as we explore further why a life of dependence on God is so important, what it looks like, and what can get in the way. It might be you are drawn to one kind of fuel more than the other. It is good to acknowledge that if it's true, but be open to God leading you to a fuller, richer fire as you seek him for every kind of fuel he wishes to give.

Why we need God's fuel

Taking a step back for a moment, though, it'll help us if we ask the 'why' question. Why is it we need to rely on God so strongly? That may seem a stupid question, bordering on the blindingly obvious! Of course, if we are to be followers of Jesus, we need to rely not on our own natural resources but on the spiritual resources he alone opens up to us. But I want to dig a little deeper than that and to explore this on two levels: the practical and the principle.

Practical: without God, you CAN'T do anything

We start here, at the surface level. If you're reading this book, I am assuming you are someone who wants to do something with your life that is valuable. This book started with a question: 'What kind of person do you need be to do the things God wants you to do?' If that question and the way we've been exploring it, has kept you reading this far, you are someone who doesn't want to waste your life. There are things God wants you to do and you want to be the kind of disciple who steps up and joins in. You want your life to achieve something with God.

In light of that, have a look at these words from Jesus:

> *I am the true vine, and my Father is the gardener. He cuts off every branch in me that bears no fruit, while every branch that does bear fruit he prunes so that it will be even more fruitful. You are already clean because of the word I have spoken to you. Remain in me, as I also remain in you. No branch can bear fruit by itself; it must remain in the vine. Neither can you bear fruit unless you remain in me. (John 15:1-4)*

The image is simple, and the message is clear. If we want to 'bear fruit', make an impact, achieve things as disciples, we must draw from the one true source. A branch disconnected from the tree doesn't grow any fruit. In case it wasn't clear enough, Jesus follows up with, "apart from me you can do nothing." (John 15:5)

The word 'nothing' is fairly strong, isn't it? In this book, we've had a focus on the Great Commission and certainly that is included in what Jesus says here. If we wish to be part of that great movement in the world to make disciples who also make disciples and multiply God's kingdom across the globe, we cannot do that without him. It's why Jesus promises he will be with us as we do it. But this is also true across the life of a follower of Jesus. Whether at home or at work, in your singleness or your marriage, as you pursue friendships or spend time alone, there is a version of all these things—the very best version—that is *only* possible when we are rooted in God and drawing on him as the very fuel we need.

These words from Jesus are clear enough, but this theme crops up again and again in the Bible. There seems to be a very human tendency, just like Peter walking across the water, to take our eyes away from the source of energy we truly need and start to rely instead on ourselves. God has to step in and correct this a lot of times in Scripture.

In Genesis 11, the story goes that everyone in the world had one language and they thought they could achieve anything. It's a great example of how unity, when directed in the wrong direction, only amplifies what is most wrong about us. In their arrogance, they say, "let us build ourselves a city, with a tower that reaches to the heavens, so that we may make a name for ourselves" (Genesis 11:4). It's quite embarrassing, really! But what are they doing? They are trying to get up to heaven and doing it with the very best bricks they can bake. What is God's response? It starts like this: "But the LORD came down to see the city..." (Genesis 11:5). Glen Scrivener comments on these verses like this:

> The Lord comes down. That's a slap in the face for those who thought they were reaching heaven. God has to stoop down to even see it. But it also shows the way of the gospel.[47]

Because the gospel is not about us reaching up to heaven, building brick upon brick until our own good work has got us there. The gospel is about heaven come *down* to us. Yes, God has to stoop to see our efforts, not in a condescending and snobbish way, but because his nature and his achievements are so much greater. He stoops in love, all the way to the cross, for us. So we can cling to our own effort, hoping it'll get there and knowing it won't, or look instead to Jesus. Scrivener lays out the challenge well:

> So today, what's it going to be? The way of Babel or the way of Jesus?
> Babel says, "Ascend to God." Jesus says, "I have come down."
> Babel says, "Make a name for yourself." Jesus says, "Take my name for yourself."
> Babel says, "Climb." Jesus says, "Receive."
> Babel says, "Strive upwards and inwards." Jesus says, "Join me—the Down and Out God—and we will reach the nations!"[48]

It's a lesson the people of God had to keep learning, though. We saw in Chapter 4 how Abram took matters into his own hands. Instead of depending on God's promises, he slept with a servant to speed things along. That's the Babel way. We saw how the people demanded a human king so they could be impressive amongst the nations, and how it was a rejection of God. They wanted to rely on a man they could see, not depend on the God who, invisible though he was, had won victory after victory for them. It's the Babel way.

The promise of Babel is that our own effort will lead us up higher and higher, but the reality is that it will leave us broken, confused and disappointed. So, again and again, God reminds his people they need to depend on him. King Solomon wrote a song for the people to sing and now we find it in the book of Psalms:

> *Unless the Lord builds the house,*
> *the builders labour in vain.*
> *Unless the Lord watches over the city,*
> *the guards stand watch in vain. (Psalm 127:1)*

It's a reminder, as the people gather to worship in song, of something they might otherwise forget. And when the people were rebuilding the temple after a return from exile, the prophet Zechariah is reminded of how the work will get done:

> *"Not by might nor by power, but by my Spirit," says the Lord Almighty.*
> *(Zechariah 4:6)*

The people were weak and their efforts so far were unimpressive. So these words are not a telling off but a word of encouragement. They need not worry, because their efforts aren't what it's all about.

So we've seen the practical reason why depending on God is so important: we cannot do anything of worth without him. This is not to say that everything will be easy and comfortable when we do rely on him. In the words we read earlier, Jesus refers to the pruning of fruitful branches that do remain close to him. I've never been a plant, but pruning doesn't sound comfortable! The purpose of the pruning is also given, though: 'so that it will be even more fruitful' (John 15:2). If we want to be fruitful, to achieve something good, we have to depend on God.

Principle: without God, you DON'T do anything

But there is a deeper reason I want briefly to explore as well. It sounds similar, but is actually a far deeper principle for us to embrace. We've said that without God you can't do anything. Now I want us to reflect on this truth: without God, you *don't* do anything.

Think about it. It's not that there are some things you are doing 'in your strength' and some that are 'in God's strength'. Not at a deep level, anyway.

What would it even mean to do something 'in your strength', anyway? It would mean using your own energy, your own intellect and your own skills to achieve your own purposes, or something like that. But where does your energy come from? Well, a mixture of the food you eat, the air you breathe and any number of other forms of energy. All of which come from…God. What about your intellect? Impressive as it might be, the brain you are using to come up with all your own ideas is a gift from God. The same is true of the skills you have. Yes, you might have put a lot of time and energy into learning and honing them, but you were made by God, designed with (to borrow from Liam Neeson) a very particular set of skills. When you use them, are you working 'in your strength', or are you just exercising the strength God has already given?

It might sound like I'm making a slightly silly point. I recognise some silliness here, but I don't actually think it's found in the point I'm making. True silliness is in thinking we are able to do a single thing that does not, in some way, draw upon the resources of God.

Remember the campfire we started this chapter with. Imagine it could think and now imagine it starts to think, 'Hmm… what shall I rely on to keep burning today? I don't really want to rely on this wood that's been assembled for me and I'd prefer not to draw on this oxygen-ripe air that's all around me. Perhaps today I will look inward and burn in my own strength. That seems far better!' It's a truly ridiculous idea. Yes, it's stupid because campfires don't think. But also because as soon as it made that decision it would cease to exist. Without fuel and oxygen, a fire simply doesn't exist.

Without God—without him creating us, breathing life into us, sustaining us—we simply do not exist. There is an arrogance in even asking whether we'll depend on God or not. We just do, whether we choose to or not!

The letter to the Hebrews starts like this:

*In the past God spoke to our ancestors through the prophets at many times and in various ways, but in these last days he has spoken to us by his Son, whom he appointed heir of all things, and through whom also he made the universe. The Son is the radiance of God's glory and the exact representation of his being, **sustaining all things by his powerful word**. After he had* *provided purification for sins, he sat down at the right hand of the Majesty in heaven. (Hebrews 1:1-3, emphasis added)*

These verses are cosmic in scale! Zooming right out, they start with the fact that Jesus is not just another messenger. He is the true message. He has authority over everything, was the creative spark in making everything and he shines forth the exact nature of God into the universe. These verses finish with a reminder that the saving work of Jesus in providing a sacrifice for our sins is complete and that he dwells now in heaven at the place of honour. It's a lot!

But tucked in the middle is a powerful statement, that he is 'sustaining all things by his powerful word.' This same Son, Jesus, whose power created the whole universe, continues to exercise that power to keep it going. At a spiritual level—that science will never have the desire or ability to measure—Jesus is what keeps the universe going. His creative work brought everything from nothing. His sustaining work stops it returning to nothing.

Everything depends on Jesus. We depend on Jesus. Without him in the past we wouldn't exist. Without him now we would cease to exist. Just like the fire without the wood. In Heaven right now, Jesus continues to speak your existence into being, along with the existence of the whole universe. You don't do anything without him, because every breath, every thought, every action cannot exist without him.

Why does this principle matter? Simply, because it gives us the chance to ask the right question. The question is not about whether we do things in our strength or his. The question is whether, having recognised that the only kind of strength we have comes from him, we will lean into that, breathe it in deeply and put all of our weight on it, or whether we will resist it and take only shallow breaths.

The people at Babel thought they were building in their own power. But the bricks were baked from earth God created and the structure stayed up because of the laws of physics God set in place.

So on one level, dependence on God isn't even a choice. Without him, we are nothing. But on another level, it is a choice. The very nature of sin is rebellion against God, rejecting him even though we need him. The opposite is to choose to lean into him, plant ourselves evermore deeply in him, draw everything we can from him. And now we turn to consider what that looks like.

Input, output, and the power of ≥

Let's stay with this idea of being 'sustained' for a moment as we think about how we lean into dependence on God. If Jesus sustains all things, including us, what does that mean? At a basic level, something is 'sustainable' if it has at least as much coming into it as it does coming out of it. It's true of our campfire, which will keep on burning as long as the supply of wood and oxygen is greater than or equal to the amount being burned up. It's true of our bank balances, which will disappear over time if we spend more than we earn. It's true for our planet, which is deteriorating because we are taking more from it than can be sustained.

Last chapter, we considered this phrase: "If your output exceeds your input, then your upkeep will be your downfall." At that point I was asking what happens when we take on more knowledge than we know what to do with. But now let's use it as a guide for what being spiritually sustained looks like. If input is the different ways Jesus gives us the resources we need and output is all the things which drain and sap us as we seek to live for him, it looks like this:

INPUT < (less than) OUTPUT = UNSUSTAINABLE
INPUT ≥ (greater/equal to) OUTPUT = SUSTAINABLE

We are going to consider some of these inputs and outputs, but before we do, take a moment to look at those two 'equations'. For your discipleship life to last, to be sustainable and healthy, you *need* your input to be at least as great as your output. Is that how you live? Are you drawing from Jesus all the fuel you need to sustain the life you live with him and for him in this world? Ponder on that for a moment.

Most of this section will consider different ways we can increase the 'INPUT' side of our spiritual sustainability equation. But first, let's be real about the 'OUTPUT' side. Life is draining, sapping our spiritual resources. There is normal life, with work, family and everything else. And it's tiring!

But also consider these three extra outputs: lies, lusts and longings. The *lies* are all the many messages we are bombarded with that are not filled with God's good news. There are many ideas and worldviews out there, some good and some bad. Sifting through to sort the truth we should hold onto from the lies to discard is a spiritual output. The *lusts* are all those moments of temptation toward things that are not good for us. Over or under-eating, deceit, sexually immoral behaviour, pride, envy… We might resist them or we might not, but either way they drain us. And the *longings*. These are the good things we desire but still wait for. Unrealised dreams, unmet expectations and long waits take a real toll on us spiritually.

And then there's the Great Commission work we know we're called to. Taking the initiative to listen to someone, serve them, share your story and how it has been changed by God's bigger story can be tiring! Yes it can be thrilling too, but it does take it out of us. Learning and teaching obedience to all that God reveals is a long journey and long journeys require fuel. It's no wonder that after giving this commission that would be exhausting, Jesus quickly followed up with "And surely I will be with you always, to the end of the age." He knew they'd need it!

So there is much that will be a very real 'OUTPUT', but Jesus sustains all things, so there must be as much or more 'INPUT' available to us. What follows here isn't an exhaustive list, but are some really vital ways for us to lean into that and depend on Jesus to sustain our lives as his disciples.

Sustained by disciplines

If we wish to lean into the sustaining power of Jesus, we need to be disciplined in creating space to seek him for it. Just as Peter needed to keep his eyes on Jesus to keep walking across the water, so we need to find ways to keep focused on him. The alternative is that we look around to other sources of strength. And while caffeine, sleep, other people or alone time (depending on whether you are more extraverted or introverted) can help, they are no replacement for Jesus himself.

If we want a Jesus-shaped life, pursuing Jesus-sized things, we need Jesus-centred habits and disciplines.

Habits like prayer or fasting are often known as 'spiritual disciplines', and there is no way around it: they are essential for putting ourselves in a place where Jesus can pour his sustenance and life into us. They are called 'disciplines' because we need to be disciplined with them. They are meant for the long term, not as one-offs. In some senses they are like the wood in the campfire because we can discover them, gather them together into our lives, assemble and arrange them as habits and see them come alive with Jesus' power. They are something we decide to do. But they aren't ultimately about us. Richard Foster, who wrote one of the great books about this, *The Celebration of Discipline*, describes it like this:

> The Disciplines are God's way of getting us into the ground; they put us where he can work within us and transform us. By themselves the Spiritual Disciplines can do nothing; they can only get us to the place where something can be done. They are God's means of grace… God has ordained the Disciplines of the spiritual life as the means by which we place ourselves where he can bless us.[49]

I want to be in the place where God can bless me! More than that, if I am truly to follow God into all the different places, tasks and opportunities out there, I *need* to be in the place where God can bless me.

That place looks like prayer. It looks like fasting. It looks like meditation on God's word. It looks like embracing simplicity and solitude and submission. It looks like the confession of my sin, to God and with others. It looks like worship, both public and private. It can look like a great many things. There is not only one right way to build a fire, but there is definitely a wrong way: without wood. If you wish to grow in dependence on God, what regular disciplines have you built into your life to lean into his sustaining power and grace?

My aim isn't to give a 'how-to guide' for each practice—there are great books like that—though we will return to prayer and fasting specifically as part of our toolkit next chapter. My aim here is simply to encourage honest reflection on where a greater investment in these holy habits could help you lean more fully into Jesus.

Sustained by the Spirit

It is not just the wood that we need. Just what we can gather and assemble will never be enough. Essential, but never enough! We need the wind of God's Spirit to blow on us, fanning into flame what would otherwise burn out and die. On his last night with the disciples before his arrest, Jesus made this promise to them:

> *And I will ask the Father, and he will give you another advocate to help you and be with you forever—the Spirit of truth. The world cannot accept him, because it neither sees him nor knows him. But you know him, for he lives*

with you and will be in you. I will not leave you as orphans; I will come to you. (John 14:16-18)

When Jesus, in the Great Commission, says "I will be with you always," what did he actually mean? He'd been with them face-to-face, but that was about to change. He could just mean with them in their memories, but that would be a bit weak. These verses from John give a much better answer. Here, Jesus says he'll send "another advocate to help you and be with you forever". How will Jesus be with us always? By sending the Spirit to be with us always! He even finishes up his description of sending the Spirit by saying "I will come to you." Having the Spirit in us *is* having Jesus with us.

But the Holy Spirit will in some ways be even closer to them: "he lives with you and will be in you." No longer just face-to-face, this will be heart-to-heart and spirit-to-Spirit. This is not second-best![50]

So how do we lean into that, instead of leaning away into our 'own strength'? We ask for it, for the regular filling with the Spirit, strengthening of the Spirit and sustaining power of the Spirit in every single thing we do. If this is a key part of how Jesus will sustain us, let's pursue that instead of ignoring it.

To be clear, I'm not suggesting some Christians have the Holy Spirit within them and others don't, depending on whether they ask or not. When we turn to receive Jesus, we are born again with a spiritual rebirth and receive the Spirit. All of us. After all, "No one can say, "Jesus is Lord," except by the Holy Spirit" (1 Corinthians 12:3). But that truth does not stop the New Testament using the language of being 'filled with the Spirit' as a recurring act as well as a one-time thing. In Acts on the Day of Pentecost the believers were 'filled with the Spirit' (Acts 2:4), and Peter promised that all those who repented and were baptized would also "receive the gift of the Holy Spirit" (Acts 2:38). Yet some of these same people, not long after, as they pray for boldness "were all filled with the Holy Spirit" (Acts 4:31).

So are we like leaky buckets gradually losing the Spirit and needing to be topped up? I don't like that language because it makes the Holy Spirit sound more like a commodity than a person to form a life-giving relationship with. So maybe it's more like a battery that needs recharging? But that reduces the Holy Spirit purely to an energy source. None of the language we might use to explain it is very satisfying, because we are trying to take a supernatural thing and force it into human language.

But just because we can't fully explain this doesn't mean we should avoid it. Jesus sends the Spirit to us, fills us with the Spirit and keeps on doing so. If he wants to give, I want to receive! We are also told to receive this, by Paul:

> Do not get drunk on wine... Instead, be filled with the Spirit. (Ephesians 5:18)

There are two things to point out here. First, being filled with the Spirit is contrasted with getting drunk because there are similarities (we see it at Pentecost, when people think the disciples *are* drunk). The similarity is that both put us 'under the influence', relinquishing control to something or someone else. Being drunk on alcohol leads to bad places. Being filled with the Spirit leads to good, beautiful places! That's why being filled with the Spirit is how Jesus sustains us: through the Spirit he leads us in ways we can't lead ourselves.

Second, this instruction to be filled is given to Christians. Paul has already told them, 'When you believed, you were marked in him with a seal, the promised Holy Spirit," (Ephesians 1:13), so they already have the Holy Spirit. But he still instructs them to be filled. In fact, the tense of the phrase 'be filled' indicate a continuous thing, that could be written as 'go on being filled'.

If an 'uninterrupted filling' of the Holy Spirit of God is offered by Jesus, sign me up! What if, each day, before each task, each conversation, each new situation we step into, we were simply to ask God to fill us anew with his Spirit? It seems we can, so let's lean into that and ask for our campfire always to be roaring as fresh wind fills us with fresh fire.

Sustained by others

The final key 'INPUT' to explore here is people. In the obedience toolkit, I shared the benefits of mentors and accountable relationships. Those are part of this, but more broadly we are designed to be sustained with Christian community. Take a burning log out of our campfire, away from the warmth of all the other logs and flames, and it will go out far more quickly than the logs still gathered together. In the letter to the Hebrews, we read this:

Let us hold unswervingly to the hope we profess, for he who promised is
faithful. And let us consider how we may spur one another on toward love
and good deeds, not giving up meeting together, as some are in the habit of
doing, but encouraging one another—and all the more as you see the Day
approaching. (Hebrews 10:23-25)

This is a high call, to hold 'unswervingly' to our faith. It is about a
deep confidence in God that is unshakeable. In lots of ways that is in
itself an 'OUTPUT' in our sustainability equation! To keep holding on
can feel like a battle in the first place. So what is prescribed to sustain
it? Christian community.

Not just being in the same room as Christians, or doing 'Christian
things'. This is an intentional community, one where people 'consider
how [they] may spur one another on'. What they do when they are
together inspires and sustains all who are present into deeper obedience, expressed through the love Jesus calls us to and the good deeds
he gives us to do. And it is a committed community, not giving up
meeting because there's something better to do. When one person
skips this time, everyone suffers.

If that doesn't sound like the kind of church community you're
part of, blame the leaders, tell them they're doing it wrong and leave!
Except, don't do that. Often that's our first reaction, though, isn't it?
The people in charge aren't providing for *my* needs properly. Things
aren't really working *for me*. But this isn't about a few people (leaders) providing a service or creating an environment for everyone else.
This is about a community looking out for and championing *one an-*
other as they follow Jesus arm in arm. So step one isn't to complain.
Step one is to commit. Get stuck in, throw yourself in and show up!
By all means ask questions and raise concerns, but do it with grace
and do it willing to be part of whatever solution is settled on.

You need Christian community around you if you are going to
depend on Jesus. It is a vital way that he extends his sustaining life
towards us, embodying around us his own love, forgiveness, power
and purposes.

Breaking down the walls

So we have seen some gifts Jesus gives for us to build and nurture
our fires of discipleship. Before we move on to our toolkit chapter,
there is something else we should be honest about. There are obsta-

cles to embracing all this. It's like sometimes the wood is damp, or there is a barrier stopping the wind coming to stir sparks into flames. A number of these obstacles come from within us and—while I don't wish to labour them—we need to notice them if we're going to seek God in overcoming them. I'll mention three.

Fear: the obstacle of security

I find this story from Lisa Rodriguez-Watson deeply challenging:

> I will always remember the comment my friend Mercy made when I lived in Nigeria: "I think it must be difficult to be a Christian in America," she said. I was perplexed. Being a Christian in America is easy with all our religious freedoms. By comparison, it is a dangerous prospect in many parts of Nigeria... Curious, I asked Mercy what she meant. Without missing a beat, she responded, "Americans don't need God because you have plenty of money. You can just fix things by paying for them."[51]

I'm not American, but I imagine Lisa's friend Mercy would say the same about the UK. I might not think my life is easy, but I'm sure a conversation with Mercy would give perspective on that. In truth, between our homes, wealth, healthcare, rights, freedoms and modern creature comforts, there is a huge degree of security in our lives. We are rich with comfort. But, as Rodriguez-Watson goes on to reflect, "affluence, often paraded as security, is in fact an idolatry that leads us away from the God who ultimately provides."[52]

A heart that longs for security and comfort will not naturally lean into God. If you feel as though you have all you need, why seek God for anything? It might be dangerous to do so, might upset the comfort you already have. What if God leads you to give more away and rely on him more, use your home differently and trust him in the discomfort that causes, or step way out of a comfort zone you've firmly established and lean heavily into him for it? All of that sounds insecure and uncomfortable. Perhaps it's just safer to take a few logs off the fire, keep it from burning too hot? Otherwise you might get burnt...

Meh: the obstacle of apathy

A second way we end up pouring water on the campfire and stopping it blazing with the fuel God wants is...boredom. It's all just become a bit routine. We turn up to church on a Sunday, hear a great sermon, feel inspired (maybe a bit challenged), enjoy a time of worship, have a coffee with our friends and…then what? Life is pretty much the same the next week as it was the week before. Maybe the sermon is to blame, because it wasn't deep/practical/short/long/ interesting enough (delete as appropriate). Or perhaps the worship wasn't 'good enough'. Or perhaps you're picking the wrong people to talk to over a coffee. Deep down, you know those aren't the real problem.

Because sermons and singing and coffee aren't the purpose, are they? And you know that. So the problem is that you've lost the energy that comes from the real purpose. Lost the big 'Wow' of the good news of Jesus. Lost the drive to live your whole life in the presence and power of Jesus, no matter what. Lost the urgency of sharing the difference Jesus has made in your life with those who need to hear it. And now it's all just a bit…meh. You're in a rut. You feel a bit like how Jesus describes the church in Laodicea near the start of the book of Revelation: "I know your deeds, that you are neither cold nor hot. I wish you were either one or the other!" (Revelation 3:15) You aren't satisfied with this, but it's become normal.

And of course when there's not a lot of urgency, when you're stuck in that cycle of apathy, there's not a lot to pull you into dependence on God. So you get out of the habit of prayer, you neglect the Bible, you are patchy with Christian community and all the ways Jesus wants to input into your life get shut off. No more wood gets put on the fire and it just stays damp.

None of this is written in judgment, by the way! I've been there. I'll likely be there again. Perhaps because of the security and comfort that can often accompany Western Christianity, we find ourselves in this place. But will we leave ourselves there, or make a choice not to settle there too long?

Pride: the obstacle of independence

And the final reason I want to highlight that the fire doesn't get the kind of fuel it needs is because we simply think we don't need it. We are fine by ourselves, thank you very much!

This is the independent spirit often admired in our world. "Isn't he strong? He doesn't need anybody to complete him." "Look at her

go, there's no stopping her and she built it all for herself!" Not only
are these things almost never true (single people still exist in community and success is hardly ever found without support), but it's a
dangerous mindset for a Christian to have.

Remember one of the ways Paul used the image of the church as
one body with many parts: 'The eye cannot say to the hand, "I don't
need you!" And the head cannot say to the feet, "I don't need you!"'
(1 Corinthians 12:21) We are supposed to rely on one another. None
of us is the complete package and that is the way it is meant to be. An
'independent Christian' is a contradiction and if we find ourselves
thinking we have all the answers, can manage by ourselves and don't
need the support and input of others, we shut ourselves off from the
sustaining power of Jesus that comes through others.

But remember, this isn't about becoming dependent *on people*. This
is about being dependent on Jesus and allowing him to sustain you
through those around you, at the same time as he sustains them
through you. Health and maturity in Christian relationships is neither total dependence on them, nor independence from them. It is
about dependence *on Jesus* expressed through inter-dependence *with
others*.

Resisting this is very natural. Having these kinds of inter-depen-
dent relationships isn't comfortable (have you met people?) so it attacks our security. It requires effort, so if we're apathetic we won't
bother. But most of all it attacks our pride. If sin is wanting things *my*
way, being lord of *my own* life, then needing to rely on others in my
walk with Jesus attacks that self-focus.

But maybe that's the point. Perhaps this is one of the reasons Jesus
works on us in community, to combat the very thing that will lead us
to pursue ourselves instead of pursuing him.

Come back to the source

We are going to step into another toolkit now, this time all about how
we can grow a deeper core of dependence on God. I hope you've seen
how vital this is. If we try to rely first and foremost on ourselves or
anything else, we are fooling ourselves and robbing ourselves.

But as we explore things like prayer, finances and how we make
decisions, let's not focus our eyes just on them. To walk on water, it
was *Jesus* that Peter needed to look at. So let's keep focused on him,

looking to him. Yes, let's receive the gifts he gives us that help us to rely on him, but let's not get so focused on the gifts that we neglect the giver.

We've thought about the firewood that we can find and assemble, but what we need above all else is for God to breathe on us by his Holy Spirit. And when he does, we must not turn away, shield ourselves or resist. We must lean into that wind, trust it to hold us, carry us and set us on fire. Then we open ourselves to the furnace of provision that God pours over us.

Chapter 6 at a glance...

In this chapter, we:

1. Introduced the image of a campfire to explore different kinds of fuel we need: the 'wood' that we can put in place ourselves, and the 'wind' that only God can provide.

2. Asked why we need to depend on Jesus, exploring two areas:

   • The practical reality that we cannot do anything of substance without God and we know this because Jesus tells us so.

   • The principle that we don't do anything without God anyway because all things come from him in the first place and he sustains everything.

3. Looked at various outputs (drains) and inputs (fuel) in our spiritual lives, using this equation: INPUT ≥ OUTPUT = SUSTAINABLE. In particular we thought about three inputs through which God sustains us:

   • Disciplines, placing ourselves before God so he can bless and work in us.

   • The Spirit, poured into us because this is how Jesus remains with us.

   • Community, Christians spurring one another on.

4. Thought about some of the obstacles that stop us depending on Jesus, in particular fear of losing security and comfort, not caring because we have become apathetic, and being so independent that we can't rely on anyone that is not ourselves.

How to lean into the wind

I like to sail. One of the reasons is that it feels almost magical to move without providing any energy. I am standing still on a boat, no engine, no paddling, no exertion, but the boat is still moving. Magical! Except it's not magic of course. It's physics. By setting the sails at the right angle, pointing the boat in the right direction and fine-tuning a number of other little things, the boat creaks into action and starts powering along. And it's not that there is no energy involved, it's just that the energy isn't something I have to create. I just have to find it and catch it, lean into it and let it fill the sails.

That is the purpose of this chapter. It's about setting our sails, tuning different parts of our lives before God so that we can harness his almighty power. As before, we'll consider decisions, postures and actions, this time geared toward growth in dependence, as we seek to lean into God.

HEAD: Dependent Decision

This time there is just one decision I am suggesting you try to make. Perhaps more than any other part of this book, dependence is less about training our mind in a new way of thinking and more choosing not to overthink and to let go of control. To extend that image of a boat catching the wind, the one decision we really need to make is to turn the engine off so the sails can do their thing.

1. 'I will not rely on myself'

This decision is not a complicated one to explain, but is a huge one to make! We have already seen why it is so important in the previous chapter as we looked at the story of Babel and at declarations like, 'Unless the Lord builds the house, the builders labour in vain' (Psalm 127:1). We saw it too when we spent time with Peter walking on the water and then realising this was too big for him. As long as he focused on what he couldn't do instead of what Jesus *could* do, the only thing he would do was sink.

But choosing not to rely on ourselves is a very hard thing to do! We can't just flip a switch and—boom—our self-reliance is gone. It isn't as simple as turning off the engine on a sailboat. To do this, you are really going to need to take stock of what it is you currently rely on and take steps to let them decrease so reliance on God can increase.

We should be clear here, because if we pursue this wrongly, we will end up doing God a disservice. Some of the things he has given you to rely on are to be found in you. He has given you a brain and it doesn't honour him not to use it. That would be like not putting up the sails on a boat and stubbornly saying, "I am relying on the *wind*, not my own sails!" But it also doesn't honour him if you assume you are always right and you don't need his perspective. This is a balancing act and you can fall off in either direction. The same is true of your personality, your gifts and abilities, your hopes and dreams and all the different experiences you have had in your life that you can draw on. Ignore them and you reject a wealth of resources God has already placed in you. Focus only on them and you forget that they're not perfect and you miss all the things that lie elsewhere.

So let's try to take stock. I will share three ways we can come to overly rely on ourselves and you can consider whether any of them are areas where you might need to turn off the motor and hoist your sails.

i. When thinking is higher than inquiring

In Joshua 9, we read the story of the Gibeonites. They lived very close to the land God's people were taking over, so they were worried. So they loaded up packs with old, mouldy bread, wineskins that had been cracked and mended and wore worn sandals and old clothes. Essentially, they dressed themselves up as if they had come on a long journey from far away. Then they went to Joshua and said they wanted to enter into a binding peace treaty. If they had been from far away, a treaty would be a good idea, but if—as in fact was the case— they were local, a treaty would limit the options Joshua had in how to deal with them. So would they be tricked? And how would Joshua check out their story? Like this:

> *The Israelites sampled their provisions but did not inquire of the Lord. Then Joshua made a treaty of peace with them to let them live, and the leaders of the assembly ratified it by oath. (Joshua 9:14-15)*

The Israelites did one thing right and one thing wrong. The right thing was using their own eyes and common sense to see if the story checked out. But the wrong thing was stopping there. They 'did not inquire of the Lord.' If they had taken time to ask God, there would be opportunity to be set straight. But they trusted their own observations to be enough and things ended up going wrong.

So this is not about never thinking and not using our own eyes, ears and common sense. It is about making sure we are also looking to 'un-common sense' which cannot come from us and needs to come from God. Where do you need to decide to make that space more deliberately.

I have a friend in church leadership who, one year, decided not to buy any new church leadership books. For him, he recognises that instead of looking first to ideas and principles in books, he needs to look more directly to God in Scripture and in prayer. It was only a year, in an effort to recalibrate. If it were for life, he would rob himself of the chance for God to lead *through* the thinking and writing of others. But for a time it's a way of increasing the inquiring in his life.

ii. When saving is higher than investing

Saving money is a wise principle. But it is not the only wise financial principle. In fact, if the reason we want to save is so we feel secure, our security is in a foolish place. What we have is meant to be invested into God's Kingdom, not to make us feel safe or be a mark of our status. Sometimes we save so we can invest into God's Kingdom in the future and sometimes we spend now to do so. But saving just to accumulate more and more for ourselves is never the point.

Jesus told a parable which gets to this point very bluntly! It's about a man who had a big harvest, so he built bigger and bigger barns to keep it in (rather than use it in more positive and less selfish ways). If he keeps it all for himself, he can secure a long and luxurious life. But Jesus concludes the parable like this:

> But God said to him, 'You fool! This very night your life will be demanded from you. Then who will get what you have prepared for yourself?'
>
> This is how it will be with whoever stores up things for themselves but is not rich toward God. (Luke 12:20-21)

That escalated quickly! This man thinks his finances were what would make him secure, but they absolutely do not. The opposite, according to Jesus, is to be 'rich toward God.' This means to find value and security in the things of God not in human possessions, and to use what possessions we do have for him instead of clinging onto them for ourselves. We will consider finances in one of our actions shortly, but for now the question is whether we will decide to focus on investing what God has given rather than depending on it and thinking it gives us security.

iii. When my plans are higher than his plans

One final sign we rely on ourselves to the exclusion of God is when we value our plans too highly. This is a big one for me, because I can be a bit of a control freak. I want to know what the plan is, want to make sure everyone else knows what the plan is, and then make sure we all stick to the plan we've all agreed. Planning isn't wrong. Idolising our plans is. Solomon, in the book of Proverbs, wrote this:

> In their hearts humans plan their course,
>   but the Lord establishes their steps. (Proverbs 16:9)

In other words, I can plan out my day, my week or my life to the last tiny detail, but unless God is in those plans and works through them, they won't amount to anything. And sometimes, God wants to change those plans, leading me in other ways because what I'd planned wasn't the best thing anyway. If you're wanting to depend on him, not yourself, you need to be willing for that.

I have a friend who is often late. Sometimes that bugs me, because I'm an 'on time person'. But often when I find myself annoyed, I have a big wake-up call when she tells me why she is late. It isn't normally because she lost track of time. Of all my friends, she is the most likely to have a story of how she met someone as she was leaving her house who needed help, or how she saw a person in distress on the way, or got a call from someone and realised she needed to give them some time.

Does she have these stories more often than me because these people and these needs are around her more often than they are around me? If not, then she's just better at noticing, less focused than I am on our plans and on being on time and able to respond as God leads her. Or maybe she genuinely does have more of those kinds of opportunities than me. If that's the case, perhaps I should ask why God puts them in her way instead of mine. Maybe because he knows she will do what needs to be done whereas I'll talk myself out of it because 'I've got plans'.

When was the last time God interrupted your plans? When did you divert because you realised there was something better? If it was quite a while ago, maybe it would be good to make a decision about that, deciding to give God permission, to rely on his leading more than your own deciding.

These three things aren't a comprehensive list. Maybe there are other ways you need to hoist your sails more and rely on the engine less. But the decision is the important thing: rely on the one with an unlimited supply of wind, not on the tank of fuel you have that will run out sooner or later.

HEART: Dependent Posture

To grow more dependent on God is all about the way we relate to him, so getting our heart towards him in the right place is vital. If we've settled into a posture that leans away from God, that needs to be addressed so we can lean more of our weight into his provision and empowering.

2. A posture of prayer and fasting

The first posture we need to adopt is a posture of prayer. And I'll suggest in a moment that adding fasting into that mix can also be a huge win. But first, let's focus in on prayer.

Think back over those three ways we've just looked at that rely more on ourselves than on God. We won't overcome them without prayer. If we need to inquire more instead of just thinking, we 'inquire' of God by praying, asking for his perspective. If we need to invest more into God's Kingdom instead of saving everything for ourselves, we need to ask him how and where to invest. And if his plans are going to redirect yours, you're going to need to pray about what those plans are.

So if you've decided to be dependent, that decision must lead you into a place of prayer. Otherwise the decision will stay in your head but never flow into your life. The deeper that prayerful dependence gets, the less it will be simply moments of praying, but a posture of prayer across our whole lives. Paul writes:

> *Rejoice always, pray continually, give thanks in all circumstances; for this is God's will for you in Christ Jesus. (1 Thessalonians 5:16-18)*

If the words 'always', 'continually' and 'in all circumstances' were removed from these verses, they would be a lot easier to follow! I can rejoice in God's goodness from time to time, pray when the mood takes me and give thanks to God when I am particularly aware of something he's done. But when you add those words into the mix, it's a huge challenge. Paul seems to think it is possible—and in fact worth pursuing—to live a life where these prayerful things are not just activities we do, but part of the people we are.

Prayer as an instinct not an afterthought. Prayer as natural as breathing in and breathing out. Prayer as a way of life, not an action on a to-do list.

Sounds wonderful, doesn't it? But I know that for many, many Christians, it is their prayer life they find hardest, decide they need to 'work on' most often and yet still feel hasn't got where they want it to be. If that is you, you're in good company. Not just because I have often found myself in that place (I doubt I classify as 'good company', anyway), but because of some words from Pete Greig that I find particularly encouraging. He founded the 24/7 Prayer movement and in his excellent book *How to Pray* shares two discoveries that led to it starting:

> The first was that prayer is pretty much the most important thing in life. And the second discovery was that my friends and I were horribly bad at it. Since that inauspicious start, we've been on an adventure of exploration into this simple, difficult, inevitable thing that beats at the heart of life and faith and culture.[53]

Prayer: massively important, but also something we can struggle with. I don't know if that resonates with you, but it does with me. But if we want to build this posture in our lives, we are going to have to take some steps to realign things so that prayer does indeed come as naturally as breathing in and breathing out. And for this let's turn to guidance Jesus gives about prayer. Just before he shares what we normally call the Lord's Prayer, he says this:

> *"And when you pray, do not be like the hypocrites, for they love to pray standing in the synagogues and on the street corners to be seen by others. Truly I tell you, they have received their reward in full. But when you pray, go into your room, close the door and pray to your Father, who is unseen. Then your Father, who sees what is done in secret, will reward you. And when you pray, do not keep on babbling like pagans, for they think they will be heard because of their many words. Do not be like them, for your Father knows what you need before you ask him." (Matthew 6:5-8)*

In these words, I see two corrections to our prayer lives that can help. One is about our routine of prayer, and the other about the language of our prayer.

Jesus tells his followers to avoid the ways of 'hypocrites'. A hypocrite is someone who pretends to be different than they really are and in prayer that meant having a routine designed more so others would notice you than to really spend time before God. In a culture with set times of prayer each day, it was possible to order your routine so you always 'just happened' to be in a public place when prayer time came. In a synagogue or on a street corner (so two whole streets could see you), you pause to pray in a loud voice, heard by everyone. Prayer as performance.

But Jesus encourages a different kind of routine. He doesn't criticise using daily times of prayer, but says to use them very differently.

He encourages a routine that makes sure prayer is protected as a space between you and God. There is nothing wrong in praying with others. Jesus does that too. But if the routine of our praying is that we *only* do it around others (either to seem holy, or because we don't know how to pray by ourselves), there is work to be done. How could you re-posture your prayer life by setting a new routine. And how can you carve out and protect that time in secret with God where he is your only audience, where you're not tempted to play up for others. I know my most honest praying is done when I am alone with God. No pretence. No masks. Just prayer.

The second example Jesus warns us to avoid is about language. He says not to "keep on babbling like pagans". Apparently they thought that if they used lots of clever words they were more likely to impress the gods and their prayers would be answered. What a relief it is that you and I do not need to impress God! We don't need big vocabularies and we don't need to pile up more and more words. As Jesus points out, God already knows what we need, so trying to lay out persuasive arguments with eloquence and wit is not the name of the game. That's how you persuade a person, because people get drawn in with things like that.

But the way to God's heart is simply to come as you are. He doesn't want your best 'prayer voice'. He wants your voice. He doesn't want lots of holy language. He wants your heart language, whatever that is. If you like big words, use them. If you don't, don't. If you express yourself with art, or poetry, or dance, bring that to God as a language of prayer. If God has given you the gift of tongues, use that before him. If you love to write, get a journal. If you prefer spreadsheets, input prayers in rows and columns. Your prayers might be loud, or totally silent. But never just try to copy someone else because you think their prayers are somehow better or more holy than yours. You won't get far trying to impress God that way.

So how can you build a rhythm of prayer that gets you alone with him regularly where you can take off all your masks? And how will you 'speak' with him when you do? Try some things, experiment with it, and have a go!

But I mentioned fasting, too. In the same passage as Jesus' teaching on prayer, he assumes people are fasting and gives similar instructions for that:

"When you fast, do not look somber as the hypocrites do, for they disfigure their faces to show others they are fasting. Truly I tell you, they have received their reward in full. But when you fast, put oil on your head and wash your face, so that it will not be obvious to others that you are fasting, but only to your Father, who is unseen; and your Father, who sees what is done in secret, will reward you." (Matthew 6:16-18)

So why fast? Why deny ourselves food (or other good things) as a rhythm in our lives? One reason is that Jesus seems to think we should, which is why he teaches about it, just as he does with prayer. The early church in Acts did it too, so I see no good reason for that to stop. But beyond that, fasting does something in us that prayer alone does not. It's obvious, but fasting makes us hungry! That hunger can do at least three things: interrupt us, remind us, and motivate us.

Hunger *interrupts* us each time our stomach rumbles and we remember why, giving us a nudge to pray about whatever it is we've decided to pray and fast for. It also interrupts us when we would normally sit down for a meal and we remember we aren't eating, creating a perfect opportunity to spend time praying instead of eating (all of this also happens if we fast something other than food). Do you see how that can help to build a posture of prayer woven into our lives?

Hunger also *reminds* us how dependent we are on God in the first place! No matter how physically fit you are, stop eating for a while and you'll notice it. You will get headaches, lose energy, struggle to concentrate, and probably find your temper is a lot shorter than normal! Perhaps you aren't so strong after all... But if Jesus really is the one who 'sustains all things', including us, a reminder of that is a good thing. John Piper puts it like this:

And the aim of fasting is that we come to rely less on food and more on God. That's the meaning of the words in Matthew 4:4, "Man shall not live by bread alone, but by every word that comes from the mouth of God." Every time we fast we are saying with Jesus, "Not by bread alone, but by you, Lord. Not by bread alone, but by you, Lord."[54]

And finally, hunger *motivates* us, making us long for something physical (food) and translating that into spiritual longing. This works because our bodies are connected to our spirits, so what we do physically relates to what we do spiritually. Whether it is kneeling before God to outwardly express an inward submission, or throwing up our hands as we sing in worship, our bodies express our spiritual desires. But not just express them, they then strengthen and motivate those desires. We fast for something to show our desire for it and as we literally hunger for it, we grow to desire it even more.

So prayer and fasting as a posture toward God is vital for a heart that depends on God. Without it, we draw away and turn back to ourselves. Where in all of this are the shifts in your posture that need to be made?

3. A posture of bravery

The second posture is a little different. If prayer is about leaning into God more fully, this second posture is about pushing back on some of the things that tempt us not to. Remember how we saw that security, apathy and independence are traps that lead us away from dependence on God? Now I want to suggest a way to push back on those: adopt a posture of bravery.

When he took over leadership of the Evangelical Alliance in the UK, Gavin Calver said he wanted the organisation to be 'braver' and 'kinder'[55]. He has returned to these themes often in his leadership. Writing in 2022, he said:

> We … are empowered to be brave if we are willing to take a stand and make the most of the possibilities in front of us. Brave steps can lead to mighty breakthroughs.[56]

I agree with him here! Notice that he says we are 'empowered to be brave' (even the courage we might have is not from within, but given to us), but then links this with being 'willing to take a stand' (we must be open to doing something with it).

Bravery doesn't come from us. But bravery does come out of us, at least that's the way it is meant to be. Remember the believers in Acts 4 praying for boldness and then, when it is *given* to them, they then all go out and *do* something with it (tell everyone around them about Jesus). And remember what it is that is meant to make the disciples dependent in the Great Commission: "I am with you always." It is very similar to the famous words Joshua gave the people of Israel:

> *Be strong and courageous. Do not be afraid; do not be discouraged, for the Lord your God will be with you wherever you go. (Joshua 1:9)*

It is God's presence with us that can make us courageous and that courage that leads us to 'be strong', which in the context is about marching forward and doing all the things God called them to do.

We break this process if we choose not to step out bravely to do the things God leads us to. When we do that, we are no longer letting anything come out of us, so we stop looking for anything to go into us. If I tie up my boat for the day and stop sailing, I very quickly stop looking to see what the wind is doing because I no longer need it. And in our lives with God, that is when apathy sets in, we become too comfortable and we embrace independence. It is safer and we settle into that safety. John McGinley puts it like this: 'Playing it safe, living within our means and abilities, means we do not express our faith and there is no adventure in our relationship with Jesus. And our faith withers on the vine and weakens and bears no fruit.'[57]

Yes, we can seek God in prayer and deepen our dependence on him, but if we do not release whatever he gives us in action, we create a blockage. The only way to break that blockage is to do something scary. What that is will vary from person to person. The things that terrify me might be your bread and butter and vice versa. In some ways it doesn't matter what it is, because anything that requires you to 'be strong and courageous' will break you out of that comfortable rut, force you to remember that 'the Lord your God will be with you' and push you back into deeper dependence on him.

HANDS: Dependent Actions

As we now turn to think about some specific things we can *do* that will help us to grow in dependence on God, there is a dilemma! The more we focus on what we can do, there is a temptation back toward self-reliance. I will try to help us resist that urge by focusing in not just on our own effort, but on two areas where we can deliberately place control and ownership into God's hands where they belong. We will look at the area of money and the decisions we make.

4. Evaluate your finances

What story do your finances tell? Here are a few that they could be telling,[58] and you'll see that the differences between them are both practical (what is done with the money) and the heart behind it (including levels of dependence):

STORY 1: I am an entitled owner. Your stuff is your stuff. You earned it, so you get to choose what to do with it. That's a mixture of spending it and saving it, but it's all within your power to decide. So that is what you do: decide what to do with it based on whatever criteria make most sense to you.

STORY 2: I am an obligated owner. Your stuff is your stuff, but you also know it wouldn't be unless God had given you it. So you know it wouldn't be right to keep and use it all for yourself and that you have an obligation to give some of it away (maybe 10%, maybe more or less). So you give that, but the rest is yours.

STORY 3: I am a generous giver. Your stuff is there to bless others. Yes, it might be in your bank account, but you are no more deserving of it than anyone else so if there is a need you'll try to meet it. You don't stick to percentages. You know it's better to give than to receive, because Jesus said so and you live that out.

These three stories have a number of differences. On the practical level, there are differences in giving. Some stories include no giving, some rigid giving and some uncapped giving whenever the need arises. There will obviously therefore be a different approach to saving and spending. These are all measurable things and there is a link between what we can measure and what is going on in our hearts. That's what Jesus is getting at when he said:

Do not store up for yourselves treasures on earth, where moths and vermin destroy, and where thieves break in and steal. But store up for yourselves treasures in heaven, where moths and vermin do not destroy, and where thieves do not break in and steal. For where your treasure is, there your heart will be also. (Matthew 6:19-21)

Taking stock of our income and outgoings shows us something of the story our finances are telling. If a sizeable chunk of income is spent on X, it stands to reason that X matters to us, we treasure X. If we treasure our family, we provide for them. If we treasure our sports team, we might buy a season ticket. If we treasure generosity, more of our income will be given away. Where we choose to put our 'treasure' both reveals where our heart already is and plants our heart there more and more firmly. So we need to check in on that.

But there is also something here about where our security comes from. As Jesus compares treasure on earth with treasure in heaven, the big contrast he makes is how durable they are. Treasure on earth is fleeting, can get taken from us or come to nothing. Heavenly treasure is everlasting and solid. But sometimes it feels the other way round. Things in our lives here and now (a car, a house, or money in a savings account) feel concrete. Jesus tells us heavenly treasure is far more secure, far more concrete, so if we are going to entrust our hearts to something, entrust it to heaven not earth. And he does that in a passage all about money. Jesus knows a major way we are going to end up trusting less in the King of Heaven is when we trust more in the things of earth. In our world that means money and possessions.

So under the surface of the practical differences between those three stories is a deeper difference and it all has to do with how much we depend on God. If we trust he will provide for us, we can order our finances in a way that isn't focused on self-preservation or personal prosperity. Of course, if what we need isn't 'enough' for us and we wish for God to provide for all we *want*, we can't trust him for that because he's never promised to give us all we want.

But if we have a heart toward God that is trusting, reliant and dependent, then the lines between giving, keeping, spending and saving start to matter less. Now your finances can start to tell a fourth kind of story.

STORY 4: I am a trusting steward. Your stuff is *not* your stuff. It is God's and the fact he has entrusted it with you does not change that. You are able to be generous not because you are wealthy, but because you trust God to provide if you are not. And every penny, whether given, spent or saved, is prayerfully considered and invested in God's purposes, not your own.

It is no longer about whether you give 5%, 10% or 15%. Because whatever you don't give is still being invested as a 'treasure in heaven'. It is invested that way when you open your home when someone needs a place to stay and do not charge them rent. It is invested that way when you spend money on a training course to equip you more fully for something God calls you to. It is invested that way when you provide for a practical need, either your own or someone else's. It is invested that way when you place money into a savings account knowing it is set aside for use in God's Kingdom. There is almost no end to the different ways your finances can be invested, but as a trusting steward you are not motivated by the 'need' to self-protect and you are not interested just in what you will enjoy, but where God is leading. Yet another reason to build that posture of prayer!

To be clear, I do believe it is right for us to give to our local church. As we invest ourselves into a local community of disciples, we are seeking for the growth of God's Kingdom here on earth through it. Part of investing into that should be through our finances. But see that as the starting point, not the upper limit.

Neil Cole, in his book *Church 3.0*, has a chapter all about money. The title of that chapter sums up perfectly what I have been trying to say: 'What about finances? From ten percent to the whole enchilada.'[59] That is the heart of a dependent steward. After all, as Cole writes,

> [Jesus] held nothing back for us. Though He was as rich as heaven, He became poor for us so that we may gain the riches of heaven (1 Cor. 8:9). He gave everything for us, not just 10 percent; we ought to respond in the same way.[60]

5. Seek guidance for a decision

What decision are you trying to make at the moment? I'm talking about a bigger kind of decision than what to eat tonight or what to do this weekend. (Those matter too, but perhaps fall into the category of 'God has already given you a mind so use that this time!') But a big decision. A career change, a relationship, whether to invest money into something or not, whether to move to a different part of the country or world, how best to care for a relative. That sort of thing.

An action we can take that will help us to grow in dependence on God is to look to him for guidance for those decisions instead of just deciding ourselves. But how do we do that? Let's start with the big picture and then dive deeper into one really important aspect.

For the big picture, I will borrow from Nicky Gumbel and the *Alpha Course*. In the video for one of the sessions, titled 'How does God guide us?', Gumbel shares five major ways God guides us.[61] I find them very helpful. (They all also have the same initials (C.S.), which I enjoy both because it means I can remember them and because some of them have clearly been shoe-horned a little to fit!). They are:

• **Commanding Scripture.** Sometimes there are clear biblical instructions or guides that will help us along the way, giving principles to apply.

- **Convicting Spirit.** Through the Holy Spirit, God can convict us, giving us a deep gut level sense about what is right to do.

- **Communion of the Saints.** We can lean on wise people around us, asking them to help us by praying and giving guidance. How does it impact on other areas of my life, and am I content with that?

- **Circumstantial Signs.** God might show us the way forward by 'opening or closing doors', lining things up for us to show us the right path.

- **Common Sense.** We have been blessed with a brain, and practical things do matter to God, so we shouldn't ignore this.

As a framework, this is a really helpful list. If you are seeking God for a decision, these are the ways he is most likely to lead you, so give time and space for each, invite God to speak through each and be on the lookout for how he does.

But in particular I want to focus in on what Nicky Gumbel calls the 'Communion of the Saints'. One of the barriers to dependence on God we've identified is having too much of an 'independent spirit'. We are not meant to become dependent on others, but to depend on Jesus and to do so partly through interdependence with other disciples. A big way we can build that kind of attitude into our lives is by inviting others into our decision-making processes.

My wife and I once did that in a very deliberate way. We were seeking God for a big decision involving a change in job and a possible relocation, all at the same time as expecting our first child. We needed God's wisdom and guidance, but we received really good advice from our friend Alex not to expect to find it by ourselves. As something of a guide, he encouraged us to draw on the example of the Antioch Church in the book of Acts:

When Barnabas and Saul had finished their mission, they returned from Jerusalem, taking with them John, also called Mark. Now in the church at Antioch there were prophets and teachers: Barnabas, Simeon called Niger, Lucius of Cyrene, Manaen (who had been brought up with Herod the tetrar-

ch) and Saul. While they were worshiping the Lord and fasting, the Holy Spirit said, 'Set apart for me Barnabas and Saul for the work to which I have called them." So after they had fasted and prayed, they placed their hands on them and sent them off.

The two of them, sent on their way by the Holy Spirit, went down to Seleucia and sailed from there to Cyprus. (Acts 12:25–13:4)

Barnabas and Saul had finished one mission and needed to know what to do next. Stay in Antioch? Return where they'd been? Go somewhere else? The answer did not come from Barnabas and Saul, though. It came through this mixed bunch of people in Antioch, with lots of different backgrounds and gifts. That is how God spoke and commissioned them and my wife and I wanted the same. So we asked a number of people to be our 'Antioch Community' (yes, we actually called it that), including family, friends, partners in ministry and people from the church we were part of. We asked them to do a number of things for us.

We asked them to (1) *pray and fast for us*. In Antioch, it was as the community were 'worshipping the Lord and fasting' that the Holy Spirit spoke. Which is what you'd expect, right? That a people who have deliberately set their focus on God are more likely to be guided by him? So over the course of a couple of months, we committed to praying intentionally, including a few set days to fast and asked if our Antioch Community would join us in that.

We also then asked them to (2) *gather and share*. They were spread out, so for us that meant a couple of online calls. After the two months of praying and fasting, we gathered and people shared different things they felt God impressing on them for us. Some of this was based on their thinking and common sense and some was what they sensed God said to them directly. It involved Bible verses, principles, specifics and all sorts. In Antioch we are told 'the Holy Spirit said...', but that would have been through human voices. We wanted to hear the Holy Spirit too, so asked people to share and weighed all that they said.

Finally, we asked this group to (3) *commission and send us*. At Antioch, this fasting, worshiping, discerning group then become a sending group. And just as it was through them the Holy Spirit spoke, now it is through them that he sends. In verse 3, it is the Antioch church that 'sent them off', but straight away in verse 4 we read that

Barnabas and Saul were 'sent on their way by the Holy Spirit'. We do not just ask others to help us discern. We also need to be cheered on and championed as we go. And as people do, God is doing so through them.

Not only has this been a hugely encouraging and enriching experience for us, but it also helped! Where some things were fuzzy for us, others could see more clearly. Where we were caught up in hurry because we were scared things might not land when we wanted, others led us back to trust in God. Where our own desires might obscure hearing from God clearly, others could take a few steps back and help us to do the same. And as clear threads emerged in what everyone was saying to us, it gave us huge confidence to push forward in certain directions, knowing we had heard the Holy Spirit in the voices of our friends. In the end, I can confidently say that we made a much bolder step than we would have by ourselves because of a deep sense that God led us there through our Antioch Community.

It is the most strongly we have ever leaned into God for a decision. And we did it not by looking inward, or even just upward. We looked outward to those around us who God has placed in our lives.

I would recommend this kind of process to anyone seeking God for a decision. You might alter it. Our version wasn't identical to Antioch in Acts, and yours might be different as well, but if dependence on God looks, in part, like inter-dependence with others, we need to lean into this kind of thing more and more in our lives.

As always, this toolkit is only useful if you take a tool out and use it. As you've been reading, are there areas that have jumped out as a place to start? If so, start there. If not, start by praying!

A reminder for you at this point as well: 'there is now no condemnation for those who are in Christ Jesus' (Romans 8:1). In my experience, particularly around our prayer lives, Christians can often feel guilty for not being good enough. We assume everyone else has a rhythm of prayer that is amazing, but that ours is not up to scratch compared with theirs. But none of this is about guilt! This is not about whether you are 'good enough' at praying, or whether your finances show total dependence on God, or anything else like that. This is about asking questions that will help us grow, not about judging ourselves. As Paul goes on to say:

And if the Spirit of him who raised Jesus from the dead is living in you, he who raised Christ from the dead will also give life to your mortal bodies because of his Spirit who lives in you. (Romans 8:11)

All of this comes from him! It is his Spirit in you that will 'give life' to you, the kind of deep life that can only come as we raise our sails to catch his wind. Seek and trust him for it, but do not let guilt set in about your own efforts. It has no place for those who are in Christ Jesus.

Chapter 7 at a glance…

In this toolkit chapter, the five tools we explored together were:

1. [HEAD:] Deciding to rely on God over ourselves, by committing to inquire of God not just trust our own thinking, invest in the Kingdom not just save up for ourselves and trust that God's ways are better than ours.

2. [HEART:] Building a posture of prayer and fasting, as a means of throwing ourselves onto God's provision and power.

3. [HEART:] Building a posture of bravery, by stepping out into situations that feel too big for us and making ourselves rely on God for them.

4. [HANDS:] Evaluating our finances and asking what story they tell in terms of how much they display trust and dependence on God.

5. [HANDS:] Seeking guidance for a decision and in particular opening ourselves up to God's voice through the community we put around us.

Becoming Effective

As with the other aspects of the spiritual genetic CODE at the heart of this book, we have a particular focus on the Great Commission and how they function there. So let's take another look, this time through the lens of dependence:

> *Then the eleven disciples went to Galilee, to the mountain where Jesus had told them to go. When they saw him, they worshiped him; but some doubted. Then Jesus came to them and said, "All authority in heaven and on earth has been given to me. Therefore go and make disciples of all nations, baptising them in the name of the Father and of the Son and of the Holy Spirit, and teaching them to obey everything I have commanded you. **And surely I am with you always, to the very end of the age.**" (Matthew 28:16-20, emphasis added)*

Jesus' words about always being with his followers are not just the end of the Great Commission. They are the end of Matthew's Gospel. These books were originally heard, not read, as someone would come into town with a copy (or with it memorised) and proclaim it in one or two sittings. And at the end of that, this is what everyone was left with: "surely I am with you always, to the very end of the age." It would have been a stirring moment and, as people gradually wandered off back to 'normality', that normality would carry this truth: 'Jesus is with me!'

That truth can do something powerful in us, too. When we applied a confidence lens to the Great Commission, we saw it could make us *willing* to join in with this great mission. With an obedience lens, we saw that when we do what it says we become *useful* in God's kingdom. But if we leave it there, we end up with two parallel tracks that never meet. Yes, Jesus has all authority to achieve this and, yes, we will get involved, but our efforts and God's power stay separate. To embrace dependence in the Great Commission is about harnessing God's resources as we obey his commands. When that happens we can become *effective*. I will suggest two ways to embrace God's power as you pursue the Great Commission.

The first is to *intentionally pray for a small group of people*. Many churches have a habit of encouraging everybody to 'Pray for Five', writing down the names of five people they wish to see become and grow as disciples of Jesus, and then regularly praying for them by name for that to happen. This is not just praying randomly as we think of people, or praying for so many that our attention is diluted. This is setting our focus on just a few people coming to life in Jesus and sticking at it till they do. This prayer (preferably daily) can also be accompanied by regular times of fasting as you commit yourself spiritually to their lives.

Most often, this will be people who do not yet know Jesus. As you pray for them, two things are likely to happen. God moves in response to prayer, so we should expect there to be shifts in these people, for things to happen or for new openness toward Jesus. The other thing is that *we* will change as we pray. Hunger and desire for their growth will make us commit to them ourselves, making space to spend time with them, striking up conversations about Jesus, offering to pray not just for them but with them.

When I've been praying for someone, I go into my time with them differently. I look for doors that God is opening. I'm bolder in responding to what look like opportunities. I am more likely to offer to pray for someone, or to be clearer about what I believe, trusting that God has been softening their heart to receive it.

While often this means praying for people who are not yet disciples of Jesus, remember the Great Commission is not just about 'getting people over the line'! If there are people you want to see grow more like Jesus, perhaps where you have a role in their life to encourage that, you can commit in the same way to them and see how the 'teaching to obey' part of Jesus' call is transformed as Jesus' presence and power fan the flame.

A commitment in prayer for someone displays dependence on God for his work in their lives, filling our Great Commission efforts with authority and power and making them far more fruitful.

The second thing I'll suggest is to *step into a conversation*, trusting Jesus to give you the words as you go. Maybe you hear someone discussing a news story at work and it's something your faith gives a particular perspective on. Perhaps someone has shared a trouble they're facing and you know God can give comfort and help. Maybe there is a moment when you could choose to share something of the difference Jesus has made in your life. The list goes on and on. There are moments when you could say something and you know you could! And there are ways we can create those moments by opening up or asking questions we know could lead in these directions.

But the moment when we actually need to say something is the hard bit! For me at least... A racing heart, a dry mouth and a mind that suddenly goes a bit blank. Of course, taking the time to think through what sorts of things to say and how to say them helps massively. Do you have a 3-minute version of your story with Jesus you can share? But whether you do or you don't, there is good news! "I am with you always, to the very end of the age."

Remember, the way Jesus is with us is that the Holy Spirit is in us. And he can take a lead on these conversations if we let him. Jesus warned his friends they will soon face much persecution and get dragged up before lots of different authorities. As an encouragement, he says:

> "When you are brought before synagogues, rulers and authorities, do not worry about how you will defend yourselves or what you will say, for the Holy Spirit will teach you at that time what you should say." (Luke 12:11-12)

Jesus is helping the disciples imagine a situation where, humanly, they are lost for words because the situation is too much for them. It is obedience that will lead them there, as they refuse to deny Jesus. They can have confidence because even before these 'authorities' they stand on behalf of the one with 'all authority'. And all of that means they shouldn't try to defend themselves, but instead lean into the

Holy Spirit who will give them the words to say. In the moment, it seems.

You might or might not ever get hauled up into this kind of situation. For most of us, we will not. But the same Holy Spirit who can give words to say when hauled up in front of rulers, law courts and authorities can give words to say at the water cooler, the pub or the school gate.

We won't necessarily know where the conversation will go, but we can decide to ask the Holy Spirit to guide us and say the first few words. "That's interesting, I was reading in my Bible recently…" Or, "I think God cares about your…" Or maybe, "There was a time in my life when…" All of those sentence starters can lead in wonderful directions as the Holy Spirit leads you. But unless those sentences are started, you'll never know.

Praying for a few people starts in a place of confidence that God can move in their lives and is about the posture of prayer we explored in the last chapter. Stepping into a conversation starts in a place of obedience, doing our bit, and cultivates a posture of bravery. But both are about leaning into dependence on God, letting him provide the power so that our actions have the chance to be effective as we pursue his Great Commission.

So maybe as we finish this whole section on dependence, you could jot down the names of five people. Or three, or six. It doesn't really matter! And pray for them, also deciding how you'll keep on doing that. And also pray for the next time you find yourself with the chance to say something, committing to him that you will and asking for the Holy Spirit's leading.

PART 4

EXPERIENCE WITH JESUS

"When they saw him, they worshiped him; but some doubted. Then Jesus came to them…"

(Matthew 28:17-18)

Acts 10:9-21

For our final spotlight, we return to the book of Acts. To understand this story, we need to understand that, since the church was born at Pentecost, two things have been a recurring fact: persecution and growth. Both fed the other. Their growth was seen as a threat, so the authorities clamped down, but the clamping down led to renewed boldness (as we saw in the confidence spotlight) and to Christians being scattered all over the place. Both resulted in growth.

That scattering was crucial in what we're about to read. Most of Jesus' life and ministry happened in very Jewish places. His disciples were Jewish. Most of his interactions were with Jewish people. And Jesus' death and resurrection and the birth of the church, all took place in Jerusalem, the centre of the Jewish world. At this point, 'Christianity' (though the word didn't exist) was very much a Jewish thing, and the earliest Christians would have followed Jewish customs. But that was all about to change, in part due to the scattering of the church geographically.

We see Philip in Samaria. We see Saul in places like Cyprus and Antioch, venturing into the Greek and Roman world. Some of this was the result of persecution and some was deliberate to reach new people, but all of it was starting to change the face of what the Jesus movement looked like. And, crucially, who was part of it.

In the middle of this, we get another story about Peter. He'd stayed in very Jewish areas, mostly Jerusalem, but this story takes place in Caesarea. We're going to look at a few sections in turn, but first go and look up the whole thing. It's Acts 10:1–11:18. We'll see again see the whole of CODE at work, but it'll also introduce how I see *experience* working in the life of disciples.

The Complete CODE

The story doesn't start with Peter. It starts with an important Roman (note: not Jewish) man called Cornelius. This is how he is introduced: "He and all his family were devout and God-fearing; he gave generously to those in need and prayed to God regularly" (Acts 10:2). This man is ticking the CODE boxes already! 'God-fearing' is all about reverence and *confidence* in God, giving generously is an act of *obedience*, and his prayer life demonstrates *dependence* in his attitude. Then he has an *experience* of God when an angel tells him to seek out Peter.

What is at stake here? We don't know how fleshed-out Cornelius's faith was, but it was likely there were plenty of gaps. It's unlikely he had responded to the gospel of Jesus Christ and more likely he had a general respect for 'God' and his people. Perhaps his soul is at stake? So when Peter has the chance to meet him, what will he do? Will he refuse because Cornelius isn't Jewish? Will he require him to become Jewish first, following all the laws and customs? Or will he see things a different way? Let's pick up the story:

> **Acts 10:9-16**
>
> *9 About noon the following day as they were on their journey and approaching the city, Peter went up on the roof to pray. 10 He became hungry and wanted something to eat, and while the meal was being prepared, he fell into a trance. 11 He saw heaven opened and something like a large sheet being let down to earth by its four corners. 12 It contained all kinds of four-footed animals, as well as reptiles and birds. 13 Then a voice told him, "Get up, Peter. Kill and eat."*
>
> *14 "Surely not, Lord!" Peter replied, "I have never eaten anything impure or unclean."*
>
> *15 The voice spoke to him a second time, "Do not call anything impure that God has made clean."*
>
> *16 This happened three times, and immediately the sheet was taken back to heaven.*

God is preparing Peter for what's coming. As a Jewish person, there were foods he simply did not eat. They were considered 'unclean' and forbidden in the Jewish Scriptures. While Jesus had challenged a religiosity about these rules (e.g. Mark 7:19), it seems Peter still thought it right to keep them. But now God gives a vision full of things he would never eat and a command to eat them!

Again, we see the strong DNA of a disciple evident in Peter. He too is praying in *dependence* on God. When he objects, it is because he doesn't want to be dis*obedient* to the law of God. At this point we must recognise, though, that his *confidence* has been knocked. In this vision, a fundamental of what he thought God had said, what confidence in God looked like, was being questioned…by God.

But this was part of God preparing Peter for the men who were about to come knocking. If these Jewish food laws were not the be all and end all he'd always thought, maybe a non-Jewish person might also be able to respond to God without adopting Jewish customs? Just maybe. The seed is planted.

A little later in the story, we see that the seed has taken root and grown. It isn't long before he is saying this:

> *"I now realise how true it is that God does not show favouritism but accepts from every nation the one who fears him and does what is right." (Acts 10:34-35)*

Peter then preaches the gospel, telling Cornelius (and other Romans) all about Jesus, his life, miraculous ministry, death and resurrection. And he commands the disciples to tell others all about it. Peter has re-found his *confidence* in the good news and come to realise it is good news for all! Then something happens that a few days earlier he would never have imagined: "the Holy Spirit came on all who heard the message" (Acts 10:44). *All* who heard the message. Not just the Jewish people in the room, but everyone. Cornelius, his family and friends. They could receive the good news of Jesus and the Holy Spirit as they were, not have to obey the Jewish laws first.

Next, they are all baptised (Acts 10:47-48). "Therefore go and make disciples of all nations, baptising them…" This experience opened up a new world within the Great Commission for Peter to discover.

Two kinds of experience

But what is it that led Peter from a shaky start to a confident finish? What actually happened in the middle? Let's read, from immediately after Peter's foodie vision:

Acts 10:17-21

17 While Peter was wondering about the meaning of the vision, the men sent by Cornelius found out where Simon's house was and stopped at the gate. 18 They called out, asking if Simon who was known as Peter was staying there.

19 While Peter was still thinking about the vision, the Spirit said to him, "Simon, three men are looking for you. 20 So get up and go downstairs. Do not hesitate to go with them, for I have sent them."

21 Peter went down and said to the men, "I'm the one you're looking for. Why have you come?"

We'll pick this up in greater detail in the next chapter, but I want to make sure we have noticed two different kinds of experience that shape Peter. God did not just send a vision. He also sent these men from Cornelius.

One kind of experience Peter has is very obviously spiritual, an *encounter with God* through a vision. And it shapes and challenges him, but the other kind does as well. That is a very human experience, in this case meeting someone. This is an *encounter with the world* that raises questions to be answered.

It is in the interaction between those two kinds of experience that Peter is shaped. Twice in these verses we hear that he is 'wondering about' or 'still thinking about the vision' as the unfolding interaction with Cornelius's men takes place. He doesn't switch off the spiritual experience so he can engage with the human, nor the other way round. He lets each inform the other. How? Peter doesn't look for answers from Cornelius' men, but he embraces the opportunity for them to raise questions ("I'm the one you're looking for. Why have you come?"). Then those questions must be answered as he takes them back to God. And those new answers open up new opportunities within the world, which will once again raise new questions, and so on…

So the final section of the book is not called 'Experience of Jesus' and only about spiritual encounters we have with God. Instead, it is called 'Experience *with* Jesus' and brings together experiencing God and experiencing the world. If our questions and answers both come from the right place, we will grow up as experienced disciples.

Don't be a big baby

I don't know you, but here are two things I know about you:

1. You used to be a baby.
2. You aren't any more.

I know. Profound. We all start the same, unable to walk, talk, sit up, eat, or do anything without help. Babies are wonderful, but useless at most things vital to being alive. But that's ok, because they're babies.

Over time, that changes. The fact you are reading this book instead of chewing on the corner and dribbling all over it means you are no longer a baby. Which means there are things expected of you. You are capable of doing those things. If as an adult we are fed from a bottle, wear nappies or get pushed around in a pram, it means something isn't how we'd want it to be.

Some things that are innocent, pure and even beautiful at one stage of life are a sign of unhealthiness at another. As Paul says when he uses a similar image, "When I was a child, I talked like a child, I thought like a child, I reasoned like a child. When I became a man, I put the ways of childhood behind me." (1 Corinthians 13:11)[62] This is not the first time Paul uses this kind of image. Earlier in the same letter, he has these quite brutal words to say:

Brothers and sisters, I could not address you as people who live by the Spirit but as people who are still worldly—mere infants in Christ. I gave you milk, not solid food, for you were not yet ready for it. Indeed, you are still not ready. You are still worldly. For since there is jealousy and quarrelling among you, are you not worldly? Are you not acting like mere humans? For when one says, "I follow Paul," and another, "I follow Apollos," are you not mere human beings? (1 Corinthians 3:1-4)

He starts by talking about their *former state*, their early days in faith and how he treated them as 'infants in Christ', giving them what they could handle. Then he turns to challenge them about their *current state* and he doesn't hold back! He is essentially saying, "But you're still like babies! You are squabbling like a bunch of toddlers instead of behaving like the grown-ups you're supposed to be. Stop being a bunch of big babies and grow up!" By this point, they should have made some progress, but their arguments show they're still 'infants in Christ'. Like big babies.

There are two things to draw out of these verses. The first is this: we are meant to grow as followers of Jesus. Paul isn't telling them off for being immature as disciples in the past. He is challenging them because they still are.

Someone who is a 'baby Christian' is not supposed to be as mature as someone who has been following Jesus for years. If you are a disciple of Jesus, that shouldn't still look the way it did in the early days of your faith and five years on from now it shouldn't look the way it does now. Healthy things grow and that's meant to be so for Christians. Just as an experienced driver is likely to be safer (hence lower insurance costs), an experienced disciple should be more mature.

These 'infants in Christ' in Corinth were whining about who the best teacher was. "My favourite preacher's better than yours!" It's childish, and a little pathetic. What is a mature response if you think you've heard great preaching? Do something with it! Be obedient to it, let it shape you, embolden you, build you up, grow you up and send you out. Not show off about it.

But the second thing to notice in these verses is what Paul says *makes them* like babies. He says it three times (I've added emphasis):

*"…but as people who are still **worldly**—mere infants in Christ."*

*"Indeed, you are still not ready. You are still **worldly**."*

*"…are you not **worldly**? Are you not acting like mere humans?"*

The thing that means they are 'baby Christians' instead of mature disciples is that they are 'worldly'. The word here is related to the word for 'flesh' (as opposed to 'spirit'). So perhaps better than 'worldly' would be to read this as 'fleshly', driven by our primal desires instead of any higher cause. Paul packs one final punch when he follows it up with "Are you not acting like mere humans?" What an awful thing to be true! That these people, made in the image of God, whose human sinfulness has been washed away, who have become a dwelling place for the Holy Spirit himself, are behaving as...mere humans. It might be worse than telling a fully-grown adult they are 'acting like a big baby'.

So the Corinthians' problem is that, instead of growing up spiritually, they leaned too heavily on the wisdom of their age, wanted to be too much like the world around them. You can see why the word 'worldly' makes quite a lot of sense. These are meant to be spiritual people, shaped by Jesus. Instead, they have settled for being fleshly people, shaped by the world.

And here we encounter a thread we will return to a number of times. If we want to grow in experience with Jesus, we must not look to the world to show us how. We saw it in Peter's story with Cornelius. Yes, an experience in the world shaped and stretched Peter's thinking and assumptions. Nothing wrong there. But he did not look to that world, or that experience, to provide the answers he needed. He did not ask Cornelius what to do about his theology. He looked to God to see what to do about Cornelius.

To grow as experienced disciples of Jesus, we must look to him before we look to the world around us. And we must come back to him after something in our world has caught our attention to ask if we're seeing it as he does.

So in this chapter we are going to spend time with both. We'll consider the nature of our experiences *of God*, what they're meant for, what they're like, and how we can make sure they really help us grow. Then we'll look at what experiences *in the world* can be like, good and bad, and how we can let them spur us on toward growth when we approach them with God. We'll finish by asking what 'growing up' actually means and what getting there requires.

Looking up: experience of God

James 4:8 says, "Come near to God and he will come near to you." What a promise! We'll look at some of the context of that verse shortly, but for now let's just hear the promise. God is willing to draw near to us, and invites us to draw near to him. We can experience and meet with God in real ways.

What do you picture when you hear the phrase 'experience God'? Perhaps you are transported into nature, to woods and forest glades, hearing the brook or feeling the gentle breeze?[63] Perhaps that is where God seems close? Or maybe you imagine a Bible open in front of you, finding God in the pages of Scripture? Or are you in a church worship service, meeting with God through songs, or preaching, or a time of prayer ministry? Or perhaps you imagine yourself serving someone else, and finding God in the faces of those you serve? Maybe you are alone and silent, hearing a 'gentle whisper'[64] as you wait on God? Or could it be you are with others, hearing his voice on the lips of others as you pray, talk and ponder the things of God to-gether? When you meet God, are you awake or asleep? Are you studying, singing, dancing, praying or thinking? Are you laughing or crying?

This is not the point where I tell you what the correct answer to that question is! I can think of good, biblical reasons for each of the answers I just listed, as well as many more. There is no one correct way to experience God. And, as with a healthy diet, a mixture of things will be good for us as we seek to draw near to God.

It is also important to be clear about something else. This is not just about the big 'mountaintop experiences' of God that blow us away. Whether that be when we go away to an event or conference, a trip with others, a divine lightbulb moment, or an experience that changes everything. They are fantastic, but most of life is not lived on the mountaintop. It is also not just about a weekly rhythm of joining with other Christians as part of a church. Again, most of life is not lived 'at church'. This is about all our experiences of God. Big, little, strange, mundane, alone, with others. The whole lot.

What happens when we meet with God?

More important than how we do it is what happens when we meet with God. If the sum total of your experiences of God is that you feel warm and fuzzy, there is a problem. Warm and fuzzy are good and I have felt both many times when I sense God's presence closely, but they are not the point. I love that God blesses us with encouragement, peace, joy and wonder as we learn to spend time basking in the gift of his own presence. I also know I can be tempted just to focus on those things. Surely God wants me to feel at peace, to be encouraged, to have joy? And he does, but that is not all he wants. So I want to paint a fuller—and perhaps less comfortable—picture of what having experiences with God is meant to lead us to.

i. We repent when we experience God

Let's return to the promise we just read from the book of James, but let's keep on reading a little further this time. It's still a wonderful promise, but you'll quickly see why only some parts of this get made into fridge magnets...

> Come near to God and he will come near to you. Wash your hands, you sinners, and purify your hearts, you double-minded. Grieve, mourn and wail. Change your laughter to mourning and your joy to gloom. Humble yourselves before the Lord, and he will lift you up. (James 4:8-10)

'Grieve, mourn and wail'. Is that what we think God wants us to do when we 'come near to' him? According to James, it should be the result at least some of the time. The promise that God will come close is quickly followed by the instruction to purify ourselves. When we encounter the perfect, holy God, we become aware of the stains on our hearts. The wrong we often gloss over gets brought into sharp focus. We see our own sin and it pains us. Where before we were laughing it off, now James describes a heart in 'mourning'. When we meet with God, the sin we know offends him begins to offend us and we know it has to change. Jackie Hill Perry draws attention to Isaiah, whose response to meeting with God was such a deep awareness of his sin that he cried out, "Woe to me! I am ruined!" Perry asks:

> Isn't it interesting how simply being in proximity to God creates a moral self-awareness in Isaiah and others? That there is something about God that is so pure, even if unspoken, that when near Him, it becomes so plain that nothing is like Him, especially in terms of righteousness.[65]

Encounters with God lead us to repentance. The best starting place in repentance is to see how dazzlingly holy and perfect God is and then to look within and know we are not. That creates an emotional response, like the one James describes, which drives us to repent, to change our minds and turn things around. If we just look at the sin, we will get cozy with it, excuse it, even justify it. But if we look at God instead, we can learn to hate that sin and expel it.

All of this is true for wrong actions, but also for wrong thinking, wrong outlooks and wrong perspectives. Our 'worldliness' can be brought to light in the presence of God as we repent of it.

But if we are honest, often it is sin in our lives that stops us from drawing near to God. We think we need to deal with it before we can meet with God, when in fact we meet with God so *he* can deal with the sin. We convince ourselves of the lie that God has grown tired of us, that we should know better by now, that he is fed up with our consistent failure. Not so! Dane Ortlund hits the nail on the head:

> When you sin, do a thorough job of repenting. Re-hate sin all over again. Consecrate yourself afresh to the Holy Spirit and his pure ways. But reject the devil's whisper that God's tender heart for you has grown a little colder, a little stiffer. He is not flustered by your sinfulness.[66]

How is it those words from James finished? 'Humble yourselves before the Lord, and he will lift you up.' This process of repentance when we come near to God is not meant to bring us low, put us down and kick us while we're there. It is to lift us up! It was only ever because of Jesus' sacrifice that we could be lifted up to new life and when we encounter God afresh today we are invited to humble ourselves once again in repentance that he might lift us up once again in forgiveness.

ii. We are changed when we experience God

Repentance is not the only thing in view when we have an encounter with God. It is also a place of deep transformation for us. Spending time with God changes us. We saw it in the lives of both Peter and Cornelius, but it is also true for us.

John, probably Jesus' closest friend among the disciples, knew the impact of time with Jesus. But as powerful and transformative as those three years were in his own life, he knew an even greater degree of transformation is waiting for all who have become God's children. In his first letter, he wrote:

> *Dear friends, now we are children of God, and what we will be has not yet*

been made known. But we know that when Christ appears, we shall be like him, for we shall see him as he is. All who have this hope in him purify themselves, just as he is pure. (1 John 3:2-3)

What he writes is simple, but profound. Right now, we are already God's children. That is a present reality, but in the present the full extent of what that looks like is not yet seen. It is still clouded and hidden. But when Jesus returns we will be like him completely, transformed to look like our big brother, fully showing the family likeness of the Son of God.

But what is it that will achieve this? John says, "we shall be like him, *for we shall see him as he is*." It is seeing Jesus fully that will make us fully like him. No barrier, fog or obstacle will get in the way. And when we see Jesus clearly, not with eyes still blurred by sin but with perfected eyes, we'll be utterly transformed. There will never be need again to grieve, mourn or wail because we fall short. In an instant all will be different around us and all will be changed in us. That is what an unfiltered experience of Jesus does.

That future can, though, reach back into our present. John isn't just telling us what *will* happen. He uses it as motivation for what *can* happen now. "All who have this hope in him purify themselves, just as he is pure". There is a direction our life is going if we are a child of God and it's toward complete Christlikeness. In light of that, we can take steps in that direction now. Our vision will be blurry, but we can still see him. And as we do we find transformation. As Paul writes:

Do not conform to the pattern of this world, but be transformed by the renewing of your mind. Then you will be able to test and approve what God's will is—his good, pleasing and perfect will. (Romans 12:2)

These words come just after an invitation to place our whole lives before God as a sacrifice, an act of worship. When we place ourselves before him, his transforming work can take hold of us. We can be led away from being like our world (like the 'big babies' of Corinth) and led into transformation as God rewires our thinking to be more like his. We grow up his way. This work will never be complete until we see Jesus as he is, face to face, but that doesn't mean it shouldn't start now.

iii. We are sent out when we experience God

Experiences of God also confirm and strengthen the things God calls us to. He does not just draw us in to be close with him. He sends us out to be active in the world. If your time with God simply leads to more time with God, if your Christian friends are always drawing on you to be with your Christian friends and if the main result of being at church is that you spend more time at church, something is likely out of balance.

We see it in the Great Commission, don't we? The disciples meet Jesus on the mountain, but what he shares as they spend time with him is not meant to keep them on the mountain. They have to "go"!

Let's return to Isaiah who, when he experiences God's presence, cried out "Woe is me! I am ruined!" In response, God does a work of transformation in his life, using a symbol of his own purifying work for Isaiah. Isaiah has a repentant heart in the presence of God and God transforms him in return. Then this happens:

> Then I heard the voice of the Lord saying, "Whom shall I send? And who will go for us?"
>
> And I said, "Here I am I. Send me!" (Isaiah 6:8)

It's quite a turnaround! Isaiah goes from "Woe is me!" to "Send me!" in no time at all. That is what time with God can do. Isaiah got it. As much as he benefited from this encounter, it was not just for him. God had plans *for* him, but those plans were not *about* him. He gives Isaiah a choice, posing a question he can respond to or not. The disciples could choose whether to follow the Great Commission and Isaiah could choose whether to go as God's messenger. But the experiences are *meant* to change them. Alan Hirsch and Rob Kelly put it like this: "In all genuinely biblical forms of spirituality, the personal encounter with God must inevitably lead to loving action in the world."[67]

And you and I can make a similar choice every time we have an experience of God. Do we keep it for ourselves? Or do we let it spur us onward and outward to the things God has in store for us? An experience of God may start with "Come!" but it always leads to "Go!"

If we will let them, these three things (repentance, transformation and sending out) can become a pattern for us as we think about our experiences with God. We will come with our own baggage, preconceptions, failures, doubts and trouble (and good things, too!). We can begin by choosing to lay those down, repenting of what needs repentance. We can then invite God's transformation, rewiring us so we are more like him. And then, armed with this, we go back into our context sent by God with fresh purpose. This process is a big part of how our experiences of God are meant to work.

What stops us?

But, if we're honest, there are many times we do not have this kind of experience of God. Or when we don't feel we experience God at all. We know he is there, but we are here and God's 'there' feels far away from our 'here'. Why is that and what can we do about it?

There are some simple reasons, which we won't dwell on but are worth touching on. Like distractedness. We are just so busy, tied up, or caught up with lots of things that it's hard to notice God at all. Let's remember, though, that is, at least in part, a choice we make. We decide how we will spend our time and whether we will carve out space in our lives to draw near to God. The world around us will make demands of us but, if we don't want to be 'worldly', we have to say 'no' sometimes so there is space to seek God.

Then there's the possibility we just don't think we need it. We read in the Psalms, "As the deer pants for streams of water, so my soul pants for you, my God. My soul thirsts for God, for the living God." (Psalm 42:1-2). And it sounds so foreign. The idea of being *that* in need of God just does not ring true for us. We just aren't that thirsty! This perhaps takes us back to the 'meh' problem (apathy) from Chapter 6. But it means we never ask the question in the very next line of that Psalm: "When can I go and meet with God?"

Those are simple reasons we might not seek God. So we skip church. We pick up the thriller from our bedside table instead of the Bible (because we actually want to be thrilled). We hit play on Netflix instead of heading outside to walk and pray. We have lie-ins more often than quiet times with God to start the day. But I also want to suggest a deeper reason, one you should be alert to. And that's falling into the trap of assuming these experiences are all about…you.

Consumers or disciples?

When we considered idols in chapter 2, we spent some time with the second of the Ten Commandments. It was the one about not setting up go-betweens that end up becoming the focus of our worship. I believe that is the problem a lot of us end up in when it comes to our experiences of God, whatever they look like.

It's a multi-stage process, that goes something like this:

1. We encounter God and want to seek him more.

2. We discover things that draw us closer to him (Scripture, church services, nature, etc.).

3. We prioritise those things, building them as habits and routines.

4. Our focus shifts and what started off helping us draw near to God starts to become the focus itself.

5. Because those things were never as good as God himself, they do not fully satisfy, so we feel frustrated.

6. We have associated those things with God so fully that we feel God has got distant, when in fact we are looking to the go-betweens, not to God.

7. We become disenchanted with God.

This is not all wrong. In fact, the first three steps are all good things! If we were never to take step 4, the rest doesn't ever need to happen. But it often will happen, because we are really good at letting our religious activities become all-important. Michael Frost and Alan Hirsch warn us that,

> …unless the worshiper is very wary, the glory of the God encounter will slowly fade, and the ritual, creeds, and rules intended to preserve the encounter will take its place. The crisis dawns when the outward forms of worship no longer match the inward experience and spiritual condition of the participants.[68]

When this has happened, what is really going on is that, instead of behaving as mature disciples, we start to be immature consumers. A mature disciple seeks God to be transformed, knowing that it's through repentance and a new vision for the world that they can step out into God's purposes. An immature consumer is stuck complaining about what isn't working *for them* now the experiences of God seem less meaningful. Our focus has shifted from being about what will grow us as disciples to what we feel we most benefit from or enjoy.

So how do we spot if we are in this place? Listen to the kinds of things you are thinking or saying. If you are getting into debates about how long a sermon needs to be instead of whether you are being transformed through God's preached word, think about why. If only a certain 'style of worship' seems to 'work for you', that could be a warning sign. If when you read the Bible there are parts you never touch, thinking 'they just aren't relevant to me' or 'I don't get anything from them', that could be a symptom of spiritual consumerism.

While this can absolutely be true of any aspect of our experiences with God, it will often show most strongly in how we think about a church we attend. So we put the blame outside of ourselves and with the church or its leaders because it is not meeting our needs anymore. Craig Groeschel has this to say about that kind of mindset:

> And the phrase "I can't find a church that meets my needs" is one of the most unbiblical statements any Christian could utter. This is the have-it-your-way mindset. We see ourselves as spiritual consumers. The church is the product. We want to find a product that meets our needs.[69]

Groeschel leads a very large church in the USA, but this mindset does not only exist in that kind of place. It doesn't matter whether your church is tens of thousands meeting in an arena or just a handful meeting in a house or under a tree. The issue is not in the set-up around us, but the heart within us, making it about my needs and how I want things to be. As he goes on to say,

> Before long, this polluted mindset creeps into our theology…We forget that we are not made to be spiritual consumers. God has called us to be spiritual contributors. And the church does not exist for us. We are the church, and we exist for the world.[70]

That is the key difference here, isn't it, that we the church 'exist for the world'? It is not the case that 'the church' is separate from me and exists for me. No, I am part of the church and it exists for the good of the world.

If that is the case, then when I gather with my church it isn't for me. When I open my Bible, it isn't for me. When I sit down to spend time with God in prayer, it isn't for me. However I seek to experience God, it isn't for me. Not primarily. Will I get things from it? Yes! Can I enjoy it? Absolutely! But if I have the heart of a mature disciple, I will always remember that isn't the main purpose. More important than my own enjoyment is that I might be called to greater depth, transformed to look more like Jesus and so be more equipped for his work in the world.

When you embrace that, if something isn't 'working for you', the first reaction won't be that it's faulty, or that God has disappeared. You'll ask first if there's something in how you're approaching it that isn't right. And you'll make sure that it never becomes an excuse for withdrawing from God because you know how much you need his transforming work.

I am aware that this is a challenging picture of what it means to experience and encounter God. As I read the Bible, I see no other way of presenting what true and life-altering experiences with God are like. It does not always appear comfortable. It seems more often to correct the course than confirm it. We are prone to water it down, make it tame, make it safe. When we do, we lose out and so does the world.

Looking out: experience in the world

So what about experiences in this world? Just as Peter was shaped by Cornelius, just as the Corinthians were shaped by Corinth, so we are shaped by the world we inhabit, people we meet, situations we face and experiences we have. We cannot avoid that. It will happen. But we can make choices about how it will happen and what kind of influence it will have. We will focus on three areas: what we do with questions the world raises, how to embrace good things and how pain can—but doesn't need to—stop us in our tracks.

Questions and answers

Let's check in again with Peter and the early church as they grappled with including non-Jewish people. A few chapters after Cornelius, the book of Acts picks up this question again, because people from the Jewish area of Judea are preaching the exact opposite of the conclusion Peter came to. A decision needs to be made about this.

The question has been raised, not just by Cornelius but far more widely, as more and more non-Jews are turning to Jesus. But where will they look for an answer. We saw how Peter took his questions from his experiences but his answers from God and now we see whole church doing the same. We read, in Acts 15, that they looked to their God-appointed leaders (v2-3), they reflected on what God had already done, focusing on his activity not their own (v4, v6-13), reflected on Scripture (v13-19) and then came to a decision. All of these were ways of looking to God for the answers, not to themselves and not to the world around them.

The result was that the church ended up more sure and more confident about what to do (v31). Where before they had been confused, now they are glad and encouraged by the clear way forward. Though we must also recognise it is rarely as simple and clean as that makes it sound. We know from Paul's letter to the Galatians that Peter himself would still struggle with this new way of seeing things that God had given. Growing in response to God's word isn't simple, clean and straightforward. It is often very messy.

The world around us is changing at a staggering pace and it isn't slowing down. All the time, new technology and new ideas are thrust at us and we must decide what to do about it. The world is asking questions about gender, sex, artificial intelligence, climate, race, economics, equality and on and on the list goes. We absolutely must not ignore these questions, but also absolutely must not look for our answers in the same places the questions come from. We can listen, learn and engage, absolutely. But if we want to know God's way forward, we must look to him and to his word.

And the same is true for the choices you are faced with on a more day-to-day level. If you are going to 'grow up' in maturity as a disciple, you need to let God answer the questions that come every day. A workplace or school with a negative culture poses a question: join in or stand out? I was speaking with a teenager recently whose friend took her to one side and told her, "You need to get better at gossip." That's the answer that was coming from her world: join in with the gossip. She knew God had a different answer to the question and has chosen to go with his!

It isn't always that blatant, of course, but our world and the people around us are constantly giving us the answers we should be looking to God for. It might be about the language we use, the priorities we have, the clothes we wear, or our sexual practices. Our world gives many answers to all those questions and more. So will we remain 'worldly', or grow up God's way?

Celebrating the wins

Sometimes, we experience things in our lives which are brilliant and we want to celebrate them. The good news is that we absolutely should celebrate them! Jesus loved a party and there's no reason we shouldn't too. If we approach them the right way, good things in life can spur us on into deeper maturity in God. If we don't, though, they can hold us back.

To explain this better, there's something that happens at a few points in the Bible when God's people experience a huge high. They set up stones as a memorial to a victory, celebrating it, so they can look back on it and let it spur them on in the future. It's a wonderful thing and one example is found in Joshua 4 when God has led the people miraculously across the Jordan river by stopping it in their tracks. This time, twelve stones are set up and Joshua explains they are:

> *"to serve as a sign among you. In the future, when your children ask you, 'What do these stones mean?' tell them that the flow of the Jordan was cut off before the ark of the covenant of the Lord. When it crossed the Jordan, the waters of the Jordan were cut off. These stones are to be a memorial to the people of Israel forever." (Joshua 4:6-7)*

There are a few things about this that can give us a great pattern for how to both celebrate and grow from the good times in our lives. I'll share three.

First, this celebration gives credit where it belongs: to God. This is a memorial to what God has done, not to their own effort. These people could have patted themselves on the back, but that wouldn't ring true when there was no way they could have crossed the river on their own. The day before, Joshua had told them, "tomorrow the Lord will do amazing things among you" (Joshua 3:5). This is God's work, not theirs.

There's a song I've sung hundreds of times in church, with the line, 'Every blessing you pour out, I'll turn back to praise.'[71] That's what the Israelites do, and it's a great habit to get into. That way our good experiences in life will always lead us to God, to celebrate with him, honour him, draw close to him.

Second, the Israelites make a choice to look back on this moment and create a way to do that. This is not just a moment, but a decision about what they will do every time they remember it. These stones are a 'memorial to the people of Israel forever', not just something for them to celebrate in the moment. The moment will pass, but they can choose to hold the memory forever. So they do.

We can do the same when we experience good things and give honour to God for them. We can frame a photograph, write in a journal, mark our calendars with anniversaries to remember. There are lots of ways of choosing to remember and when we do this over time with each blessing (big and small), it draws us closer to God and that is a place of transformation.

Finally, the Israelites then walk away from the stones. Not to forget them—they've made their choice to remember. But they do not just sit around staring at the evidence of what God *has done*. No, they press on into all the things God has *yet to do*. Crossing the Jordan was one thing, but there was a whole promised land ahead of them and God had more for them.

This is key, because the danger when good things happen is that we dwell in them for too long and forget to move forward. We still bask in the blessings God gave us years and years ago, instead of stepping forward with him into what is next. To return to the image of babies growing up, there are many milestones along the way. But no parent, when their child says their first word or takes their first step, says, 'Brilliant, job done!' There are more steps to take, more things to learn, more things to experience. Don't limit God to the level of the good things he has done so far in your life. Celebrate them, choose to remember them, but don't get stuck in them. Your best days may yet lie ahead!

The place of pain

But life is not all blessing and happiness. It is good to let the good times lead us on but we also need to know how to approach the hard times. "In this world you will have trouble," (John 16:33) Jesus warns, so we need to know what to do when it comes. In my experience, these can in fact be some of the times of deepest growth and maturing. This shouldn't surprise us, because we are told in the Bible that they can be. James writes:

> *Consider it pure joy, my brothers and sisters, whenever you face trials of many kinds, because you know that the testing of your faith produces perse-*

verance. Let perseverance finish its work so that you may be mature and complete, not lacking anything. (James 1:2-4)

I do not wish hardship on you. I really don't. But I do hope when it comes, you are able to know the joy of the work it is doing in your life and discipleship. Pain can make us more like Jesus, not just because he himself suffered, but because it can drive us onward and forward with God in ways nothing else can.

But we have to let it. Just as we look to God for answers to questions life raises, so we look to God to define us in the midst of the suffering life brings. A disciple is *never* defined by the hardship and suffering they are facing. A disciple is *always* defined by Jesus. In Exodus 6, the Israelites are in slavery in Egypt. They are suffering and there was no way out. Into that, God says this to Moses:

Now you will see what I will do to Pharaoh: Because of my mighty hand he will let them go; because of my mighty hand he will drive them out of his country. (Exodus 6:1)

This is then followed up by God with a rousing speech! In it, he makes fourteen statements about who *he* is and what *he* is going to do. The message is clear: you are not defined by your chains or your captivity because I am greater than they are. So Moses goes to the Israelites and tells them all of this, the promise of freedom and all these things God has said about himself. The response is heartbreaking:

Moses reported this to the Israelites, but they did not listen to him because of their discouragement and harsh labor. (Exodus 6:9)

They couldn't hear it. To them, their pain was louder than the truth of who God was. The good news is it didn't stop God from freeing them like he promised! God doesn't act just because we believe he will, but because he says he will. But they were robbing themselves of the opportunity to draw comfort from him and from his words at this moment.

I do not know if you are facing a hard time, but if you are it doesn't define you and you don't have to let it. When my ex-wife left me for someone else, I was plunged into pretty serious depression. I received two invaluable pieces of advice at that time. One was from a friend who'd been widowed not long before. She was also a preacher, like me. She told me not to mention what I was going through in every sermon. Mention it if relevant, but don't become 'the depressed preacher' or 'the divorced pastor'. She said this because that is not who I am! It is part of who I am, but I mustn't let it become all of who I am. The other was from my Dad, who when I first told him the news said to me, "There's a lot coming that you cannot control, but remember you can always control how you respond and behave." He wasn't giving me permission to behave poorly because I'd been treated poorly, or to lash out because I was hurt.

I thank God for both of these people and both of these pieces of advice! Both, in their own way, were telling me not to let my pain or suffering define me. There is more to me than my suffering and I am not controlled by my pain. I am defined by Jesus Christ and I follow in his way, no matter what the world throws at me. I was by no means perfect in following this advice, but because I heard it I was able not to see myself as a victim (like the Israelites did) and let what God said lead me to places of transformation and growth.

Growing up: experienced disciples

Just as babies are meant to grow up into adults, so disciples are meant to grow up into maturity in Christ. And if Jesus wants us to have the CODE we are exploring in this book, then more experience as his disciples should lead to more maturity in each part of it. We can become more confident in Jesus, regardless of what the world throws at us, because our conviction that he still has 'all authority' deepens and strengthens. We can become more obedient, choosing to live as Jesus calls us to live, not as our world does. We can live lives that are more dependent, knowing our world does not provide the answers or the strength we need but Jesus does.

All of that requires us to be disciples growing up instead of staying put. We've seen that we can be 'worldly', defined by success or failure, victories or victimhood. We can ask our world for the answers only God can give. We can seek God for affirmation but never for transformation.

Or we can grow up. That means repentance, opening ourselves up to change and being sent into our world with new and fresh purpose. It means letting him provide the answers we need to live in this world. It means submitting all our experiences, high and low, to him and letting him lead us through them all. It will not happen by mistake. We must choose to grow and put ourselves in places where God will lead us into that growth. That is what we turn to now, with our final toolkit, all about how to grow up instead of staying where we are right now.

Chapter 8 at a glance...

In this chapter, we:

1. Introduced the image of a baby growing up, seeing how Paul used it to call people to mature in faith instead of staying as spiritual infants.

2. Explored what it means to have experiences of God, including:

   - What we can expect to happen, where we focused on the process of repentance leading to change, meaning we are sent out different back into the world around us.

   - What stops us from having those kinds of experiences of God and, in particular, the difference between being a consumer and a disciple.

3. Delved into the experiences we have in the world, considering:

   - Where we allow questions to come from (anywhere) and where we look for answers (God, not the world)

   - How to celebrate the good things in life in a way that draws us nearer to God and leads to our growth rather than complacency.

   - The reality of pain and what we can do so that times of suffering are times of growth rather than setbacks in our discipleship.

4. Concluded with a call to focus on growing up into maturity with Jesus, not staying put or becoming less mature.

How to grow up

So we want to grow up. Instead of flimsy Christians, we want to be disciples of substance. That is a vision that inspires me and I hope it inspires you. In our world, it is such an important thing for followers of Jesus to commit to. These words from Richard Foster were written in 1989, but they feel like they could have been written yesterday:

> Superficiality is the curse of our age. The doctrine of instant satisfaction is a primary spiritual problem. The desperate need today is not for a greater number of intelligent people, or gifted people, but for deep people.[72]

Deep people. I agree. But depth takes time. Depth requires intentionality. Depth must be built on the right things. This isn't about being clever or talented. It is about letting ourselves grow up into the people God leads us to become, not remaining the spiritual babies we were when he found us. I want to be a deep person. If you do too, this toolkit will provide some steps to help in the constant process of growing up into maturity in Christ.

HEAD: Experienced Decisions

The idea of deciding to grow in experience and maturity is a strange one. The mustard seed Jesus speaks about (Matthew 13:31-32) does not *decide* to grow into a mighty tree. With the right conditions and time, it just will. It's the same with the babies Paul wrote about. A baby does not *decide* to grow, gain weight, develop teeth, or go through any other of the milestones parents look for. But over time, so long as the right things are provided (food, sleep, affection and so on), a baby becomes a physically and emotionally healthy toddler, child, teenager and adult. It just happens.

But seeds and babies are about physical growth. I can't decide whether, at a certain age, hair started growing from my nostrils and ears. Biology took care of that (thanks, biology…). But when it comes to other kinds of growth, in particular spiritual growth, there are decisions I can make. Let's be clear: spiritual growth is the work of the Spirit, especially as he uses God's word to do God's work in your life. But we can decide to partner with that, or get in the way. So there are a couple of decisions I encourage you to make to open up the possibilities of deep spiritual growth in your life.

1. 'I will make growth a priority'

The first decision is to care. And I really want to stress this. As with most things in life, you get out what you put in. So be honest as you answer this question: do you *want* to mature in Christ?

It might be the honest answer is 'no'. You know the right answer is 'yes', that you should want to mature, get closer to Jesus, more obedient to him, more confident sharing him with others. But you're actually pretty content with things as they are. Your Christianity does not ask too much of you, but that's ok. You aren't asking too much of it.

I write those words with no judgment at all, because I've been there many times. I remember with shame the time I told someone who was on fire for Jesus that it was a bit much and to stop 'smothering' me with him. I actually used that word: 'smothering'! I cringe as I write that. I was a Christian, but just wanted to get on with my life, without bringing Jesus into every single part of it. In other words, I wanted to remain a spiritual baby in certain bits of my life, instead of growing up with Jesus. I doubt I'm alone.

If honestly the answer is 'no' and you're settled in that, I don't have much to say. I want more for you than that, but no human persuasion will convince you to step out of comfort or strive for a deeper life with Jesus than you currently have. So I'll leave you to work that one out with God.

But maybe the answer, right now as you read these words, is 'yes'! You do want to mature in Christ, to grow up in experience as a disciple. You know there will be a cost, because he might make demands on your life that aren't comfortable, but you are up for it. Or maybe you aren't sure you want it, but you *want* to want it! I think that describes me a lot of the time.

In truth, though, we can't decide to want something, but we can decide to prioritise something, and let our desires can catch up. In particular, I want to suggest two things to prioritise that will be steps in the right direction.

i. Prioritise unlearning, not just learning

There's a sequence with anything that grows and gets stronger. A building begins with foundations and then works up through different layers and stages, finishing with final touches and detailing. A tree grows from the roots, up and out into branches, leaves and fruit. A person starts with one cell that divides over and over, eventually growing into organs, organ systems, limbs, fingernails and nostril hairs. You can't work backward from a fingernail any more than you can work backward from an apple to grow the tree on which it hangs or from a windowsill to build the foundations on which it sits.

But if there is a problem in one of those early stages, everything built on it or grown from it can be wonky, faulty or unhealthy. It's why genetic illnesses can be so hard to treat, or why a problem in a building's foundations are more worrying than a window that needs replacing. And because we aren't perfect, we all have shaky foundations of one kind of another that lead to wonky lives built on them. If we just keep learning more on top of that, it'll keep getting wonkier. As well as learning, we need to *un*learn as we go.

Alan Hirsch says it like this:

> To be able to learn something new, whether it is related to God or to other forms of learning, we need to be willing to let go of obsolete ideas and open our eyes and our hearts to being willing to grow, mature, and get back on the road of discipleship and learn again.[73]

Perhaps an experience with a human parent means your view of God as Father is a little skewed? Maybe you can't imagine different shapes or styles of church because there are assumptions you've always had even though they aren't really based on the Bible? Could it be you have learned to value things like comfort, security and ease so highly that you are unable to learn risk, adventure and discomfort for the sake of God's Kingdom? If you want to make growth a priority, that has to involve unlearning as well as learning.

ii. Prioritise the long haul, not the quick fix

A few paragraphs back, we compared the growth of a baby into an adult with the growth of a mustard seed into a tree. And in both, it was the right conditions over time that led to growth. Yes, we can set some conditions (and we'll explore a few of these in the rest of this chapter), but we also need to prioritise the other part: time.

If you think about some of the things that matter most to you, they took time. Your closest relationships did not spring up yesterday into what they are today. The same is true of the things you're most skilled in, the career you've cultivated and the passions you pursue.

We cannot fast-forward discipleship because we cannot fast-forward time. A small (or large) change to how you approach God or your life with him today will likely not make a big difference tomorrow. So if tomorrow is all you care about, I can't help. But if you care about the disciple you will be in a year, 3 years, 10 years from now, the disciple you will be and the disciples you have made when you are on your deathbed, there is good news: decisions you make now can have *huge* impact over time!

If you read one chapter of the Bible a day, you'll finish it in just over three years. Imagine the work the Spirit can do in your life through that! If you set aside 15 minutes to pray each day of your adult life, you'll have spent over 200 days in prayer.[74] Imagine the spiritual growth, answered prayer and impact of that! If you commit to deep relationships over a long time, the stage is set for sharing Jesus with others. So commit to the long haul. Growth rarely happens any other way.

2. 'I will not run from failure'

The second major decision I want to encourage as we seek to grow up in maturity and experience as a disciple of Jesus is to embrace failure, not run from it. I do not have data to prove it, but I suspect fear of failure is one of the biggest reasons we don't take steps that could enable us to grow as disciples.

I did a lot of acting when I was a teenager. Most of it was at school in various plays and as part of my Drama GCSE and A-Level. I knew the people in my class so well and we'd acted together so much that we could have a go and get things wrong without much fear. I remember trying for parts in plays that were totally wrong for me and everyone knew it, but it didn't matter. We were close, so I didn't worry they'd judge me. Then I went to university and wanted to get involved in student theatre groups and plays. I never did. Why? Auditions. The idea of getting up in front of people I didn't know and being judged terrified me. So I robbed myself of the chance to pursue something I loved, because of fear of failure.

There's something in that about the importance of church being closer to the experience I had in school, among friends and able to have a go, than at university, judged on whether we're good enough. Churches should be safe places to "spur one another on toward love and good deeds" (Hebrews 10:25). But more than that, there is something here about getting more scared of failure as we get older. The surrounding I was in had an impact, yes, but as I look back I can also see I was just more afraid of looking silly as a young adult than I was as a teenager.

There's a progression here, isn't there? Babies fail at almost everything they first try: eating, sitting, crawling, walking, even sleeping well. What an inspiration babies are—bad at almost everything, but trying anyway! Children have learned a few things and now get through the day without dribbling and soiling themselves, but in school are expected *not* to know things so they can be taught them. And as they learn one thing, they move on to other things they don't know and cannot yet do. So failure and inability are the bedrocks on which growth and learning happen. In our teenage years, that is still going on, but we also start to find our 'thing', whether that be sport, artistic pursuit, friendships, a particular skill or trade, or academic pursuits. Now we have areas of life where we *are* competent and it feels good. So we start to discard things that don't feel that way (I ditched sport, music and languages as soon as I could!) and focus on what we can do. As adults, we do that even more. We choose a career we're competent in, friends we get on with and leisure pursuits we're good at and enjoy.

So over the time the progression is clear: fail less, succeed more.

Sounds like progress, but is it? On one level, of course it is. But I suspect one of the reasons Jesus says we must "receive the kingdom of God like a little child" (Luke 18:17) is exactly this. We must embrace our non-expert nature to keep growing. Once we reject the possibility of failure, we deny ourselves the chance to mature in new ways.

I'll mention three particular kinds of failure we might fear which I encourage you not to run from if you wish to continue to grow up with Jesus: moral failure, lack of ability, and burned bridges.

First, *moral failure*. Obviously I am not suggesting we pursue sin! But pursue it or not, we will fall into it in large and small ways. Alongside asking how to reduce sin in our lives, we must ask what to do when we spot it. I believe both have the same answer: embrace it head on with God so we can repent and move on instead of getting stuck with it. We saw in the last chapter that when we experience God, repentance and transformation can come. We need that when it comes to sin and failure in our lives. Often those things mean we run from God when we need to run into his arms of love and grace. As Hirsch and Kelly say:

> Rather than feeling ashamed of losing our way from God, [repentance] is an invitation to turn in a different direction, to draw closer to God and renew our commitment to the mission of the ever-greater God we love, serve, and follow.[75]

Second, *lack of ability*. A disciple who is obedient to Jesus does things! And those things involve skills, ones we often feel we don't have. Prayer is a skill. Telling people about Jesus is a skill. Using finances for Jesus is a skill. There are hundreds of others. And whether through lack of understanding, practice or good role models, we often feel we haven't mastered these skills. But lack of mastery is not a reason not to have a go. Alex Harris and Chrissy Remsberg helpfully point this out:

> In primary school, teachers teach this important lesson to children by using the acronym for FAIL as First Attempt In Learning. The child's first attempt in learning may look like a failure but it is those failures that lead to success just as the failed seed dead in the ground leads to fruitfulness.[76]

Third, *burned bridges*. This one is about our relationships, and the fear of what will happen if we are 'too Christian' or offend people by talking about Jesus. Since this book is based on the Great Commission, this fear might have come up for you as you have thought about how you might introduce the people in your life to God. What if they reject you? What if it ruins the friendship? What if you do more harm than good? I'll give two things to consider. First, if the friendship is a real and genuine one, it is highly unlikely that talking about Jesus and what he means to you will burn those bridges. This is your friend who is interested in you, so the response is unlikely to be worse than a polite change of topic, but the positive possibilities are enormous!

But second, I'd encourage you to take an eternal perspective for a moment. I was speaking about this fear of burning bridges with someone recently, and he said something that cut me to the core: "From an eternal point of view, there is no such thing as a long-lasting relationship with someone who doesn't know Jesus." What a challenge! If my fear of burning the bridge of a friendship stops me talking about Jesus, where is my fear for that person's eternal life or for the relationship we might never enjoy in heaven together?

One final word about fear of failure before we move on. If anybody should be good at failing well, it should be Christians! We follow the crucified Jesus, who won a great victory through what looked like utter defeat and humiliation. But more than that, the basis of faith in Jesus is not being 'good enough', but receiving forgiveness and grace even though we aren't. And we are given the Spirit of God to dwell in us to bring us to maturity in Jesus because we can never get there by ourselves! So this isn't just a human encouragement to 'be ok with looking silly'. This is a call to embrace the very heart of faith in Jesus, knowing our failures are not final because his victory is enough. Embracing that can change everything!

HEART: Experienced Posture

We move now from these two related decisions to a posture of our hearts that will enable us to keep making them again and again. For me, the decision to approach discipleship with this posture has become one of the most important hallmarks of being a follower of Jesus. And it is a posture of 'reflection'.

3. A posture of reflection

'If at first you don't succeed, try, try again.' Right? Sure, it's a good motto. But there are two clarifications to make before embracing it whole-heartedly, one fairly obvious and one that's very Christian. The obvious one is that we don't just 'try, try again' by doing things the same we did the first time. We get back in the saddle, but we also ask what made us fall off the horse in the first place. Albert Einstein famously described insanity as 'doing the same thing over and over and expecting different results'.[77] So as we try, fail, try, fail, try, fail, we also reflect on things along the way.

The other, more explicitly Christian, clarification is that we must not fall into the mindset of *our* effort, *our* self-reflection and our self-improvement being the answer. We do not earn salvation and we do not independently achieve maturity. We can get in the way of it, resist it, or choose to partner with God toward it, but we mustn't start to think we make ourselves mature. That's the kind of fake tan I wrote about in the introduction of this book.

But if we wish to grow, we can choose to take stock, ask how we are doing and consider where Jesus wants us to grow. Let me suggest five ways a disciple who is maturing will be growing. There are many more, but here are five. You could use them as a checklist to take stock and ask whether there is movement in your life in any of these areas. And I'll also suggest ways you can invite the work of God into your lives to pursue growth in each.

i. Am I growing in learning?

We were clear in the section of this book about obedience that knowledge itself is not the goal. We need to work out that knowledge in obedience to God. But, as Alan Hirsch points out:

> Always remember that the word "disciple" in Greek…means learner or student, and so whatever else it means, it involves growing in wisdom and understanding. There can be no dodging or outsourcing our thinking if we are to mature as lifelong disciples of King Jesus.[78]

So are you learning? Do you feel you know or understand a particular part of the Bible, a theological idea or how God relates to a certain issue in the world better than you did a year ago? Could you better explain concepts like sin, grace or the Trinity if someone asked you? Have you stepped up your thinking in a certain area from 'intuitive' or 'inherited' to 'investigated' as we explored in Chapter 3?

Remember, part of the role of the Holy Spirit, according to Jesus, is to 'teach you all things' (John 14:26). As he dwells in us, he leads us into deeper knowledge and understanding. So as you reflect on this, perhaps there are steps he will lead you to. Maybe to devote more time to reading the Bible, or memorising parts of it. Maybe to go deep on a particular topic that is important to you. Maybe to attend a course, a training event or even some kind of formal study.

ii. Am I growing in love?

Jesus is clear: 'By this everyone will know that you are my disciples, if you love one another.' (John 13:35) Love is a mark of discipleship. We saw in the last chapter that Paul calls out the Corinthians as 'big babies'. He returns to that idea with these words later in the letter:

> When I was a child, I talked like a child, I thought like a child, I reasoned like a child. When I became a man, I put the ways of childhood behind me. (1 Corinthians 13:11)

These words are found at the end of his great description of what love is ('Love is patient, love is kind...') and a declaration that being gifted is no replacement for love. So in Paul's teaching, maturity is marked by love not just skill.

So, how's your love life? No, not like that. But is your life a life of love? Are there people you struggle to love and do you love them more than you did a year ago, or have you shut yourself off from them more since then? Since love is not just an emotion but an action, are you choosing to serve, honour, speak well of and forgive people more regularly or less regularly? Are you loving those closest to you well, or taking them for granted?

Remember, you can't muster up love for others. 'We love because he first loved us.' (1 John 4:19) So if you feel your love for others becoming stale, lukewarm or nonexistent, return to the fountain of God's love and ask him to fill you with his love for people.

iii. Am I growing in stability?

We all have wobbles. But over time, I see an expectation that maturing as Jesus-followers leads to more stability and fewer wobbles. There's another time Paul compares the immature with the mature, saying this:

> Then we will no longer be infants, tossed back and forth by the waves, and

blown here and there by every wind of teaching and by the cunning and craftiness of people in their deceitful scheming. Instead, speaking the truth in love, we will grow to become in every respect the mature body of him who is the head, that is, Christ. (Ephesians 4:14-15)

Here, maturity is spoken of in contrast to being unstable and blown around. Specifically, Paul speaks about being more stable in the face of false teaching and deceitfulness. A mature follower of Jesus is less susceptible to being hoodwinked, whether by the world, the Devil, or their own weakness. We expect toddlers to have tantrums and children to be more gullible than adults. So we should expect of ourselves that we will be more stable and less likely to be thrown by things the longer we follow Jesus.

So how wobbly do you feel? Are there things that have really thrown you in the past but which wouldn't affect you in the same way now? What storms have you weathered and what did your faith in God look like during them? How do you want it to look during the next storm? Is there something that, if it happened, you know your trust in God would be in tatters?

As you reflect on this, again resist the urge to focus on your own effort. It is not the strength of your legs, but the solidness of the ground beneath them, which means you can stand firm. In Ephesians 4, the maturity comes as the church builds on the foundations Jesus has laid and pursues him as their head. Focus less on how solid *your faith* in Jesus is and more on how solid your faith *in Jesus* is.

iv. Am I growing in holiness?

If you've received Jesus you are already holy! After all, 'if anyone is in Christ, the new creation has come: The old has gone, the new is here!' (2 Corinthians 5:17) When God looks at you, he sees the holiness of his Son given to you, no matter what you do and how you behave. It's both scandalous and incredibly good news! But it isn't a reason not to care about sin in our lives. When we stumble, God's grace covers us, leading Paul to ask (and answer) this question: 'What shall we say, then? Shall we go on sinning so that grace may increase?' 'By no means! We are those who have died to sin; how can we live in it any longer?' (Romans 6:1-2).

What about it then? How important is holiness to you? Do you treat the perfect holiness Jesus has given you cheaply or preciously?

Has it become a 'get out of jail free card' which means it doesn't matter if you fall or sin because you're covered anyway? Or does it spur you on to embrace and live out of the new and perfect identity God has blessed you with? Are there areas of sin that have increased, decreased or just stuck around in recent years? Can you point to ways in which you are holier than you were a year ago?

This is, once again, the Spirit's work in you: 'the Spirit who gives life has set you free from the law of sin and death.' (Romans 8:2) He loves to take the status God has stamped on your soul already and imprint it onto your mind, your heart, your actions, your life. He loves to turn the verdict into a lived-out reality. So ask him where he wants to do that next and open yourself up to his work.

v. Am I growing in boldness?

The final area of discipleship I want to draw out here is a vital one when it comes to the Great Commission (they all are, but this one often feels more directly so): boldness. At some point in making disciples by telling people about Jesus and leading them to him, we have to do something that carries a real risk and requires stepping out in boldness. Striking up the conversation, asking the question, telling the story, offering prayer. Whatever it is, we need the kind of boldness the early Christians prayed for before everyone was 'filled with the Holy Spirit and spoke the word of God boldly.' (Acts 4:31)

Are you naturally bold? Are you super-naturally bold? Can you think of times when you have, with heart thumping and knees trembling, taken the leap? Can you think of times when you bottled it? Are you more or less likely to talk to a colleague, neighbour, friend or family member about Jesus than you were when you first followed Jesus? Are there things others see as easy that would need a lot of boldness for you? Or the other way round?

There is a link in the Acts 4 verse above between being filled with the Spirit and speaking boldly. The boldness isn't ours, but the Spirit's given to us. These words from Paul to Timothy hint at the same idea:

> For this reason I remind you to fan into flame the gift of God, which is in you through the laying on of my hands. **For the Spirit God gave us does not make us timid**, but gives us power, love and self-discipline. (2 Timothy 1:6-8, emphasis added)

The Spirit who gave Timothy gifts did not give him timidity. He gave power (so he need not shrink back), love (so he wants others to know Jesus) and self-discipline (so he steps forward even if he'd prefer to step back). That is the Spirit's part in energising us with boldness.

But what is Timothy's part and your part? According to Paul, it's 'to fan into flame the gift of God'. This gift, in context, is about proclaiming the gospel without shame or hesitation. Yes, it is the Spirit who gives power instead of timidity, but we are to embrace, seek and pursue that, instead of ignoring it. As with all these areas for honest reflection as a disciple, we can resist the work of the Spirit, or 'fan it into flame'. If you want deeper boldness (or love, holiness, wisdom, etc.), ask God by his Spirit to make the fire roar!

HANDS: Experienced Actions

There are many other areas of maturity that an experienced disciple would want to grow in reflectively. Areas like wisdom, prayerfulness, fruitfulness, faithfulness, generosity, integrity, honesty, hopefulness, relationships and Godly character (to name ten). But rather than keep on listing and keeping on seeing how it is the work of God's Spirit in us that we must embrace to grow, I want to turn now to some of the 'how' of it all. If we are prioritising growth and being self-reflective, what can we do to actually grow? I will share two actions that might help us.

4. Set a rhythm of taking stock

The first action to encourage is taking stock in a deliberate way. This is about the long haul remember, so we need a plan to assess and reflect, to set goals and find ways forward. Just as cars need regular services and jobs have regular appraisals, so our discipleship needs regular attention if we are to grow in the ways we've seen God wants us to. There is not one way to do this, but I will suggest three layers that can be helpful: daily, weekly and annually.

i. Daily – checking in

Perhaps every day, as you spend a bit of time with God, you could add a process of reflection into the mix. Prayer and meditation on God's work as a daily habit is excellent, but so is meditation on the last 24 hours of your life as disciple. It is these 24-hour chunks that add up to the whole of your life with God, so why not take hold of each of them and reflect on them briefly.

There are a few things you could do to make this a habit (and if they are going to be sustainable, they mustn't take long!). Here are a few ideas:

- Think back over the last day (or look at a calendar if you can't remember what you did!) and note any highs or lows from it.
- Journal, reflecting on where you saw Jesus at work in your life, or anything that stands out as a moment that impacted your discipleship.
- Pray through everything you know you're going to do in the next 24 hours and commit to each of them intentionally as a disciple.
- Use a few general questions to reflect on the day (e.g. 'Where was Jesus in my day yesterday?', 'How did the truth of God impact how I lived?' or 'Was I a good witness for Jesus?').
- Ask much more specific questions geared to particular goals for growth you have at the moment (e.g. 'Did I pray for the people I've committed to pray for and look for opportunities to share Jesus with them?', 'Did I complete the Bible reading I set out to?' or 'How did I respond to temptation?').
- Set yourself a goal for the next 24 hours and write it down so you can reflect back tomorrow and see how you got on.

The aim is to increase daily awareness and intentionality as a follower of Jesus. Alongside organising your diary and planning meals, spend time looking back on your last 24 hours as a disciple and planning the next 24. Most days will not have big highs or lows, but over time a consistent approach to this can make a huge difference.

ii. Weekly – pursuing growth

For a weekly rhythm, I will borrow from what a number of movements around the world use as a pattern when Christians get together. Movements like 'BigLife'[79] adopt a 'three thirds' approach to discipleship groups, designed with obedience and growth in mind, not just knowledge or understanding. Increasingly, there are churches embracing this as the pattern for weekly meetings, often in small groups not one big gathering. In all likelihood, though, your church uses other models, so this would be something you'd need to ask one or more others to join you in as a weekly habit. Let me explain the 'three thirds'.

1. Look Back. This is the chance to reflect together on your last week. Start with how you're getting on, sharing highs or lows from the last week, what is bad or good in life at the moment and pray for those things. Then ask how you got on with what you said you'd do last week. This is always loving, not to catch each other out, but the accountability it creates is vital.

2. Look Up. Spend time together turning to God by looking at the Bible together. This can be extremely simple, just reflecting on what strikes you in a passage, or use questions or other resources as a guide. But as you look at the Bible together, think about how what you're reading impacts your real lives.

3. Look Forward. This is about setting goals. In light of what you've looked at together, what do you need to do to obey what you've read? What about it will you share with someone else? And who will you pray for and seek an opportunity to talk to about Jesus? Note all those things down (to use when you 'look back' next week), and then pray for one another as you step into them.

These kinds of communities and relationships in your life, committed to in a weekly pattern, can be game changers for your growth as a disciple! It really makes growth a high priority and does so amongst others who can spur you on, pick you up when you fall and champion you in your progress with Jesus. These people around you can help 'fan into flame' the Spirit's work within you.

iii. Annually – stepping back

Less regularly, we need to really stand back and look at our lives to ask big questions. This might mean taking a few days of retreat, going away by yourself, or with spouse, family or co-disciple. Or it might mean blocking out proper time at home to do some serious reflection. The kinds of things you might think about during these annual times of taking stock could be:

- Your growth as a disciple in areas like those mentioned in the 'Posture of Reflection section of this chapter'. What areas do you want to focus on?

- The shape of your life, including work, hobbies and relationships. Are there changes you need to make as you pray with God about these?
- Your finances and whether the story they tell are the story of the disciple of Jesus you want to be.
- Whether there are particular questions you need to ask yourself on a regular basis, maybe adding into part of a daily check in.
- What church looks like and how the community of disciples around you is or is not working toward Kingdom growth. If not, how can you shape it in a positive way?

There are lots of shapes these daily, weekly and annual layers can take. The important thing is to make a plan. If we aren't planning how we will invest in and work towards growth as disciples, it likely just won't happen.

5. Post-mortems (and pre-mortems)

A few pages ago, I suggested that an important decision is not to run away from failure as you grow in experience as a disciple. This action is one that helps you do the opposite: really engage deeply with things that have gone wrong, or things that might go wrong.

We are all familiar with the concept of a *'post-mortem'*. When someone dies, it is sometimes necessary to understand what caused their death. So a medical examiner will investigate their body and conduct various tests to work out what went wrong, or what happened to cause them to die. It's not particularly nice, but it is very useful.

The good news is that in this section we aren't talking about anybody dying, but about the reality that things will go wrong in our desire to grow up and become experienced followers of Jesus. We will fall, fail, stumble and sin. No matter how much we try not to, we still will. But that doesn't mean we settle for falling again, failing in the same way, stumbling over the same things and settling comfortably into that sin. This is where a discipleship post-mortem comes in.

Instead of looking away, look at the moment of failure and examine it. Probe it and try to understand it. Ask questions about it and then ask questions about the answers to those questions. What was going on when you acted in an unloving way? Why did you repeat the sin you'd decided the day before you'd resist? Why did you back out of the conversation when your friend asked you a question about your faith? Why haven't you picked up your Bible for a few months? What led to the crisis of faith you had last year?

I want to be extremely clear: this is *not* about shame! We do not look at our sin or our mis-steps in order to feel shame. As Christians, that wouldn't make sense anyway. We need not fear our failures. When we see how we've fallen, a Christian response is to delight even more strongly in the grace, love and forgiveness of God. It is because we're already forgiven that we can look at the ways we fall short without the sting of shame or the fear of judgment. You are forgiven! And even if you never grow in a particular area, you remain forgiven!

But if we want to grow, this is a helpful exercise and one to invite God into by his Spirit rather than to do by yourself. I find the postmortem image helpful in another way: just the bare facts aren't enough. They need to be interpreted. So the medical examiner might declare a cause of death, but a detective would then seek to establish the bigger story and who (if anyone) might have been at fault. So let's say you had a clear opportunity to speak to someone about Jesus, but you changed the topic instead. Those are the facts, but what is the story? Maybe…

- You had somewhere else you needed to be.
- You imagined where the conversation would go and felt you didn't have good answers to questions that might come up.
- You didn't care enough about the other person to really want to talk about it.
- You had actually lost confidence in the good news of Jesus yourself so didn't feel you'd be the right person to speak to anyway.
- You hadn't had a lot of sleep the previous night and were too tired for what you knew would be an intense conversation.
- You were worried about the consequences (perhaps you were at work and weren't sure what you were allowed to say in that context).[80]

The important thing is not just to understand *what* went wrong, but *why* it went wrong. Because only then can you think about what could help next time. Real life and discipleship is not general but specific. So the question isn't, 'What helps people talk about Jesus?' but rather, 'What would help *you* talk about Jesus with greater confidence next time?' There's no point reading endless books if what you really needed is better sleep. And there's no point brushing up on your rights as a Christian in the workplace if actually you just don't love the other person (or love Jesus) enough to care in the first place. It might be the reason was genuinely unavoidable, so there isn't really any area to grow—knowing that is pretty useful (and reassuring) too! But once you've investigated, you can make a plan to grow.

Don't do this for everything, but if you want to grow in a particular area, this kind of tool can be valuable. And it tends to get even more useful if you ask someone to help you think, pray and work it through. They can ask the kinds of questions you wouldn't think of, remind you of the grace of God when you don't feel it and lovingly walk with you as you grow in experience and maturity as a disciple of Jesus. You could offer to return the favour, too.

Before we leave this idea behind, I want to suggest a variation of it. Instead of a 'post-mortem', you could conduct a 'pre-mortem'. This is an exercise used in the business world quite often, but can also be helpful as a disciple. It requires more imagination and is about avoiding failing before you actually do. For a 'pre-mortem', you imagine a future where something has gone wrong and ask what the most likely reasons would be to end up there. It is a way of leaning into the fact that, often, we actually know what it is that would help us grow in a certain area, but never do it. Imagining the reality of a future where that thing was never done can help kickstart decisions in the present so that future never comes.

So whether pre- or post-mortem, these exercises can really help us get beneath the symptoms of our mis-steps as disciples, and dig into the root causes. What we find might be surprising, painful, encouraging, weird or very mundane. It might or might not be particularly nice, but it is very useful.

This brings us to the end of the final 'toolkit' of the book. In the next few pages, we will reflect on what growth of experience with the Great Commission itself might look like, but I want to invite you first to pause. Maybe flick back through what you've just read in this chapter. How will you intentionally pursue growth with God? How will you not sit and settle where you are, but seek him for more? What decisions, re-posturing or actions are needed?

> *Therefore, since we are surrounded by such a great cloud of witnesses, let us throw off everything that hinders and the sin that so easily entangles. And let us run with perseverance the race marked out for us, fixing our eyes on Jesus, the pioneer and perfecter of faith. (Hebrews 12:1-2)*

Inspired by those who've gone before us and with eyes always on Jesus, our call is to throw off sin and all that holds us back and to run onwards with perseverance. These are the acts of intentional, disciplined, focused disciples. It isn't something we do in our own strength (he marked out the race for us and he perfects the faith he pioneered in us), but it also isn't something we do passively. So what are the things you know need to shift or change in order for you to grow up in Jesus? Whatever they are, do them.

Chapter 9 at a glance…

In this toolkit chapter, the five tools we explored together were:

1. [HEAD:] Committing to growth as a key priority, including un-learning when we need to and being focused on long-term development not just quick fixes.

2. [HEAD:] Deciding not to run from failures, but letting them shape and form us, with a particular focus on moral failure, lack of ability and worry about burning bridges with people as we share Jesus with them.

3. [HEART:] Building a posture of reflection, evaluating our growth in key areas, including learning, love, stability, holiness and boldness.

4. [HANDS:] Setting a rhythm of taking stock of how we are growing, with ideas of daily check-ins, weekly goals and annually taking a step back.

5. [HANDS:] Conducting post-mortems on times we feel we've failed, and pre-mortems so we can take action before failures come along.

Becoming a Disciple-Maker

As we have done three times already, we return now to apply all we've explored to the Great Commission. There are many areas of life with Jesus where we can grow up in experience: prayer, the gifts God gives, Godly character and so on. But if the purpose of the church (and of each of us as disciples) is found in the Great Commission, we should ask whether or not we are growing in experience of living it out. So, let's read it one more time:

> Then the eleven disciples went to Galilee, to the mountain where Jesus had told them to go. **When they saw him, they worshiped him; but some doubted. Then Jesus came to them** and said, "All authority in heaven and on earth has been given to me. Therefore go and make disciples of all nations, baptising them in the name of the Father and of the Son and of the Holy Spirit, and teaching them to obey everything I have commanded you. And surely I am with you always, to the very end of the age." (Matthew 28:16-20, emphasis added)

The words I've put in bold describe an experience the first disciples had of Jesus. These experiences of Jesus after his resurrection must always have been filled with wonder and amazement. They'd seen him crucified! I doubt that ever got old. But this was also a very honest and human experience, where their doubts were not put to one side but very much in the mix of things. It's in this state of wonder and wondering that 'Jesus came to them'. And he came in order to fill them with all that this book has been about: a confidence in his authority, an obedience to his commands (including this one), and a dependence on him for it all. That was their experience of Jesus.

What I couldn't put in bold is the other aspect of experience we've explored: experience in the world. To do that, I'd need to include the whole of the book of Acts! Because this Great Commission did not stay up on the mountain as theory. It came down and went out and then kept going further and further out. Along the way there were amazing moments of success and awe (like the Day of Pentecost), as well as trials, struggles and confusion (prison and persecution, disagreement and death). These disciples and those that came after would return many times to Jesus with more wonder and more wondering, only to be sent back out again.

And this is how I see that the Great Commission is meant to work in your life and mine. Because we have met Jesus, we are filled with confidence, commit in obedience, lean on him in dependence and 'go'. And as we go, all sorts of things will happen. Highs, lows, success, failure, clarity, confusion, hope, despair, excitement, apathy. And each of those will inform how we go about this amazing task Jesus has given us to do, so we return to him to help us make sense of it all, only to go again.

And as we become more and more experienced in the life of Great Commission discipleship, we will grow. Not just willing. Not just useful. Not just effective. We might actually become disciple-makers, just as we were called to be. And, as we commit to the process, to the long haul, to the command to go, we might even get better and better at it.

So what about you? What are your experiences of following this command to go, to make disciples, to baptise and to train in obedience to Jesus? Take a moment to look back. Have you led someone to faith in Jesus? Have you helped someone to re-shape their life in obedience to him? Have you baptised someone? Have you gone deliberately somewhere in order to be Jesus' light and voice in that place? And how has it gone? On a scale from glorious success to total car crash, where do your disciple-making efforts sit?

I ask this simply to get you to reflect honestly on your past and current life as a Great Commission disciple, on your experience in this area. That is your starting point. And whether it drives you to worshipful wonder or doubtful wondering, it is where you are. The question is whether you will take a step forward from where you are, or whether you will stay where you are (or even go backwards).

In truth, as I reflected on in Chapter 1, it is often newer followers of Jesus who display energy and drive to make Jesus known and follow the Great Commission. Over time, many of us become settled, comfortable or cynical. Or we end up with a life that so revolves around Christians and the church that we don't meaningfully know non-Christians to 'go' to. Or we get busy. Or we start to believe that, since we haven't led anyone to Jesus so far in our lives it's unlikely we ever well. Or we come to the conclusion that disciple-making is for other people, not us.

But none of those takes seriously the commission Jesus gives or our responsibility to live it out. If we wish to grow in experience from where we are, we must get rid of those kinds of thinking, and step forward in following Jesus' call. But I can think of two big things that might stop us: we don't know how, or we still don't want to.

If you don't know *how* to follow the Great Commission in your life, this book won't have helped much! Remember the question we started with: what kind of person do you need to be to do the things God wants you to? This hasn't been a 'how to' guide, but more of a 'who to become' guide. It's about what *kinds* of disciples Jesus forms through the Great Commission, not how to do it today. But if you find yourself in that place, don't stay there. If we want to grow in skill and experience in something, we look for those who know what they're doing and learn from them. Find someone who feels like a 'Great Commission disciple' and watch them, learn from them, ask questions. Read other books that do give you the answer to your questions.[81] Find training courses, or a mentor, or do the things your church leaders encourage you to do but you've never really put into practice before.

But if you don't *want* to grow in experience as a Great Commission disciple, no amount of technique or training will help. I suspect that if you've made it this far in this book, you want to at least a little bit. But maybe you feel you would like to want it a little more.

I can't change your heart on this one, but Jesus can.

It was the experience, the encounter with Jesus that set this whole thing off in motion. The hallmarks of discipleship we've looked at have not been confidence, obedience, dependence and experience. They have been confidence *in Jesus*, obedience *to Jesus*, dependence *on Jesus* and experience *with Jesus*. Unless it all flows from him and returns to him again and again, we're just going through some motions and hoping they'll get us somewhere. But always knowing they won't. So if you want to step forward and become experienced not just as a disciple but as a disciple-*maker*, do whatever you need to do to let Jesus come to you, bowl you over and commission you afresh.

God isn't make-believe. You didn't invent him. You didn't decide what he should or shouldn't ask of you. And as a result, it is us who get transformed by him, not the other way round. We can keep him at arms-length, or put everything on the table and let him come and do whatever he wants. Andrew Wilson puts it far better than I could:

> A made-up God will leave your world undisturbed, conveniently aligning with your priorities without displacing anything, because ultimately you are more glorious than it is. The real God, however, will land in the middle of your life like an elephant crashing through the ceiling, displacing your sin, changing all your priorities, and forcing you to reorient yourself around the weight of glory.[82]

So whatever your experience has been with Jesus and his Great Commission so far, he has the power to crash in, get rid of what needs to go, change what matters to you most and reorder everything. He did it on a mountain 2,000 years ago in eleven lives. He has done it in my life and your life before. He can do it again. And if you want to grow from disciple to disciple-maker, to become more experienced in living out the Great Commission, that might just be exactly what you need.

Will you climb the mountain?

Confidence. Obedience. Dependence. Experience.

Four parts of a healthy discipleship DNA that Jesus wanted to form as he climbed a mountain to give those eleven worshiping, doubting disciples a life-altering task. And four qualities he still wants to form in his followers today, qualities that shape our pursuit of the Great Commission, but also so much more.

He wants us to be *confident*, not just so we will be willing to entertain the Great Commission in our lives, but so we might stand firm on the glacier of his love.

He wants us to be *obedient*, not just so we are useful in carrying out the Great Commission, but so we can live in ways that bring life, light, joy and spiritual health.

He wants us to be *dependent*, not just so we are effective as we go about the Great Commission, but so we can harness his power in every part of who we are and how we live.

He wants us to be *experienced*, not just so we make disciples instead of merely knowing we should, but so we become more and more like him.

So as we come to conclude our exploration of these four big ideas, I want to go on one last journey up and down this mountain and it's a journey that will involve a little imagination on all our parts.

Approaching the mountain

We need some imagination because there are two bits of this story we never hear. We know the eleven disciples went 'to the mountain where Jesus had told them to go.' But we don't know how he told them to go there. Did he tell them in person or through a messenger or vision? Is this what was meant by the message Jesus gave through the women who first saw him resurrected: 'go to Galilee; there they will see me.' (Matthew 28:10) Or was it at another point? Did others know, or was it a secret just for them? Which mountain even was it?

The other thing we don't know is what happened as they came down from the mountain. Did Jesus stay up there, or walk down with them? Did they continue in worship, or get silenced by the huge task they'd been given? Did they still have doubts, or had the encounter with Jesus washed them all away? Did they start to plan how they'd do what Jesus asked, or just sit with it for a while? Who spoke first? (Probably Peter. It was normally Peter...)

I want to use the final pages of this book to invite you to respond. As we imagine how these two 'gaps' in the story could have played out, I will invite you to go on your own journey, first approaching the mountain of the Great Commission and then coming down from it into your actual life.

So we begin by approaching the mountain. It's a good image because the Great Commission is a mountain of a task. It is huge in its scope, covering every nation and requiring obedience to everything Jesus commanded. It asks so much of us that we can feel tiny, staring up at the Everest of what Jesus tells us to do, feeling we'll never be able to scale it. I draw courage and comfort from the equally huge scope of Jesus' declarations that 'all authority' rests with him and that he will be with us 'always, to the very end of the age'. Yes, the task is huge, but so is he!

But, especially because the task feels so mountainous, I am nervous as I invite you to respond and step into the life of a Great Commission disciple more fully. I am always nervous inviting response to the truth of God's word because I don't want you to respond to me, or to this book, or to anything other than Jesus himself. My deep desire is that in reading what I've written you would be led to respond to Jesus and that *he* would bring you into the life he wants and specifically the life of the Great Commission he gives.

Because nothing other than Jesus will bring the level of transformation needed to approach and scale this kind of a mountain. Jackie

Hill Perry powerfully declares what we all know to be true: No matter how passionate the preacher is, how good the gospel is, or how true the Bible is, none of them will bring about change. We are too resistant for that. Only God himself will bring us to life. This is how she puts it:

> The preacher may say, "Live!" And we will not budge. The casket is our home and we are too dead to leave it anyhow. The gospel may beckon us to "Feel" but we can't. The affections are so entrenched in sin, so in love with hell, that they refuse to give their love to God... The Scriptures may cry, "Think!" but until God says, "Let there be light," there will not be (2 Cor. 4:6). A dead person's mind can't concern itself with the thoughts of the living, and if it tried—as we do before we are raised—it is unable to accept such things.[83]

This is why each section of a book about what kind of disciples *we are* has tried to call attention to the truth of who *God is*. As we sought the confidence not to tiptoe but to dance, it was the glacier *of God* we could do that on. As we sought to play Twister with obedience, it was the voice *of God* whose instructions we listened out for. As we sought dependence on a fire to warm and protect us, it was fuel *from God* that we made it from. And as we sought to grow in experience from the babies we were to the mature disciples we can be, it is *God our Father* who gave birth to that new life and leads us to grow.

So I am asking you to consider how you will respond, but want to be clear that it is your response *to God*, to the Great Commission *that Jesus gave*, that matters. This is between you and him, so be attentive to him as you read what follows.

But which mountain?

The importance of responding to God instead of me or anyone else is why I am so captured by the fact we don't know anything about this mountain except that it was 'the mountain where Jesus had told them to go.' I can imagine there being lots of different responses a reader of this book could make, and they'd all be good. But the mountain you should climb is very simply the one that Jesus asks you to.

So I have a few suggestions as to where you might start to respond when you close this book in a few minutes, but they are only suggestions. There are seven of them and they are different from one another so you can't start with all of them! I include them not so you can do them all, but to get your own imagination going and prompt you to ask God which of these routes (or which other route) up the mountain of what I've been calling 'Great Commission discipleship' you should set out on.

1. Start where Jesus wants

At the risk of repeating myself, I will repeat myself: starting where Jesus is asking you to is what matters most. So if something in particular has really stood out as you've read this book, take note of that. It could be that by his Spirit Jesus has been highlighting an area to focus on or take action in. Paul, who had so many places he could go and things he could do said this: 'I press on to take hold of that for which Christ Jesus took hold of me.' (Philippians 3:12) He only wanted to take hold of, to do, the things that Jesus had taken hold of him for.

So while my other six suggestions are things that might be right, this first one is one that definitely is. So pray, asking God to nudge, prod or shove you to take the steps up the mountain of Great Commission discipleship that he wants you to. It might be something I say below that he highlights and directs you to, or it may be something completely different. Why not pray now? I can wait.

2. Start where it is least comfortable

One thing you could do is focus on the aspect of discipleship you know you find hardest right now. Perhaps you lack confidence in God, because of experiences you've had, parts of the Bible you struggle with, or something else entirely. Maybe it is obedience that is hardest, because there are things you know God wants you to change but you aren't ready to. It could be that you're a driven, self-reliant, independent person who knows that stops you from leaning in dependence on God. Or you could have settled into a comfortable routine and don't want to grow up into deeper maturity because it could upset what you have now.

In truth you know that until you have dealt with the thing which will be hardest to start with, none of the rest really matters. If so, biting the bullet and staring the difficulty in the face until you resolve it could serve you well.

3. Start with experience

While you could start anywhere in the spiritual genetic CODE we've explored, there are two ways I suspect will often be helpful and the first is to start with the experience element of it. This is helpful because it starts honestly with where we are (our experiences of life in the world) and seeks to submit all of it to God as we ask him to encounter us there. So we can start where we are and find a pathway with God from there into a new and better place. The cycle of reflection and growth we explored in those chapters can lift us out of being stuck and move us forward into greater maturity.

So perhaps you need to capture where you are right now, what the nature of your experience with God has been and what things you're encountering in the world. And then ask God to help you make sense of it and give you fresh experiences of himself to lead you in repentance, transformation and being sent out once again into the world.

4. Start with obedience

The other place in CODE I would recommend to begin is a new commitment in the area of obedience. Why? Because that includes things you can actually decide to *do*. It can become tangible very quickly. Of course obedience is rooted in confidence that God's ways are best and fuelled by dependence on him to live in them, but you are the one who is obedient or not. So if there is a command or principle in Scripture you know you aren't obedient to, change that. Just obey.

Obey, and see what you learn as you go, about yourself, about God and about the world. How does it change your experiences with others when you stop getting drunk or swearing, or start honouring your parents or giving financially to God's work? Let those experiences kick off a cycle of reflection that leads you back to God and forward on a process of growth.

5. Start by picking up a tool

Almost half of this book has been given to tools that can help us bed in the four big ideas we've explored. They've focused on our heads (decisions to make), hearts (postures to adopt) and hands (actions to take). In total, there have been twenty of them, and each one represents a way you could start your journey up the mountain of Great Commission discipleship. Perhaps as you were reading one of those sections there was something you thought would be good to focus on, consider further, or do. But then you moved on because there was more book to read. Well, soon there will be no more book, so you could get back to it.

To help, there is an Appendix at the back of this book with a table summarising each of the 20 'tools' so you can see them at a glance and prayerfully consider which could be good to pull out and use.

6. Start with the Great Commission itself

This book has not strictly been *about* the Great Commission. We have come back to it many times and it's been the foundation of it all, but it's been a launchpad to leap from not the whole of our journey. We've taken qualities of a disciple which Jesus forms through it and considered how they can come alive across our whole lives. But that should not mean we leave the Great Commission itself behind.

Maybe you really need to step up your personal engagement with Jesus' command to be his witness and to make disciples, with all that entails. If so, the brief reflections on the Great Commission at end of each section could be worth revisiting.

7. Just start somewhere!

At the risk of sounding rather unspiritual, just do something. There have been lots of ideas, theory and theological concepts in this book, but I have tried to write it in a practical way as well. I'm sure I haven't got the balance right on that, but my belief is that theory and practice should go hand in hand. And I think that is God's heart too, which is why obedience is such a prominent theme in the Bible. What I've written isn't the Bible (obviously!), but if it contains any truth at all, then it's right to respond to that truth by doing something with it.

So I started these seven recommendations by encouraging you to climb the mountain Jesus leads you to. And I end them by saying that even if you aren't sure what that is, do something anyway.

Coming down the mountain

Moving on now from the ascent, we now consider what it means to descend the mountain where we hear Jesus give us the Great Commission. Although Matthew finishes his book with the disciples still up there, we know they came down. But what kinds of people were they when they did? What did the experience of Jesus giving the Great Commission do to them, and what can it do to us?

As I've already said, we don't know because Matthew doesn't tell us what happens next. But I have hopes for what it might look like. My hope is that reading this book has given a glimmer of what the disciples encountered up that mountain and that as you finish it, something will be different. Different *in you* and also different *around you* as things flow from you.

That hope is birthed from another story in the Bible, at another mountain. It's found just after Moses has returned from Mt. Sinai where God has spoken to him on behalf of the people. But Moses of course finds that the people have already turned from God to worship a golden calf they've made. He is caught up between this amazing experience of God on the mountain and the reality of life below. You can hear the desperation as he turns to God in this snippet of the story:

> *Moses said to the Lord, "You have been telling me, 'Lead these people,' but you have not let me know whom you will send with me. You have said, 'I know you by name and you have found favour with me.' If you are pleased with me, teach me your ways so I may know you and continue to find favour with you. Remember that this nation is your people."*
>
> *The Lord replied, "My Presence will go with you, and I will give you rest."*
>
> *Then Moses said to him, "If your Presence does not go with us, do not send us up from here. How will anyone know that you are pleased with me and with your people unless you go with us? What else will distinguish me and your people from all the other people on the face of the earth?"*
>
> *And the Lord said to Moses, "I will do the very thing you have asked, because I am pleased with you and I know you by name." (Exodus 33:12-17)*

It's another CODE passage, isn't it? All the elements are there. Utter confidence in God, that what he says is true ('You have said') and that the only thing that sets him apart is God ('I know you by name and you have found favour with me'). A desire to live in obedience as they move on from this place ('teach me your ways'). The desperate need to depend on God's presence and empowering, or it's all for nothing ('If your Presence does not go with us, do not send us up from here.') And the grappling of Moses between what God has said and what he is currently experiencing ('You have been telling me … but you have not let me know'), which ultimately leads to a fresh experience God gives Moses that shapes his outlook going forward. Because in the verses that follow God gives Moses exactly what he asks for and more: Moses gets to physically see the glory of God in a way nobody else ever has!

This is a man who met God and was changed by him. He displays all the hallmarks Jesus would later inspire his eleven friends with on another mountain. May we catch that too, because we have met with God!

But then we see this intensify and ramp up even further. In the part of the story we just read, Moses is actually between two mountaintop experiences. In anger at the golden calf, he has smashed the tablets containing the law, so needs to receive them afresh. Up the mountain once more, into God's presence once more and then down the mountain once more. And this time, the impact of his experience with God is so strong that he is physically different: 'his face was radiant because he had spoken with the Lord.' (Exodus 34:29) In fact he had to veil his face when he was around other people.

So my hope that you will not just be informed but transformed as you 'come down the mountain' now is based on this simple fact: that is what meeting God does. It is what meeting with God has always done. For Moses. For the eleven disciples. For us. The Great Commission is given by God and our exploration of it has drawn us into the heart and mind of God, so I feel confident in hoping we will leave transformed by the experience.

But the best news is that, unlike Moses, we do not have to hide it and veil our faces. In an age when the holy and radiant presence of God was too much for sinful people to handle, the face of one who'd been with God was too much.

Not so for us who stand on the other side of the cross, the empty tomb and the outpouring of the Spirit. We can approach the throne of God, bask in his glorious presence, ascend the mountain to hear his voice, and then we can descend into our world, our lives and our realities with faces unveiled. We can radiate the glory and presence of Jesus, transformed from the inside out and infused with the spiritual genetic CODE of the Great Commission. Paul, after reflecting on the veil that Moses once wore, said this:

> *But whenever anyone turns to the Lord, the veil is taken away. Now the Lord is the Spirit, and where the Spirit of the Lord is, there is freedom. And we all, who with unveiled faces contemplate the Lord's glory, are being transformed into his image with ever-increasing glory, which comes from the Lord, who is the Spirit. (2 Corinthians 3:16-18)*

So place your confidence firmly in Jesus, who takes away sin and shame so that the 'veil is taken away'. Lean strongly into the Spirit, discovering not only that 'there is freedom', but that true freedom is found in obedience to the one who made you, knows you and loves you. Live a life of dependence, where you do not rely on yourself but instead 'contemplate the Lord's glory,' knowing that in him you have all you need. And as you do, enjoy the process—step-by-step and bit-by-bit—of becoming more and more experienced with him, 'being transformed into his image with ever-increasing glory'.

Visit my Website
www.davecriddle.com

For more content, head to my website and sign up to my newsletter. You'll get more resources to accelerate your discipleship growth, including a Personal Learning Journal to make the most of this book, and my free discipleship training video series.

THE 1234 OF HEALTHY DISCIPLESHIP

A free four-part video series, unlocking four vital aspects of following Jesus:

1 Lord: why treating Jesus as King changes everything

2 Priorities: discover the true purpose of life with Jesus

3 Ways to Build: overcome imbalance and embrace the whole of discipleship

4 Threads of Discipleship DNA: The CODE of a healthy spiritual life

Available only from my website.

Acknowledgments

I've wanted to write a book for a long time, but always said I wouldn't until I actually had one worth writing. It's my sincere hope that having come to the end of this one you feel it was. But while I always wanted to write a book, I've never been sure I'd know how. I'm still not sure I know how to write a book, but I do know how this one came to be and it wasn't all by myself! So I want to take a few pages to say thank you to those who have helped.

I want to start by thanking people who have taught me what it means to follow Jesus. It is as a disciple that I've written this book about discipleship and the progress I have made in that it is because of those who have guided along the way. So I thank those who have led me as my church leaders, especially Keith Wilson, Will Pearson-Gee, Malcolm Duncan and Stephen Walker-Williams. Your finger-prints are on this book because of how you've shaped my walk with Jesus. There are lots of others who have shaped me as a disciple, but special thanks go to Sam Cox, Sally Pettipher, Jim Graham (who I miss very much), Alex Harris and the whole Bitternes Afloat family.

But discipleship happens in community and I have been blessed to be part of some wonderful churches. I can pinpoint in my own disci-pleship the impact each of those churches has had and I am so grate-ful. So thank you to all at Lower Earley Baptist Church, St Andrews in North Oxford, Buckingham Parish Church, Gold Hill Baptist Church and now Pathway Church, where I have the absolute honour of leading a group of disciples who have counted the cost and stepped out in brave ways.

Absolutely the top of the list of those who have discipled and sown into my life are my parents, Graham and Jo. Mum and Dad, thank you! Thank you for the constancy, love, care, encouragement and challenge (and knowing which I needed when). Thank you for the ways you raised Richard and me. But above all thank you for teaching me about Jesus and helping me as I took my own first steps as his disciples. My gratitude will be literally eternal.

This book began as a phrase I sensed God whispering to me in May 2019: "I want to recode my church." I was at a retreat for leaders, surrounded by many who I felt were far more impressive and deserving of being there than I was. It was there that God spoke and I think I was able to hear because of the environment cultivated by those leading it. So thank you to Emma Jeffries, Anthony Delaney and Rich Robinson for setting the stage and valuing me as a leader when I wasn't sure I deserved it. I have benefitted enormously from each of you and your ministries, at that retreat and many times since.

As I've said, I've been deeply helped by others as I've written, so to those who have read and given feedback and guidance along the way: thank you. I am also extremely grateful to those who been willing to lend their name to my work with an endorsement. So thank you Anne Calver, Andy Glover, Nic Harding, Jason King and Phil Moore. And a huge thank you to Alex Harris who has championed this project from the first time I told him about it, and was kind enough to write the foreword. You continue to teach me so much!

There are five people I particularly want to highlight, whose contributions during this process have been utterly invaluable. I'll list them in reverse order of when their contributions took place, starting with the most recent.

So first is Simon Holley, who you can find at therawleader.com. Simon has guided me through the process of getting this book out there. There's a strong chance you read this book because of something he did or got me to do. I hate self-promotion, but Simon has pushed and guided me and its been invaluable. As a result the book went from something I wrote to something people can actually read. Thanks Simon.

Second, Laura Best. Laura, you are an incredible friend. I will never forget you and the tribe who surrounded me when I most needed it and how much you champion Natalie and me (and now the wee man Jed). Laura helped with this book's design. I cringe now when I look back at my first attempts before you got your hands on them, so thank you for rescuing me. On top of that, Laura helped with all my social media, which I'm bad at and she isn't!

Third, the reason there are as few typos in this book as there are is simple: Kirsty Allen. Kirsty hasn't just caught typos, she's helped it all make more sense. I've ended up deep in the weeds with every page and paragraph, so a fresh set of eyes made all the difference. And what a set of eyes! An eye for detail, for consistency and for clarity. But above all that, an eye for Jesus! Your discipleship is inspiring and I love what you've brought to this book. There's an irony in the fact that even these words thanking Kirsty will be put under her lens and Kirsty rest assured I am typing extra slowly and carefully right now. I really mean it when I say thank you for picking up the pen.

Fourth, my dad: Graham Criddle. I've thanked you and mum for the impact you've had on my faith and that's the biggie. But you also read and re-read I don't know how many drafts, given detailed and considered comment, questioned things, celebrated things, told me what was good and what wasn't and always told me you thought what I was doing was a good thing. You are definitely the person who's had the most impact on the final text of this book and I honour and thank you for that. (You've also been good at changing the topic when I've been going on about the book too much when Natalie and I meet up with you and mum and I've needed that too!)

And finally, Stephen Walker-Williams. Your impact on my life has been huge, there at my darkest moment and at many of the most joyful. You have taught me so much by your words and example, and I cherish our partnership in ministry. But as well as all that, you let me write this book! You allowed me to take something we always thought would be a course for the church and make it a book with my name on. Not just allowed, but championed me in it simply because you believed me when I said God had told me to. You also helped by nudging me to give time to it, looking at early drafts, praying and writing an endorsement. Thank you for all of it.

So that's the tribe that has resulted in this book. And every single thank-you is heartfelt. But there is one more person who I want to give the biggest, loudest and most heartfelt thank-you: Natalie.

This book has been a sacrifice of time and energy. Most of that sacrifice has been carried by you. Thank you for your patience. Thank you for not begrudging the hours I shut myself away to pray, plan and write. Thank you for sending me to do it when I was feeling lazy. Thank you for putting up with my mind wandering because I'd had a thought about the book. Thank you for doing that even when it meant I wasn't with you and Jed on a family day off. Thank you for helping me shape the ideas, for challenging imposter syndrome when it kicked in and for believing that people should read it. That kept me writing it. Without others, this book would be worse. Without you, it wouldn't exist.

But more than all that, thank you for being the most dazzlingly wonderful wife, mum and follower of Jesus. You are the real deal! I learn so much about being a disciple through you and I doubt I'll ever know how much. It is the greatest joy and honour to partner with you in life, marriage, parenting and mission. Thank you.

Appendix:
Toolkit at a Glance

For easy reference, this table gives a summary of the 'tools' suggested in the toolkit chapters of this book:

SECTION	HEAD: decisions	HEART: postures	HANDS: actions
Confidence: Chapter 3	1. 'I will see idols for what they are' 2. 'I will trust God's word not my own'	3. A posture of submission 4. A posture of trust	5. Give authority back
Obedience: Chapter 5	1. 'I will let God call the shots' 2. 'I will not value knowledge over obedience'	3. A posture of response	4. Imitate someone worth imitating 5. Become accountable to someone
Dependence: Chapter 7	1. 'I will not rely on myself'	2. A posture of prayer and fasting 3. A posture of bravery	4. Evaluate your finances 5. Seek guidance for a decision
Experience: Chapter 9	1. 'I will make growth a priority' 2. 'I will not run from failure'	3. A posture of reflection	4. Set a rhythm of taking stock 5. Post-mortems (and pre-mortems)

Notes

Introduction: No more fake tan

1   Alan Hirsch, *The Forgotten Ways* (Grand Rapids: Brazos Press, 2016), 110.

2   Cris Rogers, *Making Disciples* (Uckfield: Essential Christian, 2018), 13.

CODE – The DNA of the Great Commission

3   https://licc.org.uk/resources/questions-jesus-asked-the-power-of-the-question/
#:~:text=Even%20as%20a%20boy%2C%20he,183%20questions%20he%20is%20asked. "Jesus is recorded as asking 307 questions in the Gospels. In contrast, he directly answers only three of the 183 questions he is asked." This is a statistic quoted quite often. I have not counted Jesus' questions and answers, but these ratios ring true of the Jesus I see in the Gospels.

4   Matthew 6:5-15; Luke 9:1-6; 10:1-12.

5   Mark 8:31-38 13:1-36.

6   John 16:1-33.

7   Mark 8:33; Luke 9:51-56.

8   Jesus used long, evolving stories like the Parables of the Sower, the Good Samaritan, and the Lost Sons (Luke 8:1-15; 10:25-37; 15:11-31). But he would also sum up big truths simple as in, "Ask and it will be given to you; seek and you will find; knock and the door will be opened to you," and, "do to others what you would have them do to you" (Matthew 7:7, 12).

9   I choose this cross-section not because they are all equally accurate as translations—some are not even translations, but paraphrases or expansions of the text. I choose them because, I hope, they will open up the text for us in ways that will be less familiar and provoke thoughts and questions we might otherwise miss. If I have not included your favourite version, go and look it up there as well!

1. Healthy Discipleship Confidence

10 Glen Scrivener, https://www.christthetruth.net/2014/10/06/thingamy-jiggery-pokery/

11 Glen Scrivener, https://www.christthetruth.net/2010/02/04/faith-is-not-a-thing-thawed-out-thursday (emphasis added).

12 Exodus 3:13-14; 7:14-18; Joshua 1:9; 1 Samuel 17:45-47; Proverbs 3:5-6.

13 Genesis 3:1-7; Exodus 32:1-6.

14 Mike Reeves, *The Good God* (Bletchley: Paternoster, 2019), 56-57.

15 John Stott, *The Cross of Christ: 20th Anniversary Edition* (Nottingham: Inter-Varsity Press, 2008), 261.

16 Andrew Wilson, *Unbreakable: What the Son of God Said About the Word of God* (Croydon: 10Publishing, 2014), 25.

17 I write from a Protestant perspective. In Jewish and in Catholic traditions, the Ten Commandments are broken up differently, and do in fact group these 'first two' as one commandment. But however they are divided, there are clearly two related but different aspects to these words about idolatry.

18 Tim Keller, *Counterfeit Gods* (London: Hodder & Stoughton, 2009), xvii.

19 https://www.warc.com/content/feed/global-advertising-to-top-1-trillion-in-2024-as-big-five-attract-most-spending/en-GB/8558

20 https://konmari.com

21 This idea was first articulated by Augustine, describing sin as 'homo incurvatus in se', which means 'the human being curved in on itself'.

22 Jackie Hill Perry, *Holier Than Thou* (Nashville: B&H Publishing, 2021), 5.

23 Glynn Harrison, *The Big Ego Trip* (Nottingham: Inter-Varsity Press, 2013), 59-60.

24 Ibid., 61.

25 Ibid., 147.

2. Confident Disciple's Toolkit

26 Andrew Wilson, *God of All Things* (Grand Rapids: Zondervan, 2021), 162.

27 https://www.youtube.com/watch?v=nYuWlxnqa4o

28 Wilson, *God of All Things*, 180 (emphasis added).

Great Commission Confidence

29 https://joshuaproject.net/people_groups/statistics, though they recognise (https://joshuaproject.net/resources/articles/how_-many_people_groups_are_ there) that these numbers can be counted in different ways. As a definition of 'People Group, Joshua Project uses this from the Lausanne Committee Chicago meeting: 'For evangelization purposes, a people group is the largest group within which the Gospel can spread as a church planting movement without encountering barriers of understanding or acceptance.'

30 https://joshuaproject.net/help/definitions#unreached

4. Healthy Discipleship Obedience

31 John Goldingay, *Genesis for Everyone, Part 1: chapters 1–16* (London: Society for Promoting Christian Knowledge, 2010), 37.

32 Genesis 4:1-16; 5:1-32; 6:5–8:22; 11:1-9.

33 Packer, 'Obedience', 680.

34 Hirsch, *The Forgotten Ways*, 132.

5. An Obedient Disciple's Toolkit

35 Perry, *Holier Than Thou*, 42.

36 John McGinley, *The Church of Tomorrow* (London: Society for Promoting Christian Knowledge, 2023), 19.

37 Ibid., 21.

38 I first heard this from Canon J. John, but it seems to be one of those phrases that many have used in various forms, and the original source (if there is just one) is unknown.

39 Michael Frost & Alan Hirsch, *ReJesus* (Cody: 100 Movements Publishing, 2022), 144.

40 Ibid., 148.

41 Available at www.youtube.com/goldhillbc, then search for 'Kids Church'.

42 Søren Kierkegaard, *The Journals of Søøren Kierkegaard*, Trans. Alexadrer Dru. (London: Oxford University Press, 1938), 324.

43 Richard Foster, *Celebration of Discipline* (London: Hodder & Stoughton Ltd., 2008), 188.

44 Neil Cole, *Church 3.0*, (San Francisco: Jossey-Bass, 2010), 133-134. Cole records these questions used by 'Life Transformation Groups' as part of the 'Church Multiplication Associates' movement:
1. Have you been a testimony this week to the greatness of Jesus Christ with both your words and actions?
2. Have you been exposed to sexually alluring material or allowed your mind to entertain inappropriate sexual thoughts about another this week
3. Have you lacked integrity in your financial dealings, or coveted something that does not belong to you?
4. Have you been honouring, understanding, and generous in your important relationships this past week?
5. Have you damaged another person by your words, either behind the person's back or face to face?
6. Have you given in to an addictive behaviour this week? Explain.
7. Have you continued to remain angry toward another?
8. Have you secretly wished for another's misfortune?
9. What is your personal accountability question?
10. Did you finish your Bible reading this week and hear from the Lord? What are you going to do about it?
11. Have you been completely honest with me?

45 Bobby Harrington & Alex Absalom, *Discipleship that Fits* (Grand Rapids: Zondervan, 2016), 174.

Great Commission Obedience

46 https://talkingjesus.org/2022-research/

6. Healthy Discipleship Dependence

47 Glen Scrivener, *Reading Between the Lines, Vol. 1: Old Testament Daily Readings* (Leyland: 10Publishing, 2018), 87.
48 Ibid., 88.
49 Foster, *Celebration of Discipline*, 8.
50 Cf. John 16:7, where Jesus indicates it is perhaps even better to have the Holy Spirit within than to have him there in person. He tells the disciples it is *'for your good'* that he goes, precisely because that way the Spirit can be sent to them.
51 Lisa Rodriguez-Watson, "The Mouth of a Shark," *Red Skies* (Cody: 100 Movements Publishing, 2022), 143-144.
52 Ibid., 144.

7. A Dependent Disciple's Toolkit

53 Pete Greig, *How to Pray* (London: Hodder & Stoughton, 2019), 3.
54 John Piper, *A Hunger for God* (Wheaton: Crossway, 2013), 57.

55   https://premierchristian.news/en/news/article/new-ceo-gavin-calver-promises-a-braver-and-kinder-evangelical-alliance

56   https://www.eauk.org/news-and-views/brave-and-kind

57   John McGinley, *The Church of Tomorrow*, 64.

58   These are based on a talk from Chris Goulard (Saddleback Church) at LAUNCH Conference 2020.

59   Neil Cole, *Church 3.0*, p241.

60   Ibid., p252.

61   https://alpha.org.uk/blog/2016/1/19/alpha-film-series, but note that a log-in is required to access the videos.

8. Healthy Discipleship Experience

62   Paul's argument here is not actually about his former self, though. He is using the principle to point out that some of the things they do now (including use of certain spiritual gifts), will one day seem childish when viewed from an eternal perspective. Love, on the other hand, is never something they will 'outgrow', so should be a greater focus for them now than things that will one day fade.

63   Borrowed from the second verse of 'How Great Thou Art' by Stuart K. Hine.

64   1 Kings 19:12.

65   Perry, *Holier Than Thou*, 28.

66   Dane Ortlund, *Gentle and Lowly* (Wheaton: Crossway, 2020), 194.

67   Alan Hirsch & Rob Kelly, *Metanoia* (Cody: 100 Movements Publishing, 2023), xxvii.

68   Frost & Hirsch, *ReJesus*, 94.

69   Craig Groeschel, *Divine Direction* (Grand Rapids: Zondervan, 2017), 128.

70   Ibid., 128.

71   From 'Blessed Be Your Name' by Matt Redman.

9. An Experienced Discipleship Toolkit

72   Foster, *Celebration of Discipline*, 1.

73   Alan Hirsch, *5Q* (Columbia: 100M, 2017), xxvii.

74   Based on a life expectancy of 80, it works out as 235.7 days of prayer.

75   Hirsch & Kelly, *Metanoia*, 14. They use the Greek word 'metanoia' instead of 'repentance', as it is the core concept (and title) of their book. But since I have not explored that in the same way, I have used 'repentance' for clarity.

76 Alex Harris & Chrissy Remsberg, *On This Rock* (Firestarters Network, 2023), 81.

77 As with many 'famous quotations', it's questionable whether the source here is really Einstein. It has also been attributed to Benjamin Franklin, and has popped up in many other places. Perhaps it doesn't have just one source, because it is so obvious that lots of people came up with it independently.

78 Hirsch & Kelly, *Metanoia*, 84.

79 www.big.life. In the resources section of their website, you can find a fuller description of the 'three thirds' model for discipleship groups.

80 For a UK context, this guide from the Evangelical Alliance outlines legal rights and protections, to give confidence in this area: https://www.eauk.org/current-affairs/upload/Speak-Up-Brief-Guide.pdf

Great Commission Experience

81 My two favourite, because of how intensely practical they are, are:
- Dave and Jon Ferguson, *B.L.E.S.S.: 5 Everyday Ways to Love Your Neighbor and Change the World* (Washington D.C.: Salem Books, 2021).
- Sam Chan, *How to Talk About Jesus (Without Being THAT Guy)* (Grand Rapids: Zondervan, 2020).

82 Andrew Wilson, *God of All Things*, 19.

Conclusion: Will you climb the mountain?

83 Jackie Hill Perry, *Holier Than Thou*, 130.

Printed in Great Britain
by Amazon